1999

# Managing Healthcare Compliance

## Scott C. Withrow

# Managing Healthcare Compliance

## Scott C. Withrow

Health Administration Press
Chicago, Illinois

03  02  01  00  99        5  4  3  2  1

**Library of Congress Cataloging-in-Publication Data**
Withrow, Scott C.
    Managing healthcare compliance / Scott C. Withrow.
        p.    cm.
    Includes bibliographical references and index.
    ISBN 1-56793-096-4 (alk. paper)
    1. Medical care—Law and legislation—United States.    2. Insurance, Health—
    Law and legislation—United States.    3. Medicare—Law and legislation.
    I. Title
    KF3821.W58    1999
    344.73'0226—dc21                    9847637
                                        CIP

The paper used in this publication meets the minimum requirements of American National Standards for Information Sciences—Permanence of Paper for Printed Library Materials, ANSI Z39.48–1984.™

Health Administration Press
A division of the Foundation of the
    American College of Healthcare Executives
One North Franklin Street
Chicago, IL 60606
312/424-2800

# TABLE OF CONTENTS

# Part III: Managing the Compliance Program . . . . . . . . 81

## Chapter 12    Implementing a Compliance Program. . . . . . 83

## Chapter 13    Billing Compliance . . . . . . . . . . . . . . . . . . 93

## Chapter 14    Anti-Kickback and
##                         Self-Referral Compliance . . . . . . . . . . . . 111

# EXHIBITS

# Compliance Programs
# in Healthcare

1

# INTRODUCTION

ompliance with healthcare laws and regulations has been a concern to
healthcare providers since the days of Ancient Babylon. Under the Code
of Hammurabi, which was adopted in 1750 B.C. and is thought to be
the oldest promulgation of laws in human history, a doctor who was convicted
of inept surgery was punished by amputation of his hands. Some 3,750 years
later in the United States, new fraud-fighting laws combine with a confound-
ing system of healthcare reimbursement to punish inept healthcare practices in
a similarly unforgiving manner. Healthcare compliance is the most perilous
and compelling topic that today's healthcare providers and executives face.

A series of well-publicized compliance investigations, the most notorious
involving the hospital giant Columbia/HCA, have resulted in criminal indictments and staggering fines for alleged failures to comply with healthcare laws
and regulations. One impetus for the federal government's increased focus on
healthcare compliance is the political dilemma faced by America's elected officials—how to ensure the availability of modern and often costly healthcare services to an aging population without raising taxes. Federal officials have seized
on wild guesses regarding the extent of healthcare fraud, such as the U.S.
General Accounting Office estimate in 1992 that healthcare fraud amounted
to approximately 10 percent of total national healthcare expenditures, or up to
$100 billion annually.[1] Politicians suddenly blamed "fraudulent" healthcare
providers for the nation's healthcare crisis.

More fuel was thrown on the fire by the report released in 1997 by the
Office of Inspector General of the Department of Health and Human Services
(OIG) on the first financial statement audit of the Health Care Financing

Administration (HCFA), the federal agency that administers the Medicare and Medicaid programs, for the fiscal year ended September 30, 1996.[2] Because HCFA's records were in such disarray, the OIG's report concluded that no audit opinion could be rendered on major balance sheet items such as Medicare accounts payable. Nevertheless, the OIG's report estimated that $23 billion in Medicare payments were improper, for reasons ranging from inadvertent mistakes to outright fraud and abuse.

The U.S. government has characterized healthcare fraud as the "crime of the nineties."[3] New legislation passed in 1996 and 1997 altered the legal standards, making it easier for the government to prove violations of the technical requirements for reimbursement under federally funded healthcare programs. In addition, Congress and the president greatly increased resources devoted to enforcing healthcare laws and regulations, including the hiring of 167 attorneys, paralegals, investigators, and support staff for healthcare fraud enforcement and the enlisting of the Federal Bureau of Investigation in actions against healthcare providers.[4] In addition, state governments, private payors, plaintiffs' attorneys, and individual citizens are focusing their attention on enforcement.

In an open letter to all healthcare providers published in early 1997,[5] the OIG declared a zero tolerance for fraud and asked healthcare providers to adopt and maintain compliance programs to assist the U.S. government in eliminating healthcare fraud. The OIG released its Model Compliance Program for Clinical Laboratories in 1997 and its detailed Compliance Program Guidance for Hospitals in February 1998. As a result, a whole new industry of healthcare consultants, information systems experts, accountants, attorneys, and ethicists has emerged to assist healthcare providers in their compliance efforts. The healthcare compliance officer is now viewed as a vital member of any provider's senior management.

Will government enforcement officials and/or private plaintiffs bankrupt providers with monetary fines and lawsuits? Will the U.S. government begin to impose the economic death penalty of exclusion from federally funded healthcare programs on a widespread basis? Will providers need armies of compliance consultants, accountants, and attorneys to protect themselves against enforcement actions? Or will providers comply themselves out of business by exhausting all their resources in a futile attempt to achieve a zero error rate in the numbingly complex healthcare reimbursement system?

The increased level of scrutiny over healthcare compliance is a fact of business in today's world. Providers are already devoting vast resources to comply with the requirements of the Medicare/Medicaid reimbursement system, healthcare insurers, and other private payors. Competitive pressures within the healthcare industry and limited government funding of healthcare constrain the additional resources that can be allocated to compliance issues. To survive the present firestorm, management must make wise use of its resources, focus on the hot spots, and enlist all members of the organization in the modern-day bucket brigade: the compliance program.

All healthcare providers can benefit by adopting, implementing, and maintaining an effective compliance program. This book will assist healthcare executives in understanding and managing compliance issues by explaining how to design, implement, and maintain a focused healthcare compliance program that addresses current government requirements. The basic compliance principles discussed in this book apply equally to all kinds of healthcare providers, including hospitals, physicians, home health, skilled nursing facilities, outpatient centers, clinical laboratories, mental health facilities, practice management companies, and fully integrated providers. Part I (Chapters 1 and 2) provides a brief review of the present focus on healthcare fraud, the government's encouragement of compliance programs, and the reasons to adopt a compliance program.

Part II (Chapters 3 through 11) explains what a compliance program is and how to design a written compliance program. Chapter 3 describes the background of compliance programs and the impact of the United States Organizational Sentencing Guidelines. Individual chapters then discuss each of the seven basic elements required for an effective healthcare compliance program, according to the OIG:

1. written standards of conduct;
2. designating a compliance officer;
3. effective education and training;
4. audits and other evaluation techniques;
5. internal reporting processes (such as a hotline);
6. disciplinary mechanisms; and
7. investigation and remediation.

Part III (Chapters 12 through 16) explains how to manage the compliance process, from design to implementation to maintenance, including specific advice on government searches and public relations. Individual chapters provide detailed information about how to comply with three areas of high exposure to modern healthcare providers:

1. billing (including coding and clinical documentation issues);
2. anti-kickback and self-referral; and
3. antitrust.

The book includes numerous practical aids to assist the reader, including:

- form of healthcare compliance program (Appendix A);
- copy of OIG's Compliance Program Guidance for Hospitals, cross-referenced to relevant sections (Appendix B);
- organizational chart showing compliance functions (Figure 5.1);

- compliance questionnaire designed to evaluate a provider's current compliance program (Form 12.1);
- summary tables comparing federal anti-kickback safe harbors and self-referral general exceptions (Appendices 14.1, 14.2 and 14.3); and
- synthesis of antitrust safety zones (Table 15.1).

The book also lists recommended compliance action items at the end of each of the following chapters and summarizes all recommended compliance action items at the conclusion of the book in Form 16.1. Healthcare executives are urged not only to become knowledgeable about compliance issues by reading the book, but also to act immediately to implement and maintain an effective compliance program for the organization.

## Notes

1. Report to Chairman, Subcommittee on Human Resources and Intergovernmental Operations, U.S. House of Representatives, *Health Insurance: Vulnerable Payers Lose Billions to Fraud and Abuse*, United States General Accounting Office (GAO/HRD-92-69), Washington, D.C., May 1992, p. 1.

   Notwithstanding the estimate contained in this report, a subsequent General Accounting Office report declared that "no reliable estimate of the cost of fraud to the Medicare program exists." Report to the Ranking Minority Member, Subcommittee on Labor, Health and Human Services, Education, and Related Agencies, Committee on Appropriations, U.S. Senate, *"Medicare: Antifraud Technology Offers Significant Opportunity to Reduce Health Care Fraud,"* United States General Accounting Office (GAO/AIMD-95-77), Washington, D.C., August 1995.

2. U.S. Department of Health and Human Services, Office of Inspector General. *Report on the Financial Statement Audit of the Health Care Financing Administration for Fiscal Year 1996* (CIN: A-17-95-00096), Washington, D.C., July 1997.

3. U.S. Department of Justice. *Health Care Fraud Report—Fiscal Years 1995 & 1996.* Washington, D.C., August 1997.

4. U.S. Department of Health and Human Services and Department of Justice. *Annual Report of the Attorney General and the Secretary Detailing Expenditures and Revenues Under the Health Care Fraud and Abuse Control Program For Fiscal Year 1997,* Washington, D.C., January 1998.

5. June Gibbs Brown, inspector general of Department of Health and Human Services to healthcare providers, open letter, February 1997.

# FOCUS ON FRAUD AND COMPLIANCE PROGRAMS

## 2.1 Legislation Against Fraud and Abuse

The Health Insurance Portability and Accountability Act of 1996 (HIPAA),[1] which became effective on January 1, 1997, adopted a number of important legal changes and additions in the area of healthcare fraud and abuse. HIPAA amended the civil fraud provisions of the Social Security Act to specifically prohibit claims based on incorrect coding or medically unnecessary services. HIPAA added an objective legal standard (i.e., the provider knows or should know) that holds the provider responsible for any pattern of presenting a claim if the provider "knows or should have known" that the claim will result in a greater payment to the provider than the amount actually allowed under the complex federal reimbursement rules.

HIPAA also created the new criminal offense of healthcare fraud, which applies to all claims under all health benefit programs, regardless of whether government funded or privately funded, and is punishable by up to ten years imprisonment. HIPAA defines healthcare fraud broadly to include any scheme to obtain the money or property of any healthcare benefit plan by means of false or fraudulent pretenses, representations, or promises.

The Balanced Budget Act (BBA) of 1997,[2] which became effective in August 1997, mandated permanent exclusion from participation in federally funded healthcare programs of those convicted of three healthcare-related crimes ("three strikes and you're out"). BBA also created new civil monetary penalties for violations of federal anti-kickback laws of up to $50,000 per violation, plus three times the illegal remuneration giving rise to the anti-kickback law violation. These civil anti-kickback penalties may be imposed if the government proves by a simple preponderance of the evidence that a violation of the anti-kickback laws occurred, a legal standard much easier to satisfy than the beyond-a-reasonable-doubt standard applied in criminal matters.

HIPAA provided substantial new enforcement funding for the OIG to combat healthcare fraud and abuse: $100 million in fiscal year 1997, increasing to $240 million by fiscal year 2003. In addition, civil monetary penalties and assessments resulting from government enforcement efforts may be used to fund activities under the fraud and abuse control program established by HIPAA. Government fraud fighters are thus financially motivated to perpetuate their own existence.

## 2.2 Enforcement

The OIG uses these additional resources in its enforcement efforts. For the fiscal year ended September 30, 1997, the OIG reported 215 convictions of individuals or entities for crimes or violations of federal healthcare program legislation or regulations and 1,255 civil settlements, netting OIG more than $1.2 billion in investigative receivables.[3] In addition, the OIG excluded 2,719 providers from participation in federal healthcare programs during fiscal year 1997, a 93 percent increase over the prior fiscal year. Not to be outdone in criminal convictions, state Medicaid fraud control units reported a total of 341 convictions for the six-month period ending September 30, 1997.

The OIG proudly announces its larger settlements in media advisories and on a web page.[4] The cost of settling with the OIG and other parties can be staggering. SmithKline Beecham Clinical Laboratories paid $325 million to settle claims relating to unbundling clinical laboratory tests, billing for tests not performed or not medically necessary, inserting false diagnosis codes to obtain reimbursement, paying kickbacks to physicians for patient referrals, and double-billing for laboratory tests for patients with end-stage renal disease. Caremark International paid $250 million to settle public and private claims relating to alleged illegal financial relationships with referring physicians.

Even with their significantly expanded resources to combat fraud and abuse, the OIG and HCFA cannot review all 800 million Medicare claims filed annually. HCFA currently reviews about 9 percent of all Medicare claims either on a prepayment or postpayment basis.[5] Whenever possible, such review is automated to avoid the costs associated with manual documentation review. However, many possible errors in claims for reimbursement cannot be discovered without some form of manual review of supporting medical documentation external to the claims.[6] Providers are not required to routinely submit full medical documentation with each Medicare claim, although providers must furnish such supporting documentation upon specific request.

## 2.3 Background of Compliance Programs

The OIG and HCFA are seeking the help of the provider community to take more responsibility for identifying and eliminating the allegedly "widespread" fraud and abuse in healthcare. In an open letter to all providers published in February 1997, the OIG recommended that all providers adopt compliance programs to protect their operations from fraud.[7] The OIG stated that the provider's compliance efforts will be considered in determining the level of sanctions, penalties, and exclusions that will be imposed if violations nevertheless occur. Simultaneous with the publication of the open letter to providers, the OIG issued a so-called *Model Compliance Plan for Clinical Laboratories* (Model Lab Compliance Plan)[8] and promised to issue other model programs shortly thereafter. Despite its name, the Model Lab Compliance Plan does not contain a model written compliance plan for providers to adopt; it only discusses the various areas that the OIG believes should be covered by a written program.

Compliance programs have been widely used for some time in the defense industry, another large component of the federal budget. The adoption of the *United States Organizational Sentencing Guidelines* (Sentencing Guidelines) in 1991 by the United States Sentencing Commission greatly increased the importance of compliance programs because the existence of "an effective program to prevent and detect violations of law" ensured a measurable reduction in any sanctions imposed under the Sentencing Guidelines.[9] A 1996 Delaware court case arising from the fraud investigation of Caremark even suggested that corporate directors now have a fiduciary duty to ensure that a corporate information and reporting system, such as a compliance program, is in place.[10] This case also implied that directors might be personally liable for losses that might have been prevented had such a compliance program been in place.

In February 1998, the OIG released its long-promised *Compliance Program Guidance for Hospitals* (Hospital Guidance).[11] Unlike the Model Lab Compliance Plan, the Hospital Guidance readily admits that it is not in itself a compliance program. Rather, it is a set of guidelines for a hospital interested in implementing a compliance program to consider. The Hospital Guidance was largely followed by the OIG's *Compliance Program Guidance for Home Health Agencies* (Home Health Guidance) released in August 1998.[12] The OIG has indicated that compliance guidance for other types of healthcare providers will be forthcoming. This book focuses on the compliance principles set forth in the Hospital Guidance, the principles of which will be generally applicable to all healthcare providers. But why should the honest provider who already expends significant resources to comply with healthcare laws and regulations be interested in implementing an elaborate compliance program?

## 2.4 Benefits of Compliance Programs

Adoption and implementation of an effective compliance program will afford a number of benefits to the provider, such as:

- identifying and preventing illegal and unethical conduct;
- increasing awareness of and compliance with reimbursement requirements for federal health programs;
- deterring private plaintiffs from suing on behalf of the U.S. government for false healthcare claims (*qui tam*);
- documenting preventive action by officers and directors in discharging their organizational fiduciary duties;
- reducing the level of sanctions, penalties, and exclusions that might be imposed if violations nevertheless occur; and
- following the directive of the OIG.

Another financial reason to voluntarily adopt a compliance program is specifically mentioned in the OIG's Hospital Guidance. Current HCFA reimbursement principles provide that certain costs associated with the creation of a voluntarily established compliance program may be allowable on the cost reports of certain types of hospitals and other providers, to the extent such costs are reasonable and are related to patient care.[13] In contrast, however, costs specifically associated with implementing a corporate integrity agreement (which is essentially a government-imposed compliance program) in response to a government investigation that results in a civil or criminal judgment or settlement are not allowable under current HCFA reimbursement guidelines.

## 2.5 Risks of Compliance Programs

Adopting and implementing an effective compliance program requires a substantial commitment of time, energy, and resources by senior management and the provider's governing body. Programs hastily adopted without appropriate implementation and ongoing monitoring are likely to be ineffective. In addition, many of the standards suggested in the OIG's Model Lab Compliance Plan, the Hospital Guidance, the Home Health Guidance, and other general statements by the OIG about ethical conduct in the healthcare industry establish standards of conduct that are higher and more difficult to satisfy than applicable legal standards. Providers should be very careful not to establish such higher standards in writing without the organizational commitment and practical ability to achieve such standards.

A number of technical points suggested by the OIG in the Hospital Guidance may be objectionable to hospitals for legal or other reasons. For example, the OIG suggests that the compliance officer should not be subordinate to the general counsel or the chief financial officer. This structure may not be possible in smaller organizations or advisable for organizations with in-house counsel because of concerns about maintaining attorney-client privilege over compliance communications. The recommendations of the OIG in the Hospital Guidance and other published statements about compliance programs should be critically analyzed by a provider to ensure that each element is appropriate for that provider under its particular circumstances.

## 2.6 Immediately Adopt a Written Compliance Program

In light of the increased penalties and enforcement of healthcare laws and regulations and the ease with which technical violations can occur, the benefits of having a compliance program easily exceed the associated costs and risks. Prudent providers should undertake the compliance process *immediately*.

The compliance process, as reflected in the Hospital Guidance, involves a wide variety of compliance issues that will be extensively discussed in this book. Attempting to deal with all of these issues at once can lead to paralysis over the actual adoption of a written compliance program. The Hospital Guidance recognizes that "full implementation of all elements will not be immediately feasible for all hospitals. However, as a first step, a good faith and meaningful commitment on the part of hospital administration, especially the governing body and the CEO, will substantially contribute to a program's successful implementation."

To take the first step in exhibiting a meaningful commitment to compliance, the governing board of every healthcare provider should formally resolve to adopt a compliance program and assign responsibility to one or more specific officers of the organization to develop and implement a compliance program. Form 2.1 contains an example of resolutions that should be included in the official minutes of the governing board to document its commitment to compliance.

The officers responsible for implementing the compliance program should then quickly customize and adopt a simple written program focused on high exposure areas such as the form healthcare compliance program contained in Appendix A (the form compliance program). Some customization of the form compliance program will be required to make the document appropriate for the individual provider. Adoption of a simple written compliance program will

**FORM 2.1   Resolutions of Governing Board Adopting Compliance Program**

The undersigned, being the Board of Directors of the [Name of Provider] (the Provider), do hereby unanimously adopt the following resolutions:

**RESOLVED,** the Board of Directors of the Provider desires to affirm its commitment to ensure that the Provider operate its business in full compliance with all laws and regulations of the United States and the State of [name of state of jurisdiction];

**RESOLVED FURTHER,** it is in the best interest of the Provider to adopt a formal compliance program to prevent, detect, and correct any instances of noncompliance;

**RESOLVED FURTHER,** that the position of Compliance Officer is hereby created within the organizational structure of the Provider and that [Name of Compliance Officer] is hereby appointed to said position;

**RESOLVED FURTHER,** that the Compliance Officer is hereby given full authority and directed to draft, manage, run, and do all other things necessary and expedient to develop and implement an effective compliance program for the Provider that meets the criteria of the United States Organizational Sentencing Guidelines;

**RESOLVED FURTHER,** that the Compliance Officer is directed to establish committees as he/she sees fit to assist in drafting and implementing a compliance program;

**RESOLVED FURTHER,** that the Compliance Officer shall be authorized and directed to report to the Chief Executive Officer and the Board of Directors about the compliance activities at least annually and more frequently as may be necessary or advisable under the circumstances.

**IN WITNESS WHEREOF,** the undersigned have caused this consent action to be executed the ___ day of _____, 199___.


_____          _____
Director                                                      Director


_____          _____
Director                                                      Director

at least provide tangible evidence that the provider is taking compliance seriously in the event violations occur before all elements of the compliance program can be fully implemented. The basic written program can be refined and expanded over time as the provider works through the compliance process described in this book.

The following chapters will summarize the basic elements necessary for an effective written compliance program, show how those elements can be worked into a simple written compliance program, and critically analyze the details in the OIG's published statements on compliance programs to assist providers in determining whether to adopt each aspect recommended by the OIG.

---

### Action Items

1. Make the decision to adopt and implement a compliance program.
2. Quickly customize and adopt a simple written compliance program such as the form compliance program in Appendix A.
3. Commit substantial time, energy, and resources of senior management to implement and maintain the compliance program appropriately.

---

## Notes

1. Public Law 104-191 (1996).
2. Public Law 105-33 (1997).
3. U.S. Department of Health and Human Services, Office of Inspector General, *Semi-Annual Report*, April 1, 1997–September 30, 1997, pp. iii-iv.
4. *www.hhs.gov/progorg/oig/medadv/medadv.html.*
5. House Committee on Ways & Means, Subcommittee on Health, statement of Bruce C. Vladek, Administrator, Health Care Financing Administration, on "Chief Financial Officers Audit, FY 1996," July 17, 1997.
6. See, e.g., U.S. Department of Health and Human Services, Office of Inspector General, *Using Software To Detect Upcoding of Hospital Bills*, OEI-01-97-00010, August 1998.
7. June Gibbs Brown, inspector general of Department of Health and Human Services to healthcare providers, open letter, February 1997.
8. U.S. Department of Health and Human Services, Office of Inspector General, *Model Compliance Plan for Clinical Laboratories*, February 1997.
9. United States Sentencing Commission, *Sentencing Guidelines for United States Courts*, promulgated pursuant to 28 U.S.C.A. § 994(a) (West 1997) (hereinafter Sentencing Guidelines).
10. *In Re Caremark International, Inc. Derivative Litigation*, 698 A.2d 959, 970 (Del. Ch. 1996).
11. U.S. Department of Health and Human Services, Office of Inspector General, *Compliance Program Guidance for Hospitals*, February 1998, 63 Fed. Reg. 8987 (1998) (hereinafter Hospital Guidance).

12. U.S. Department of Health and Human Services, Office of Inspector General, *Compliance Program Guidance for Home Health Agencies*, August 1998, 63 Fed. Reg. 42410 (1998) (hereinafter Home Health Guidance).

13. Hospital Guidance, 63 Fed. Reg. 8987, 8989, footnote 7 (1998). See generally 42 U.S.C.A. § 1395x(v)(1)(A) (West 1997) (definition of reasonable cost); 42 C.F.R. §§ 413.9(a), (b)(2) (1996) (costs related to patient care).

# Elements of a Compliance Program

# WHAT IS A COMPLIANCE PROGRAM?

## 3.1  Simple Definition

In its most simple form, a compliance program is intended to prevent and detect violations of law. The Sentencing Guidelines expand on this basic notion as follows:

> An "effective program to prevent and detect violations of law" means a program that has been reasonably designed, implemented and enforced so that it generally will be effective in preventing and detecting criminal conduct. Failure to prevent or detect the instant offense, by itself, does not mean that the program was not effective. The hallmark of an effective program to prevent and detect violations of law is that *the organization exercised due diligence in seeking to prevent and detect* criminal conduct by its employees and other agents (emphasis added).[1]

## 3.2  Impact on Organizational Culpability

While the general notion of compliance programs has existed for more than 30 years, the promulgation of the Sentencing Guidelines in 1991 significantly altered the legal approach to judging organizational culpability and specifically mandated mitigation of sanctions for organizations having effective compliance programs. Organizations can act only through agents. Under federal criminal law, organizations are vicariously liable for offenses committed by their agents. At the same time, individual agents are responsible for their own criminal conduct. Federal prosecutions of organizations therefore frequently involve individual and organizational codefendants. Convicted individual agents of organizations are sentenced in accordance with a distinct set of sentencing guidelines. The Sentencing Guidelines applicable to organizations are designed so that the sanctions imposed on organizations and their agents, taken together, will provide just punishment, adequate deterrence, and incentives for organizations to maintain internal mechanisms for preventing, detecting, and reporting criminal conduct.

Under the Sentencing Guidelines, the range of fines is determined by a complicated process affected by two major factors: (1) the seriousness of the offense and (2) the culpability of the organization. The seriousness of the offense is represented by a base monetary fine. The base fine can be computed in a number of different ways, but in most cases, the base fine is the loss caused by the offense.[2] In other words, the organization is required to make full restitution for the illegal conduct and then must pay an additional fine based on culpability.

As for determining the portion of the fine relating to culpability, the Sentencing Guidelines provide a complex method for assigning "culpability points." The starting point for every organization is five culpability points.[3] From there, "aggravating" factors may increase this culpability score from five points to as high as 17 points. The aggravating factors include:

- *Level of authority and size of the organization.* If a high-level official of a large organization was involved in the offense or somehow tolerated this offense occurring, then that organization is more culpable. High-level involvement and large size (more than 5,000 employees) will increase the culpability points anywhere from one to five additional culpability points.[4]
- *Prior history of the organization.* Did the organization have a previous criminal, civil, or administrative adjudication for similar conduct? If so, the organization is more culpable and culpability points will increase by one or two points, if the prior adjudication was within ten and five years, respectively.[5]
- *Violation of a court order, injunction, or probation.* Did the organization violate a court order, injunction, or a condition of probation by committing this offense? If so, the organization is more culpable and it will pick up additional culpability points—one point for violating probation or two points for violating a court order or injunction.[6]
- *Obstruction of justice.* Did this organization obstruct the investigation or the prosecution of this offense in any way? Three culpability points are added for this factor.[7]

## 3.3 Dramatic Reductions in Fines for Compliance and Cooperation

The Sentencing Guidelines also identify mitigating factors that may decrease the culpability score as follows:

- *Effective program to prevent and detect violations of law.* If the offense occurred despite an effective program to prevent and detect violations of law, the organization may subtract three culpability points.[8]
- *Self-reporting, cooperation, and acceptance of responsibility.* If more than one applies, use the factor with the greatest number of points:
  1. If the organization (a) prior to an imminent threat of disclosure or government investigation and (b) within a reasonably prompt time after becoming aware of the offense reported the offense to appropriate governmental authorities, fully cooperated in the investigation, and clearly demonstrated recognition and affirmative acceptance of responsibility for its criminal conduct, the organization may subtract five culpability points; or
  2. If the organization fully cooperated in the investigation and clearly demonstrated recognition and affirmative acceptance of responsibility for its criminal conduct, the organization may subtract two points; or
  3. If the organization clearly demonstrated recognition and affirmative acceptance of responsibility for its criminal conduct (i.e., pleads guilty), the organization may subtract one point.[9]

Once the culpability points are determined as described above, the Sentencing Guidelines establish the range of additional penalties by assigning minimum and maximum multipliers of the base fine.[10] Multipliers range from a minimum of 0.05 for zero (or less) culpability points to a maximum of 4.0 for ten or more culpability points. Table 3.1 contains an example to demonstrate how this process would operate on an organization that has committed a pervasive healthcare fraud costing the federal government $10 million.

To summarize, the combination of an effective compliance program, cooperation, and acceptance of responsibility reduces the organizational fine in the example by $9.5 million at the minimum, and $18 million at the maximum, or between 90 percent and 95 percent of the fine. Thus, programs to prevent, detect, and self-report violations of law can have a dramatic effect on the organizational penalties imposed under the Sentencing Guidelines.

## 3.4 Commentary on Organizational Culpability

The increased culpability scores for aggravating factors under the Sentencing Guidelines are based on three interrelated principles. First, an organization is more culpable when individuals who manage the organization or who have substantial discretion in acting for the organization participate in, condone, or are willfully ignorant of criminal conduct. Second, management participating in, condoning or willfully ignoring criminal conduct increasingly is seen as a breach of trust or abuse of position as the organization becomes larger and its management becomes more professional. Third, as the organization increases

**TABLE 3.1**   Examples of Fines Under U.S. Organizational Sentencing Guidelines

Assume a provider has committed a pervasive healthcare fraud that costs the federal government $10 million. The provider would be required to pay restitution of $10 million, plus an additional fine as follows:

| Aggravating/Mitigating Factors | Culpability Points[1] | Multiplier Range[2] | Range of Fine (Multiplier times base fine of $10 million) |
|---|---|---|---|
| No aggravating or mitigating factors | 5 | 1.00 to 2.00 | $10 million to $20 million |
| No aggravating factors, effective compliance program only | 5 − 3 = 2 | 0.40 to 0.80 | $4 million to $8 million |
| No aggravating factors, effective compliance program, and full cooperation in investigation and affirmative acceptance of responsibility | 5 − 3 − 2 = 0 | 0.05 to 0.20 | $0.5 million to $2 million |

1.   Sentencing Guidelines, § 8C2.5 (1997).
2.   Sentencing Guidelines, § 8C2.6 (1997).

in size, the risk of criminal conduct beyond that reflected in the instant offense also increases whenever management's tolerance of that offense is pervasive.

The Sentencing Guidelines reflect a prosecutorial approach to the notion of compliance largely because they deal only with situations in which an offense has already occurred. The punishment and reward of the Sentencing Guidelines depend mainly on enforcement procedures such as detection, self-reporting, cooperation, acceptance of responsibility, violation of orders, and obstruction of justice. Indeed, an organization that simply self-reports, cooperates, and accepts responsibility receives a greater reward in terms of the reduction of its monetary fine (five-point culpability reduction) than an organization that merely has an effective program to prevent and detect violations (three-point culpability reduction).

This prosecutorial focus is misplaced when compliance is analyzed from a management perspective; prevention is the critical topic for managers. Management should allocate its limited resources to compliance elements that emphasize prevention to avoid the need to self-report, make restitution, and then plead for mercy from the possibility of exorbitant fines.

## 3.5  Is a Compliance Program a Trojan Horse?

The major mitigating factors for both the effective compliance program and for self-reporting may prove illusory for organizational defendants. For the fiscal year ended September 30, 1996, the United States Sentencing Commission reported 94 cases that assessed whether the mitigating factor for the effective program to prevent and detect violations was applicable. Every one of these cases allowed no culpability reduction because the court determined that the organization did not have an effective program.[11] Likewise, in the 92 cases reported over the same period that assessed whether the self-reporting mitigating factor was applicable, 100 percent allowed no culpability reduction for self-reporting.[12] Minor culpability reductions were allowed for cooperation (one point) in 50 percent of the cases and for acceptance of responsibility (one point) in 26 percent of the cases.[13]

The Sentencing Commission data does not distinguish between cases in which no compliance program existed at all versus situations in which a compliance program existed but was deemed ineffective. The data only considers sentencing by the courts after a criminal proceeding. Government prosecutors may be more mindful of good faith compliance attempts in choosing to prosecute or settle civil or administrative offenses, which are not punishable by imprisonment. Nevertheless, the data suggests that where blatant criminal conduct occurs, the organization will have a difficult time showing that its program to prevent and detect violations was effective and that it reported the offense to the appropriate governmental authorities in a timely manner.

If, in fact, the promised rewards for adopting a compliance program are not forthcoming when violations occur, adoption of a compliance program may resemble the Trojan horse, with federal prosecutors sneaking through the walls of the organization by means of detection and self-reporting mechanisms—essential elements of the compliance program. While the compliance program may benefit the organization by preventing violations from occurring, it also may detect and report inadvertent violations that might have otherwise gone unnoticed.

The detection and reporting elements of a compliance program do contribute to the goal of prevention by deterring premeditated illegal conduct with the threats of discovery by auditors or whistle blowers and the resulting discipline. Also, the OIG retains a great deal of discretion in the prosecutorial process, and it has clearly stated its desire for healthcare organizations to adopt compliance programs that include detection and reporting elements. For these reasons, detection and reporting mechanisms should be included in compliance programs. Management should concentrate its efforts and resources on preventive elements such as extensive training, rather than costly, retrospective audits (see Chapters 6 and 7).

## 3.6 Application of Compliance Programs to Healthcare

The purposes of a compliance program under the Sentencing Guidelines are straightforward: prevention, detection, and self-reporting of violations of law.

The OIG has significantly expanded these purposes in its compliance guidance to healthcare providers. Purposes for compliance programs, as articulated by the OIG in the Hospital Guidance, include:

- developing effective internal controls that promote adherence to applicable federal and state law, and the program requirements of federal, state, and private health plans;
- advancing the prevention of fraud, abuse, and waste in these healthcare plans; and
- furthering the fundamental mission—to provide quality care to patients—of all hospitals.[14]

With stated purposes extending beyond compliance with laws to include issues of private payor contracts and quality of patient care, healthcare executives face a daunting challenge in designing compliance programs as suggested by the OIG. Implementing any program that tries to encompass all these areas would be extremely difficult, if not impossible. The average employee would be overwhelmed by all the implications of such an expansive program. To be comprehensible and usable by employees, the written compliance program must stay focused on central concepts such as prevention, detection, and self-reporting of violations of law as emphasized in the Sentencing Guidelines.

The government has also undertaken massive investigations, such as the initiative involving physicians at teaching hospitals (see Section 13.10) and the DRG 72-hour window project (see Section 13.11), in areas where providers believe the applicable rules and regulations are unclear. Indeed, the 72-hour window project is expected to include 4,660 hospitals,[15] out of roughly 5,100 acute care, nongovernment hospitals in the United States that are reimbursed under the prospective payment system.[16] Such widespread alleged noncompliance with the DRG 72-hour rule cannot reflect premeditated fraud by nearly every hospital in the United States. The reality is that the Medicare reimbursement system is outrageously complex and much of the "noncompliant" conduct is simply inadvertent—not premeditated.

This aspect of widespread, but inadvertent, conduct that is possibly noncompliant under the federal healthcare reimbursement system presents special challenges for designing appropriate compliance programs. The deterrent effect of detection, reporting, and disciplinary mechanisms, as discussed above, is lessened because providers may not even recognize that their conduct is noncompliant. The judgment about what is or is not compliant must be carefully considered before detection and reporting compliance processes are brought to bear. In this atmosphere, the compliance program must employ extraordinary procedures first to define what noncompliant conduct is and then to educate all parties involved. Only then can detection, reporting, and disciplinary mechanisms of a compliance program be fairly employed.

## 3.7 Basic Elements of a Compliance Program

The basic elements of a healthcare compliance program, as set forth in the OIG's Hospital Guidance, largely track the basic elements of an effective program to prevent and detect violations of law as defined in the Sentencing Guidelines. Table 3.2 illustrates the similarities and differences:

To summarize Table 3.2, the Sentencing Guidelines and the Hospital Guidance share seven basic elements:

1. written standards of conduct;
2. designating a compliance officer;
3. effective education and training;
4. audits and other evaluation techniques;
5. internal reporting processes (such as hotlines);
6. disciplinary mechanisms; and
7. investigation and remediation.

The only significant difference is that the Sentencing Guidelines, but not the Hospital Guidance, include as a separate element a requirement that the organization must have used due care not to delegate substantial discretionary authority to individuals who the organization knew, or should have known through the exercise of due diligence, had a propensity to engage in illegal activities. However, the Hospital Guidance does specifically recommend the provider's new employee policy include a background check to disclose any propensity to engage in illegal activities.[17]

## 3.8 Beyond the Basics

The seven basic elements of a compliance program outlined in the Hospital Guidance should be addressed in the organization's overall written compliance policy. The form compliance program included in this book provides an example of the incorporation of these basic elements into a concise written compliance policy. The OIG goes far beyond the seven basic elements in its Model Lab Compliance Plan, Hospital Guidance, and Home Health Guidance, all of which could be described as extensive wish lists from the OIG for very detailed policies and procedures in specific areas of healthcare.

Providers are thus left with a dilemma. Should providers satisfy the relatively basic elements of an effective compliance program under the Sentencing Guidelines, or should they try to establish all the detailed policies and procedures suggested by the OIG in its published compliance guidance?

Providers are advised to follow the OIG's guidance in most respects to have the best chance at any possible leniency should a violation occur. The Sentencing Guidelines technically govern just criminal violations, not civil violations (which are not punishable by imprisonment). The Social Security Act and other

**TABLE 3.2** Essential Elements of an Effective Compliance Program[1]

| Federal Organizational Sentencing Guidelines (1991)[2] | OIG Compliance Program Guidance for Hospitals (1998)[3] |
|---|---|
| (1) The organization must have established **compliance standards** and procedures that are reasonably capable of reducing the prospect of criminal conduct, to be followed by its employees and other agents. | (1) The development and distribution of **written standards of conduct**, as well as written policies and procedures **that promote the hospital's commitment to compliance** (e.g., by including adherence to compliance as an element in evaluating managers and employees) and that address specific areas of potential fraud, such as claims development and submission processes, code gaming, and financial relationships with physicians and other healthcare professionals. |
| (2) **Specific individual(s) within high-level personnel** of the organization must have been assigned overall responsibility **to oversee compliance** with such standards and procedures. | (2) The designation of a **chief compliance officer** and other appropriate bodies (e.g., a corporate compliance committee) charged with the responsibility of operating and monitoring the compliance program and that report directly to the CEO and the governing body. |
| (3) The organization must have used due care **not to delegate substantial discretionary authority to individuals** whom the organization knew, or should have known through the exercise of due diligence, had a **propensity to engage in illegal activities**. | Not specifically mentioned. |
| (4) The organization must have taken **steps to communicate effectively its standards** and procedures to all employees and other agents (e.g., **by requiring participation in training programs or by disseminating publications** that explain in a practical manner what is required). | (3) The development and implementation of regular, effective **education and training programs** for all affected employees. |
| (5) The organization must have taken reasonable steps to achieve compliance with its standards (e.g., by using **monitoring and auditing systems** reasonably designed to detect criminal conduct by its employees and other agents **and by having in place and publicizing a reporting system** whereby employees and other agents could report criminal conduct by others within the organization without fear of retribution). | (6) The use of **audits and/or other evaluation techniques to monitor compliance** and assist in the reduction of identified problem areas; and<br><br>(4) The maintenance of a **process such as a hotline to receive complaints**, and the adoption of procedures to protect the anonymity of complainants and to protect whistle blowers from retaliation. |
| (6) The standards must have been enforced consistently through appropriate **disciplinary mechanisms**, including, as appropriate, discipline of individuals responsible for the failure to detect an offense. Adequate discipline of individuals responsible for an offense is a necessary component of enforcement; however, the form of discipline that will be appropriate will be case specific. | (5) The development of a system to respond to allegations of improper/illegal activities and the enforcement of appropriate **disciplinary action** against employees who have violated internal compliance policies, applicable statutes, regulations, or federal healthcare program requirements. |
| (7) After an offense has been detected, the organization must have taken all **reasonable steps to respond appropriately to the offense and to prevent further similar offenses**—including any necessary modifications to its program to prevent and detect violations of law. | (7) The **investigation and remediation of identified systemic problems** and the development of policies addressing the nonemployment or retention of sanctioned individuals. |

1. Numbers in parentheses correspond to the numbering used in the respective source documents.
2. Sentencing Guidelines, 8A1.2, Application Note 3(k)(1)-(7) (1997).
3. 63 Fed. Reg. 8987, 8989 (1998).

federal laws and regulations governing healthcare providers contain draconian civil penalties, including huge monetary fines and the economic death penalty of exclusion from participation in federally funded healthcare programs. The OIG has stated that the existence of an effective compliance program will be considered in determining the level of sanctions, penalties, and exclusions that will be imposed on the provider for both criminal and civil violations.[18] As the compliance focus is relatively new in healthcare, it remains to be seen whether the OIG will deliver on its promises of leniency in both criminal and civil matters. Nevertheless, management should attempt to reduce the organization's exposure to the severe civil sanctions available to federal prosecutors by following the reasonable compliance recommendations of the OIG.

## 3.9 Critical Analysis Required of OIG's Compliance Guidance

Although it is advisable to follow the OIG's guidance in most respects, the OIG's guidance makes onerous demands of providers far beyond the basic elements established by the Sentencing Guidelines. The OIG has derived many of the specific provisions from corporate integrity agreements, which were crafted by prosecutors and imposed on offending providers as part of the settlement of an OIG prosecution. Now that the Model Lab Compliance Plan, Hospital Guidance, and Home Health Guidance have been officially issued, providers must critically analyze the OIG's compliance guidance. They should follow such guidance when appropriate but decline or modify such guidance if it is impractical or inadvisable for the provider. By no means should the OIG's guidance be viewed as the exclusive authority of the advisable provisions in a compliance program. Even the OIG recognizes that "the development and implementation of compliance programs in hospitals often raise sensitive and complex legal and managerial issues."[19]

Chapters 4 through 10 critically analyze each of the seven basic elements of compliance and the technical points suggested in the OIG's compliance guidance that go beyond the basic elements. The OIG's guidance is acceptable on many points and is often helpful in considering specific healthcare compliance issues. Some technical points suggested by the OIG in its published guidance are inadvisable, however, and have not been included in the form compliance program for reasons that are explained in the following chapters.

---

**Action Items**

1. Emphasize the preventive elements of the compliance program, such as extensive training and concurrent oversight.
2. Include elements necessary for an effective compliance program, such as retrospective audits, reporting mechanisms, and appropriate disciplinary procedures.
3. Critically analyze the OIG's guidance before adopting all of the OIG's demands.

# Notes

1. Sentencing Guidelines, § 8A1.2, Application Note 3(k) (1997) (emphasis supplied).
2. Sentencing Guidelines, § 8C2.4 (1997).
3. Ibid., (a).
4. Ibid., (b).
5. Ibid., (c).
6. Ibid., (d).
7. Ibid., (e).
8. Ibid., (f). and Official Commentary thereto. The reduction for an effective program to prevent and detect violations of law is subject to two provisos. First, the reduction does not apply if an individual within high-level personnel of the organization, a person within high-level personnel of the unit of the organization within which the offense was committed (where the unit had 200 or more employees), or an individual responsible for the administration or enforcement of a program to prevent and detect violations of law participated in, condoned, or was willfully ignorant of the offense. Participation of an individual within substantial authority personnel in an offense results in a rebuttable presumption that the organization did not have an effective program to prevent and detect violations of law. Second, the reduction does not apply if, after becoming aware of an offense, the organization unreasonably delayed reporting the offense to appropriate governmental authorities. The organization will be allowed a reasonable period of time, however, to conduct an internal investigation, and no reporting is required by this proviso if the organization reasonably concluded, based on the information then available, that no offense had been committed.
9. Ibid., (g). (1997).
10. Ibid. § 8C2.6. (1997).
11. United States Sentencing Commission, *1996 Sourcebook of Federal Sentencing Statistics*, Table 47.
12. Ibid.
13. Ibid.
14. Hospital Guidance, 63 Fed. Reg. 8987, 8987-8 (1998).
15. United States General Accounting Office, Report to Congressional Requesters, *Medicare—Application of the False Claims Act to Hospital Billing Practices*, GAO/HEHS-98-195, July 1998, p.9.
16. U.S. Department of Health and Human Services, Health Care Financing Administration, Office of Strategic Planning, *1997 HCFA Statistics*, HCFA Pub. No. 03403, October 1997, Table 17 (5,118 hospitals under PPS as of March 1997, with a declining trend [see Table 15]).
17. Hospital Guidance, 63 Fed. Reg. 8987, 8996 (1998).
18. June Gibbs Brown, inspector general of Department of Health and Human Services to healthcare providers, open letter, February 1997.
19. Hospital Guidance, 63 Fed. Reg. 8987, 8989 (1998).

# ELEMENT ONE: WRITTEN STANDARDS OF CONDUCT

## 4.1 Legal and Ethical Standards

On the subject of written standards of conduct, the OIG instructs hospitals to

> develop standards of conduct for all affected employees that include a clearly delineated commitment to compliance by the hospital's senior management and its divisions, including affiliated providers operating under the hospital's control, hospital-based physicians and other health care professionals (e.g., utilization review managers, nurse anesthetists, physician assistants and physical therapists). Standards should articulate the hospital's commitment to comply with all federal and state standards, with an emphasis on preventing fraud and abuse.[1]

This straightforward notion is addressed by Article I of the form compliance program (Appendix A), as follows:

> _____ (the Hospital) has a policy of maintaining the highest level of professional and ethical standards in the conduct of its business. The Hospital places the highest importance on its reputation for honesty, integrity, and high ethical standards. This Policy Statement is a reaffirmation of the importance of the highest level of ethical conduct and standards . . . . Employees must be cognizant of all applicable federal and state laws and regulations that apply to and affect the Hospital's documentation, coding, billing, and competitive practices, as well as the day-to-day activities of the Hospital and its employees and agents. Each employee who is materially involved in any of the Hospital's documentation, coding, billing, or competitive practices has an obligation to familiarize himself or herself with all such applicable laws and regulations and to adhere at all times to the requirements thereof.

## 4.2 OIG's Areas of Special Concern

The form compliance program contains a clearly delineated commitment to comply with all federal and state standards, with emphasis on the areas of documentation, coding, billing, and competitive practices, areas where the OIG is particularly concerned about fraud and abuse. Things would be simple if the analysis could end here. However, the Hospital Guidance goes on to list 18 different areas of "special" concern that have been identified by the OIG through its investigative and audit functions.[2] The Home Health Guidance is even more unfocused, identifying 31 areas of "special" concern.[3] The areas of special concern are randomly mentioned, without further grouping or references to legal authority. The OIG's shotgun approach to special areas of concern in the Hospital Guidance and Home Health Guidance makes it difficult to delineate clearly and concisely the written standards with which the provider must comply. Tables 4.1 and 4.2 attempt to group the OIG's areas of special concern into categories relating to the operations of hospitals and home health agencies, respectively.

**TABLE 4.1**   OIG's Areas of Special Concern—Hospitals

| Operational Category | OIG's Area of Special Concern[1] |
| --- | --- |
| Billing (including documentation and coding) | • Billing for items or services not actually rendered<br>• Providing medically unnecessary services<br>• Upcoding<br>• DRG creep<br>• Outpatient services rendered in connection with inpatient stays<br>• Teaching physician and resident requirements for teaching hospitals<br>• Duplicate billing<br>• Unbundling<br>• Billing for discharge in lieu of transfer |
| Relationships with physicians/other providers | • Hospital incentives that violate anti-kickback rules<br>• Joint ventures<br>• Financial arrangements between hospitals and hospital-based physicians<br>• Stark physician self-referral law |
| Patient care | • Patients' freedom of choice (e.g., choice of home health providers on discharge)<br>• Knowingly failing to provide covered services or necessary care to members of an HMO<br>• Patient dumping |
| Accounting | • False cost reports<br>• Credit balances—failure to refund |

1.   Compliance Program Guidance for Hospitals, 63 Fed. Reg. 8987, 8990 (1998).

**TABLE 4.2** OIG's Areas of Special Concern—Home Health Agencies

| Operational Category | OIG's Area of Special Concern[1] |
| --- | --- |
| Billing (including documentation and coding) | • Billing for items or services not actually rendered<br>• Billing for medically unnecessary services<br>• Duplicate billing<br>• Billing for services provided to patients who are not homebound<br>• Billing for visits to patients who do not require a qualifying service<br>• Overutilization and underutilization<br>• Knowingly billing for inadequate or substandard care<br>• Insufficient documentation<br>• Billing for unallowable costs of home health coordination<br>• Billing for services provided by unqualified or unlicensed clinical personnel<br>• False dating of amendments to nursing notes<br>• Falsifying plans of care<br>• Untimely and/or forged physician certifications on plans of care<br>• Forging beneficiary signatures on visit slips/logs<br>• Inadequately managing subcontracted services, which results in improper billing<br>• Billing for unallowable costs associated with the acquisition and sale of home health agencies<br>• Knowingly misusing provider certification numbers, which results in improper billing<br>• Failing to adhere to home health agency licensing requirements and Medicare conditions of participation |
| Relationships with physicians/other providers | • Home health incentives to actual or potential referral sources that violate anti-kickback rules<br>• Joint ventures between parties, one of whom can refer Medicare or Medicaid business to the other<br>• Stark physician self-referral law<br>• Improper patient solicitation activities and high-pressure marketing of unnecessary services<br>• Compensation programs that offer incentives for number of visits performed and revenue generated<br>• Improper influence over referrals by hospitals that own home health agencies |
| Patient care | • Patients' freedom of choice (e.g., choice of home health providers on discharge)<br>• Discriminatory admission and discharge<br>• Patient abandonment<br>• Knowing or reckless disregard of willing and able caregivers (such as family members) who can provide the needed services without the agency |
| Accounting | • False cost reports<br>• Credit balances—failure to refund<br>• Knowingly failing to return overpayments |

1. Home Health Guidance, 63 Fed. Reg. 42410, 42413-5 (1998).

When the special areas of concern to the OIG are categorized by the operational areas they affect (Tables 4.1 and 4.2), executives can glean which operational areas deserve special attention in a hospital compliance program, arguably in the following order of importance:

1. billing (including documentation and coding);
2. relationships with physicians/other providers;
3. patient care; and
4. accounting.

## 4.3 Commentary

From the provider's viewpoint, the OIG's unfocused and expansive approach to formulating written standards may not be the most effective way to design a healthcare compliance program. The OIG professes "special" anti-kickback concerns with respect to hospital financial arrangements with hospital-based physicians that compensate physicians for less than the fair market value of services they provide to hospitals, citing an obscure 1991 OIG *Management Advisory Report*.[4] An example of such arrangements that may violate the anti-kickback statute according to the OIG is token or no payment for Part A supervision and management services. In fact, hospitals rarely attempt to quantify and pay a fair market value for Part A supervision and management services. As one commentator to the 1991 OIG *Management Advisory Report* explains:

> Why, pray tell, should the Federal Government care about this issue when there is no direct relationship between patient flow and hospital-based physicians in connection with these contracts, nor indeed will the Federal Government be spending one nickel more whether the physicians agree to provide support to hospitals or whether they do not.[5]

The terms "upcoding," "DRG creep," and "unbundling" are all media buzzwords without direct statutory or regulatory authority. The OIG's own 1992 *National DRG Validation Study Update*[6] concluded that "DRG creep" had been eliminated. The study found that DRG coding errors divided approximately evenly between errors that had overreimbursed the hospital and underreimbursed the hospitals. More specifically, the study attributed overreimbursement to the hospitals aggressively resequencing patient diagnoses to obtain higher reimbursement. Underreimbursement was attributed to attending physicians selecting their patient diagnoses with caution, earning their hospitals less reimbursement than they should have received. By using terms such as "upcoding" and "DRG creep," the OIG is encouraging providers to focus only on overreimbursement to the exclusion of the underreimbursement problem. Providers cannot afford to focus only on one side of the equation from a financial standpoint.[7]

And finally, what is the point of rewriting standards of conduct that already are written into statutes or are well-understood tenets of ethical conduct? Dr. Mark Pastin, president of the Council of Ethical Organizations, presented the results of an extensive survey exploring the effectiveness of written compliance standards at the 1995 symposium *Corporate Crime in America: Strengthening the "Good Citizen" Corporation,*[8] which was sponsored by the United States Sentencing Commission. Approximately 750,000 employees in 203 large companies, roughly Fortune 650 companies, responded to the survey over five years ending December 1994. After rejecting unscorable responses, the study included 660,000 scorable surveys, an average of about 3,500 employees per company.

The study concluded that codes of conduct were generally ineffective as compliance tools. In particular, 86 percent of the codes in effect in the responding companies were viewed as not effective, 8 percent as effective, and 6 percent were in the category of "effectiveness not determined." The study found that codes of conduct were largely viewed by employees as legalistic and one-sided in favor of the company, and such codes actually increased the likelihood that employees would exhibit behavior that the company identified as unethical or illegal. Only those codes of conduct that were viewed by employees as straightforward, informative, and evenhanded were found to decrease the likelihood that employees would exhibit behavior they viewed as unethical or illegal. In light of this research, written standards should be straightforward, informative, and focused on a manageable number of areas requiring truly special compliance efforts.

## 4.4  Legal Standards

The form compliance program attempts to cover the more important areas of concern to the OIG, with one major modification. Rather than throwing out a nebulous buzzword such as "upcoding," the form compliance program relates the area of special concern to the applicable legal standard. By relating the compliance standard to the actual legal requirement, readers of the form compliance program get a more accurate statement of what the law requires in each area, and the program does not establish standards in excess of what the law requires.

For example, the terms "upcoding" and "DRG creep" are not defined or even found in the Social Security Act provisions concerning illegal claims. The exact legal standard prohibits presenting a claim "for a medical or other item or service that such person knows or should know was not provided as claimed, including a *pattern or practice* of presenting or causing to be presented a claim for an item or service that is based on a code that such person *knows or should know* will result in a greater payment to the claimant than the code such person *knows or should know* is applicable to the item or service actually provided (emphasis added)."⁹ The "pattern or practice" requirement excludes inadvertent errors from the scope of the legal standard. The "know or should know" language requires proof that the provider either acted in deliberate disregard of the truth or falsity of the information or acted in reckless disregard of the truth or falsity of the information. In the Hospital Guidance, the OIG ignores these important requirements that must exist before the conduct becomes illegal. Chapter 13 provides a more detailed discussion about the legal standards affecting documentation, coding, and billing.

By incorporating the precise legal elements into the written standards of conduct, the form compliance program makes an intentional compromise with the concurrent goal of straightforwardness. The Hospital Guidance suggests that written standards of conduct should be translated into other languages and written at appropriate reading levels, where appropriate.¹⁰ However, the laws with which providers must comply are written in very complex English and are subject to varying interpretations. An important part of the compliance process is to educate personnel about the legal complexities inherent in healthcare. While written standards should be straightforward to the extent possible, oversimplification may be detrimental to compliance efforts because employees may not appreciate how the legal complexities affect their job responsibilities. For example, billing personnel should understand that while some inadvertent errors may not constitute a pattern so as to be unlawful, they must exercise heightened diligence in ascertaining what coding and billing rules apply, because the legal standard has been broadened recently to include both the rules that they actually know and ones they should know.

## 4.5 Reduced List of Areas Needing Special Compliance Attention

After relating the OIG's areas of special concern to applicable legal standards, the form compliance program reduces the 18 areas of special concern in the Hospital Guidance to the following areas, which should be highlighted by most types of healthcare providers for special compliance attention:

1. improper claims;
   a. item or service not provided as claimed;
   b. false claim;
   c. service by unlicensed physician;
   d. excluded provider;
   e. not medically necessary;
2. false statement in determining rights to benefits;
3. conspiracy to defraud;
4. patient dumping;

5. provision of care to contract HMO patients;
6. healthcare fraud/false statements relating to healthcare matters;
7. physician self-referral;
8. anti-kickback;
9. antitrust; and
10. failure to report violations to compliance coordinator.

Items 1, 2, 3, and 6 cover most of the OIG's areas of special concern in the areas of billing and accounting. Patient issues are covered by Items 4 and 5. Items 7, 8, and 9 cover relationships with physicians and other providers. Item 10, the obligation to report to the compliance coordinator, is an area of special concern to the provider for two important reasons. First, a major goal of the compliance program should be to encourage the internal disclosure and self-reporting that are rewarded under the Sentencing Guidelines as discussed above. Second, the obligation to report internally undercuts the legal position of a potential whistle-blower who may report alleged violations to the government rather than the compliance coordinator because of the monetary motivation to share in any recovery under the *qui tam* provisions of the False Claims Act (see Section 8.3). The OIG ignores these provider-oriented dynamics in its compliance guidance.

Providers may, of course, customize and update the form compliance program from time to time to include or exclude any other areas of particular concern to their organization. Providers should stay focused on matters that truly involve special risk in healthcare so that the written standards of conduct are concisely delineated in a manner understandable by the readers of the written compliance standards—namely, all the employees of the organization.

The OIG recognizes that not all standards, policies, and procedures need to be communicated to all employees. However, the OIG believes that the bulk of the standards that relate to complying with fraud and abuse laws and other ethical areas (such as covered by Items 1–10 above) should be addressed and made part of all affected employees' training.[11] More detailed compliance policies and procedures can be disseminated on a departmental or other basis to address specialized matters affecting only smaller groups of employees.

---

### Action Items

1. Develop written standards of conduct for the compliance program that are straightforward and understandable by all employees.
2. Avoid using media buzzwords such as "upcoding" in a written standard; instead, refer to the applicable legal requirement for a precise statement of the applicable standard.
3. Distill the OIG's areas of "special" concern to a concise number of areas that truly require special compliance attention by the provider.

# Notes

1. Hospital Guidance, 63 Fed. Reg. 8987, 8989-90 (1998) (footnotes omitted, emphasis supplied).

2. Ibid. 8990 (footnotes omitted).

3. Home Health Guidance, 63 Fed. Reg. 42410, 42414-5 (1998) (footnotes omitted).

4. Hospital Guidance, 63 Fed. Reg. 8987, 8990, footnote 25 (1998); U.S. Department of Health and Human Services, Office of Inspector General, *Management Advisory Report: Financial Arrangements Between Hospitals and Hospital-Based Physicians*, OEI-09-89-00330, October 1991.

5. American Hospital Association to Richard P. Kusserow, Office of Inspector General, dated March 11, 1991, comment letter on *Management Advisory Report: Financial Arrangements Between Hospitals and Hospital-Based Physicians*, OEI-09-89-00330, October 1991.

6. U.S. Department of Health and Human Services, Office of Inspector General, *National DRG Validation Study Update: Summary Report*, OEI-12-89-00190, August 1992.

7. See also, U.S. Department of Health and Human Services, Office of Inspector General, *Using Software to Detect Upcoding of Hospital Bills*, OEI-01-97-00010, August 1998, Appendix E, endnote 8 (OIG's own study of hospitals identified by software as "upcoding" finds 4.73 percent of claims were undercoded).

8. United States Sentencing Commission, Proceedings of the Second Symposium on Crime and Punishment in the United States, *Corporate Crime in America: Strengthening the "Good Citizen" Corporation*, "A Presentation of Empirical Research on Compliance Practices: What Companies Say They Are Doing—What Employees Hear, A Study of Compliance Practices in 'Compliance Aware' Companies" September 8–9, 1995.

9. 42 U.S.C.A. § 1320a-7a(a)(1)(A) (West 1997).

10. Hospital Guidance, 63 Fed. Reg. 8987, 8990 (1998).

11. Ibid. footnote 10.

# ELEMENT TWO: DESIGNATING A COMPLIANCE OFFICER

## 5.1 Attorneys as Compliance Officers

Designating a compliance officer with the appropriate authority is critical to the success of the compliance program. The OIG believes that a high-level official with direct access to the provider's governing body and the chief executive officer (CEO) should be the compliance officer.[1] In organizations with in-house counsel, the first thought is often to designate the general counsel as the compliance officer. The general counsel would typically have direct access to the provider's governing board and the CEO. The general counsel would have the legal training helpful in understanding and analyzing the complex statutes, regulations, rules, and case law affecting healthcare. Another major factor favoring selection of the general counsel as compliance officer is that compliance communications with the general counsel may be protected from involuntary disclosure by the attorney-client privilege, an evidentiary rule designed to encourage truthful communications between client and counsel. To appreciate the significance of the privilege issue, some legal history is required.

## 5.2 Attorney-Client Privilege

The attorney-client privilege is the oldest of the privileges for confidential communications under common law (i.e., nonstatutory law created by court decisions over the years). Its purpose is to encourage full and frank communication between attorneys and their clients and thereby promote broader public interests in the observance of law and administration of justice. The privilege "is founded upon the necessity, in the interest and administration of justice, of the aid of persons having knowledge of the law and skilled in its practice, which assistance can only be safely and readily availed of when free from the consequences or the apprehension of disclosure."[2] Courts have routinely recognized the attorney-client privilege when the client is a corporation.[3]

The leading case on the organizational use of the attorney-client privilege, *Upjohn v. U.S.*,[4] involved an internal investigation by Upjohn to determine whether any of its employees had violated the Foreign Corrupt Practices Act by making improper payments to foreign officials. In-house attorneys for Upjohn prepared and distributed a questionnaire for area managers asking them to provide full information concerning questionable payments. The managers completed the questionnaires and, as a result of the investigation, the company filed reports with the Securities and Exchange Commission and the Internal Revenue Service (IRS) as required by law. When the IRS received the report, it issued a summons to Upjohn seeking access to all the underlying questionnaires as well as all interview notes with company employees.

The U.S. Supreme Court held that Upjohn could assert the attorney-client privilege under the circumstances. The Court stated:

> The narrow scope given the attorney-client privilege by the court below not only makes it difficult for corporate attorneys to formulate sound advice when their client is faced with a specific legal problem but also threatens to limit the valuable efforts of corporate counsel to ensure their client's compliance with the law. In light of the vast and complicated array of regulatory legislation confronting the modern corporation, corporations, unlike most individuals, constantly go to lawyers to find out how to obey the law, particularly since compliance with the law in this area is hardly an instinctive matter.[5]

The *Upjohn* case set forth the following factors for federal courts to consider in assessing the applicability of the attorney-client privilege when the client is an organization:

1. whether the communications were made for the purpose of securing legal advice;
2. whether the employees making the communications were acting at the direction of corporate superiors;
3. whether the employees were aware that the communications were intended to aid in obtaining legal advice;
4. whether the communications concerned matters within the scope of the employees' duties;
5. whether the information obtained from the employees could have been given by higher level management;

6. whether the employees were informed that the communications were to be treated as highly confidential; and

7. whether such confidentiality was in fact maintained by the corporation.[6]

Privileges are often narrowly construed and may be invoked only when clearly warranted.[7] In addition to satisfying the above-mentioned factors, organizations claiming the privilege with respect to communications with in-house counsel must demonstrate that such counsel was providing strictly legal advice and not business advice, which is not protected by the attorney-client privilege. This distinction can be difficult to draw.

## 5.3 No Fifth Amendment Privilege

Even if the attorney-client privilege can be asserted by an organization, the privilege has limited usefulness because it only protects disclosure of communications between attorney and client; it does not protect disclosure of the underlying facts by those who communicated with the attorney. For example, in the *Upjohn* case, the IRS was free to question the employees who completed the questionnaires or communicated with Upjohn's attorneys. While it would have probably been more convenient for the IRS to secure the results of Upjohn's internal investigation by simply subpoenaing the questionnaires and notes taken by Upjohn's attorneys, the IRS could have obtained the same information by directly posing the same questions to the employees.

Although the Fifth Amendment of the U.S. Constitution protects individuals from having to give compelled, incriminating testimony, it does not do the same for corporations or any other collective entities beyond a simple sole proprietorship.[8] Moreover, an agent of a corporation may not refuse to turn over corporate records that have been subpoenaed even when the content of those records may incriminate the agent himself.[9] As a result, the benefit of the attorney-client privilege for organizations is largely undercut by the lack of a Fifth Amendment privilege against self-incrimination in matters involving organizations.

## 5.4 Conflicts of Interest

The lack of a Fifth Amendment privilege for the organization creates a raging conflict of interest for any in-house attorney who serves as the compliance officer. An employee/perpetrator may disclose information to the attorney thinking a confidential attorney-client relationship exists. As the representative of the organization, the attorney/compliance officer must disclose the offense to the CEO and governing board for investigation, corrective action, and appropriate discipline. The perpetrator's confidence is broken. Furthermore, the organization is motivated to discipline the perpetrator and disclose the perpetrator's actions to government authorities to obtain possible mitigation of organizational sanctions offered by the Sentencing Guidelines for voluntary disclosure and acceptance of responsibility.[10]

John A. Meyers, who was senior vice president, associate general counsel, and special counsel to the CEO of Tenet Healthcare Corporation, formerly known as National Medical Enterprises (NME), experienced the complexity of this attorney conflict. From 1991 to 1994, NME and its psychiatric hospitals were the target of one of the most thorough federal investigations in healthcare history. One of the sanctions imposed on NME was a corporate integrity program, or a government-designed compliance program. At the 1995 symposium sponsored by the United States Sentencing Commission, shortly after leaving Tenet and returning to private practice, Mr. Meyers commented:

> Finally, I wanted to just touch on this. It's the most difficult area. It's the disclosure requirements under the imposed program. As an in-house lawyer, I found it became ever more necessary to Mirandize employees, to tell them, "I am not your lawyer; I am the corporation's lawyer. Things that you tell me that indicate that we have violated law, I must report to our management, and our management must make a decision about what to do with that, given the constraints of the corporate integrity program."
>
> This has a tendency to make your employees less willing to talk to their lawyers. They formerly thought of you as their lawyer, and now they wonder whether they need a lawyer to talk with their ex-lawyer. We tried to solve this problem a number of ways, but I don't really believe that there is a good solution to this problem. I think there is an inherent tension, and I tell you this from personal experience; it played no small role in my decision to leave the corporation, because I believe that in some circumstances I could more effectively represent it from the outside.
>
> And this segues into another notion, which is the role of the attorney. For those of you who are lawyers out there, when you have an imposed program, it will raise issues that will surprise you in their complexity. These issues will make you search for who your client is within the organization, wonder about your function, wonder whether or not your duty is to disclose or to defend under client-attorney privilege, and whether or not to resign. I think it adds a great deal of complexity to operating inside.[11]

Attorneys sometimes use a joint defense agreement, whereby the attorney receiving the disclosure agrees before the disclosure is made to represent the interests of both the organization and the individual making the disclosure, in an attempt to keep the disclosure within the attorney-client privilege. It is hard to imagine a situation in which it is in the interest of the organization, as distinct from an individual with a Fifth Amendment privilege, not to correct and discipline conduct that blatantly violates the law. However, a joint defense agreement may be useful if a good faith question exists about whether the conduct violates any legal standard at all. Even so, the conflict between the interests of an individual perpetrator and the organization puts an attorney/compliance officer in a very difficult situation.

## 5.5 OIG's Hostility Toward Attorneys as Compliance Officers

The OIG has traditionally been hostile to designation of the general counsel or other in-house attorney as the compliance officer. In the Hospital Guidance, the OIG suggests that there is some risk to establishing an independent compliance function if that function is subordinate to the hospital's general counsel, comptroller, or similar chief financial officer (CFO).[12] The OIG believes that by separating the compliance function from the key management positions of general counsel or CFO (where the size and structure of the hospital make this a feasible option), a system of checks and balances is established which more effectively achieves the goals of the compliance program.

Of course, the checks and balances rationale used by the OIG still applies if the compliance function is subordinate to any officer in the organization, including the CEO. This issue is routinely faced by any sort of internal auditor (typically a subordinate of the CFO) within an organization. The system of checks and balances for the internal auditor is generally established by giving the auditor a direct reporting line to the governing body of the organization or a subcommittee thereof (such as the audit committee). Likewise, a system of checks and balances for the compliance officer can be created by providing the compliance officer with a direct reporting line to the governing body of the organization.

Although not specifically addressed in the Hospital Guidance, the OIG must be concerned that when an attorney is the compliance officer, the assertion of the attorney-client privilege for compliance communications may impede the OIG's prosecutorial duties. Asserting the attorney-client privilege for compliance communications may also frustrate the self-reporting component of compliance programs emphasized by the Hospital Guidance and the Sentencing Guidelines.

In today's environment, providers must constantly consult attorneys for legal advice about the vast and complicated array of healthcare laws and regulations. The OIG cannot legitimately expect providers to voluntarily forgo this crucial advice in the course of adopting compliance programs. Providers have the right to appoint a lawyer as the compliance officer or at least involve a lawyer in the prevention, detection, and self-reporting processes of a compliance program. The suggestions by the OIG in the Hospital Guidance and other compliance proclamations that providers should not involve lawyers in the compliance process are not realistic.

## 5.6 Non-Attorneys as Compliance Officers

Providers may also consider non-attorneys for the role of compliance officer. As long as the non-attorney receives a high-ranking position with direct lines of reporting to the governing board and CEO, the non-attorney can have the same management access as the general counsel. One major advantage of the non-attorney may be significant training, experience, and understanding in the high-risk areas of healthcare, such as documentation, coding, physician relations, and patient care issues. These highly technical areas are difficult for even full-time healthcare attorneys to master.

Good organizational relations is another key attribute of any compliance officer. The compliance officer must be able to coordinate the diverse groups and individuals within the organization to implement and maintain an effective compliance program. Also, size of the organization and available resources will affect compliance officer selection. While Columbia/HCA hired a compliance czar, Alan Yuspeh (an attorney), many providers lack the size and/or resources to justify the addition of another high-ranking official to the payroll to handle compliance affairs exclusively. On the other hand, even providers with limited resources must give compliance a high priority in the current environment and must expect that implementation and maintenance of an effective compliance program will require a substantial time commitment for the designated compliance officer.

## 5.7 Who Should Be the Compliance Officer?

Many large organizations already have compliance programs in place and have selected compliance officers. A survey of 200 such large organizations with compliance officers compiled the background of the individual officer. The most common areas of expertise were as follows (presented in order, percentages given if available):

1. general business management (31 percent);
2. legal (26 percent);
3. audit and finance; and
4. human resources.[13]

In conclusion, while the attorney-client privilege can be an asset, the privilege should not drive the decision of who should be the compliance officer. If the provider has an in-house counsel and that counsel is familiar with documentation and coding issues (probably the most likely area for compliance concerns), and that counsel has the organizational relationships and the time necessary to implement and maintain an effective compliance program, the general counsel can be a wise choice as the compliance officer. The general counsel has the legal background often needed to analyze compliance issues and may use the attorney-client privilege when appropriate, although the attorney/compliance officer will face conflicting legal interests between the organization and its individual employees.

Otherwise, the most senior executive in the organization (including the CEO) who is familiar with documentation and coding issues and who has the organizational relationships and the time to oversee the compliance process, should be the compliance officer. If a non-attorney is selected as the compliance officer, he or she should have access to legal counsel as needed.

## 5.8 Compliance Committee(s)

The OIG's Hospital Guidance recommends that a compliance committee (note the singular) be established to advise the compliance officer and assist in the implementation of the compliance program.[14] Furthermore, the OIG believes that the compliance committee will benefit from the perspectives of individuals with varying responsibilities in the organization, such as operations, finance, audit, human resources, utilization review, social work, discharge planning, medicine, coding, and legal, as well as employees and managers of key operating units.[15]

While various perspectives can indeed improve the compliance process, such a diverse compliance committee may also paralyze compliance efforts if the compliance officer must obtain committee-level approval of all elements of the compliance plan. Imagine dozens of meetings, hundreds of viewpoints, and no conclusion being reached on some very pressing compliance issues.

Instead, the compliance officer should be empowered by the governing board of the organization to immediately design and implement a basic written compliance program, such as the form included in this book (see page 161). After implementation of a basic written compliance program, the compliance officer can then constitute committees (subordinate to the compliance officer) to assist the compliance officer in developing and implementing specific guidelines and training in specialized areas. These committees can focus on some of the more detailed and specialized compliance policies recommended by the OIG at the appropriate departmental level. Although the compliance officer should have general authority with respect to implementing the compliance program, the compliance officer should be subject to normal financial budgets and would still report to the governing body of the organization and the CEO. Figure 5.1 depicts the organizational chart for this approach to the compliance officer and compliance committees.

The form compliance program emphasizes this notion of empowerment by giving the person in charge of the compliance program the title of compliance coordinator and authorizing that person to create one or more committees to advise and assist in the implementation of the compliance program. For example, the compliance coordinator may establish the following committees:

**Figure 5.1**  Compliance Organizational Chart

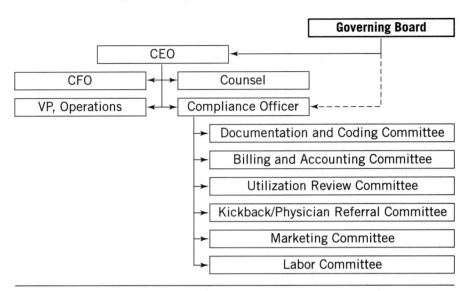

A.  *Documentation and Coding.* Including representatives from health information management (HIM)/medical records, coding, nurses, and physicians to focus on documentation and coding issues such as standards of documentation (timely, descriptive, legible); standards of coding (medical record support, official coding guidelines, no upcoding incentives); special procedures for outpatient services rendered in connection with inpatient stay (DRG 72-hour window), laboratory services, physicians at teaching hospitals (PATH); and definitions of medical necessity.

B.  *Billing/Accounting.* CFO, billing staff, accounting staff, and outside auditors to focus on billing requirements, cost reports, bad debts, credit balances, and tax issues.

C.  *Utilization Review.* Case managers, operations executives, medical staff representatives to focus on patient dumping, discharge, HMO contracts.

D.  *Kickbacks/Physician Referral.* CEO, CFO, legal counsel, and physicians to focus on structures for physician ownership and compensation arrangements to fall within safe harbors and exceptions to anti-kickback and self-referral laws.

E.  *Marketing.* CEO, marketing director, legal counsel to focus on structuring joint ventures, mergers, acquisitions, and other marketing practices to comply with antitrust laws and other ethical standards.

F.  *Labor.* Director of human resources, departmental managers, and labor counsel to focus on labor issues such as equal opportunity, sexual harassment, the Americans with Disabilities Act, and background checks.

In summary, any compliance committees should be subordinate to the compliance officer, or the organization's compliance efforts may be paralyzed.

These committees should also do more than parrot current federal and state statutes and regulations regarding specific healthcare areas. These committees should assist in establishing meaningful written policies and setting the agenda for substantive education.

## 5.9 Duties of the Compliance Officer

The duties and responsibilities of the compliance officer should include the following:

- preparing written guidelines on specific legal and regulatory issues and matters involving ethical and legal business practices;
- developing and implementing an educational training program for personnel to ensure understanding of federal and state laws and regulations involving ethical and legal business practices;
- handling inquiries by employees regarding any aspect of compliance;
- investigating any information or allegation concerning possible unethical or improper business practices and recommending corrective action when necessary;
- providing guidance and interpretation to the governing body of the organization, the CEO, and other personnel, in conjunction with the organization's legal counsel, on matters related to the compliance program;
- developing policies and programs that encourage managers and employees to report suspected fraud and other improprieties without fear of retaliation;
- planning and overseeing regular, periodic audits of operations to identify and rectify any possible barriers to the efficacy of the compliance program;
- preparing at least annually a report to the governing body of the organization and the CEO;
- coordinating personnel issues and background checks with the human resources office (or its equivalent);
- ensuring that independent contractors and agents who furnish medical services to the provider are aware of the provider's compliance program; and
- performing such other duties and responsibilities as the governing body of the organization may request.

The OIG suggests in the Hospital Guidance that the compliance officer be empowered to independently investigate and act on matters related to compliance, including the flexibility to design and coordinate internal investigations (e.g., responding to reports of problems or suspected violations) and take any resulting corrective action with all hospital departments, providers and subproviders, agents, and, if appropriate, independent contractors.[16] Notwithstanding the OIG's recommendation, it would not be prudent for any organization to empower a single individual to direct corrective action—which may involve legal sanctions and expenditures of large sums of money—without due review and approval by the legal counsel, the CEO, and the governing body of the organization. While the compliance officer should have a direct reporting line to the governing body, the compliance officer should be subject to a system of checks and balances as well to ensure the compliance officer appropriately discharges his or her duties.

---

### Action Items

1. Select a compliance officer who is knowledgeable about technical compliance issues, has good organizational relationships, and can devote the time necessary to implement and maintain the compliance program. A legal background is helpful but not required.
2. Understand the limitations of the attorney-client privilege with respect to compliance communications.
3. Organize compliance committees that are subordinate to the compliance officer to avoid paralysis in implementing the compliance program.

---

## Notes

1. Hospital Guidance, 63 Fed. Reg. 8987, 8993 (1998).
2. *Hunt v. Blackburn*, 128 U.S. 464, 470 (1888).
3. *Upjohn Co. v. U. S.*, 449 U.S. 383, 389-90 (1981).
4. Ibid.
5. Ibid. 392-93 (citations omitted).
6. Ibid. 394-5.
7. *United States v. Nixon*, 418 U.S. 683, 710 (1974).
8. *Hale v. Henkel*, 201 U.S. 43 (1906) (corporation has no Fifth Amendment privilege); *United States v. White*, 322 U.S. 694 (1944) (labor union unprotected by Fifth Amendment).
9. *Braswell v. United States*, 487 U.S. 99 (1988).
10. Sentencing Guidelines, § 5K1.1. and § 5K2.16. (1997).
11. United States Sentencing Commission, Proceedings of the Second Symposium on Crime and Punishment in the United States, *Corporate Crime in America: Strengthening the "Good Citizen" Corporation.* "Where Theory and Reality Converge: Three Corporate Experiences in Developing 'Effective' Compliance Programs, A Study of Organizational Practices and Their Effect on Compliance," September 8-9, 1995.
12. Hospital Guidance, 63 Fed. Reg. 8987, 8993, footnote 35 (1998).
13. United States Sentencing Commission, Proceedings of the Second Symposium On Crime and Punishment in the United States. *Corporate Crime in America: Strengthening the "Good Citizen" Corporation.* "A Presentation of Empirical Research on Compliance Practices: What Companies Say They Are Doing—What Employees Hear, A Study of Compliance Practices in 'Compliance Aware' Companies," September 8–9, 1995.
14. Hospital Guidance, 63 Fed. Reg. 8987, 8994 (1998).
15. Ibid. footnote 39.
16. Ibid., 8994.

# *6*

# ELEMENT THREE: EFFECTIVE EDUCATION AND TRAINING

## 6.1 Subject Matter of Education

Of the seven basic elements of a compliance program, the requirement for effective education and training is the most important element from a healthcare management perspective because it can actually prevent violations from occurring. The rules and regulations applicable to healthcare, particularly with respect to documentation and coding, anti-kickback and anti-referral, are perplexing and voluminous. Even the most altruistic and conscientious employees require extensive and continuous education in the various requirements to achieve full compliance in healthcare.

The OIG's Hospital Guidance appropriately recognizes the importance of education and training, stating that all relevant levels of personnel should be made part of various educational and training programs of the hospital. The Hospital Guidance also succinctly summarizes the proper focus of a hospital training program: "These training programs should include sessions highlighting the organization's compliance program, summarizing fraud and abuse laws, coding requirements, claim development and submission processes and marketing practices that reflect current legal and program standards." [1]

More specifically, the Hospital Guidance lists certain items that the training program should cover:

- government and private payor reimbursement principles;
- general prohibitions on paying or receiving remuneration to induce referrals;

- proper confirmation of diagnoses;
- submitting a claim for physician services when rendered by a nonphysician (i.e., the "incident to" rule and the physician physical presence requirement);
- signing a form for a physician without the physician's authorization;
- alterations to medical records;
- prescribing medications and procedures without proper authorization;
- proper documentation of services rendered; and
- duty to report misconduct.[2]

## 6.2 Focus on Documentation and Coding

Except for the duty to report misconduct, all of these listed items relate to documentation, coding, and authorization issues. Similarly, the areas of special concern to the OIG summarized in Tables 4.1 and 4.2 focus on documentation and coding issues. The OIG also highlighted inadequate documentation and incorrect coding as leading causes of improper Medicare payments in its financial statement audit of HCFA for the fiscal year 1996. Table 6.1 summarizes this data.

The OIG identified inadequate or no documentation as the leading type of error found in the HCFA audit, accounting for 47 percent of the improper payments. The government's rule is that if it is not written down, it did not happen. The OIG considers payments to be improper even if the service was provided and was medically necessary but the medical documentation does not so reflect. As a result, accurate documentation becomes absolutely critical to support healthcare billings.

**TABLE 6.1**   Categories of Improper Medicare Payments

| Type of Improper Payment | All Medicare | Hospital Inpatient | Physician | Home Health |
|---|---|---|---|---|
| Insufficient/No Documentation | 47% | 20% | 55% | 46% |
| Lack of Medical Necessity | 37 | 63 | 12 | 53 |
| Incorrect Coding | 9 | 17 | 21 | 0 |
| Noncovered Services | 5 | 0 | 7 | 0 |
| Other | 2 | 0 | 5 | 1 |
| Totals—Improper Payments | 100% | 100% | 100% | 100% |

*Source:* U.S. Department of Health and Human Services, Office of Inspector General. *Report on the Financial Statement Audit of the Health Care Financing Administration for Fiscal Year 1996* (CIN: A-17-95-00096). Washington, D.C., July 1997.

The OIG noted lack of medical necessity as the second most common error, accounting for 37 percent of the errors in all of Medicare and 63 percent of the errors in hospital inpatient services. In many cases, lack of medical necessity is really a subset of inadequate documentation. Generally, physicians are ethical professionals who do not knowingly order medically unnecessary services for their patients; rather, the medical records often do not fully reflect the reasons that the services were necessary in the physician's opinion. Recently adopted federal and state physician self-referral laws significantly limit the occasions in which physicians would benefit financially from their own referrals for ancillary healthcare services. Managed care also provides incentives to physicians not to overutilize services without medical necessity. Often, the problem is simply that the reviewer does not appreciate the medical necessity based on the information (or lack thereof) contained in the medical record.

Inadequate documentation and lack of medical necessity errors combined account for 84 percent of errors in Medicare as a whole, 83 percent in hospital inpatient (the single largest category within Medicare), and 100 percent in home health. In the physician category, incorrect coding errors caused 21 percent of the errors, but even so, the combination of inadequate documentation and lack of medical necessity errors account for two out of every three physician errors identified in the OIG audit. This data confirms that documentation and coding, including the subset issue of medical necessity, should be the primary focus of any compliance program.

## 6.3 Training: Who and How Much?

The organization must provide compliance training programs that explain in a practical manner the specific requirements relating to the areas of special concern in healthcare, particularly documentation and coding. This training must be provided to all affected employees, physicians, independent contractors, and other significant agents.[3] The OIG recognizes that not all standards, policies, and procedures need to be communicated to all employees. Certain employees, such as the janitorial and cafeteria staffs in a hospital, may not require any compliance training at all. The OIG believes, however, that the bulk of the compliance standards relating to fraud and abuse laws and other ethical areas should be made part of all affected employees' training.[4]

The OIG suggests that affected persons be required to receive a minimum number of educational hours per year. In its compliance integrity agreements imposed in settlements of government prosecutions, the OIG usually requires a minimum of one to three hours annually for basic training in overall compliance matters and more training for specialty fields such as billing, documentation, and coding.[5] The organization may elect to establish formal educational credentialing in these important areas. Periodic training updates are critical, especially in operational areas with high employee turnover.

Because documentation and coding are so important in healthcare, compliance programs must involve all healthcare professionals who participate in the documentation and coding process, whether such individuals are direct employees of the provider, nonemployed members of the medical staff, or independent contractors. The Hospital Guidance explains this connection: "Accurate coding depends upon the quality and completeness of the physician's documentation. Therefore, the OIG believes that active staff physician participation in educational programs focusing on coding and documentation should be emphasized by the hospital. . . In addition, where feasible, the OIG believes that a hospital's outside contractors, including physician corporations, should be afforded the opportunity to participate in, or develop their own, compliance training and educational programs, which complement the hospital's standards of conduct, compliance requirements, and other rules and regulations."[6]

## 6.4 The Underreimbursement Issue

Involvement of physicians in documentation and coding education is absolutely critical from management's perspective. According to the OIG's own *1992 National DRG Validation Study Update*,[7] DRG coding errors divided approximately evenly between errors that overreimbursed the hospital and underreimbursed the hospital. More specifically, the study attributed overreimbursement to hospital billing departments aggressively resequencing patient diagnoses to obtain higher reimbursement. Underreimbursement was attributed to physicians generally selecting patient diagnoses with caution, earning their hospitals less reimbursement than they should have received.

Of the DRG coding errors identified in the study, 63 percent resulted from physician misspecification in attesting to the narrative diagnoses in the medical records. These errors on balance significantly underreimbursed the hospital. Among the examples of misspecification are (1) the physician selecting the wrong principal diagnosis and (2) including or excluding a complication, comorbidity, or operating room procedure.

With better knowledge about the technical requirements of specifying diagnoses and procedures, physicians may better document the acuity of illness actually handled by the hospital so that the hospital receives the appropriate reimbursement under the Medicare system. If healthcare managers are going to adopt compliance programs to correct any cases of overreimbursement, it is only appropriate that they correct cases of underreimbursement as well.

Including the issue of underreimbursement within the scope of a compliance program may neutralize the overall revenue impact on the provider from strict adherence to documentation and coding standards.

## 6.5 Legal Concerns about Involving Nonemployed Physicians

The need to involve physicians and other outside contractors in compliance training raises several major legal concerns. First, the furnishing of documentation and coding training to physicians may be characterized as an inducement to refer business to the provider in violation of federal anti-kickback law. Second, the training may be characterized as compensation that is prohibited under the federal physician self-referral law and possibly state-level laws. Third, involvement of independent contractors in the compliance process may be viewed as sufficient control over the independent contractors by the provider so as to obscure the distinction between employee and independent contractor status, possibly making the provider legally liable for the actions of independent contractors (for example, making a hospital liable for an independent physician's malpractice).

As for the federal anti-kickback and self-referral concerns, the requirement that physicians and other contractors receive compliance training should not be considered remuneration or compensation under those statutes, but rather the discharging of a duty to comply, which is entirely consistent with the express directions of the OIG. The fallback position (see Section 14.15) is to provide all compliance training pursuant to a written agreement with the nonemployed physicians and other contractors that fits the arrangement into applicable safe harbors and exceptions to the federal anti-kickback and physician self-referral laws. The physician acknowledgment attached to the form compliance program is an example of such a written agreement.

The employee/independent contractor issue is not easily solved. Documentation and coding issues are closely related to quality of care issues. The new legal requirement of medical necessity involves clinical considerations beyond the issue of whether the service was rendered or not. By including physicians and other independent contractors in compliance training, providers will impair their legal defense to malpractice by their independent contractors. Unfortunately, providers have no other logical choice. To exclude nonemployed physicians from compliance training would leave the provider totally exposed in the number one area of improper Medicare payments as identified by the OIG. The best way to manage the employee/independent contractor issue is to require all contractors to maintain minimum acceptable levels of malpractice and general liability insurance, with standard additional insured provisions for the provider, so that the provider is only at risk for claims in excess of the minimum insurance limits.

## 6.6 Effective Training Methods

Extensive training in all of the areas of special concern to the OIG would require a major investment of time and resources. Managers will be tempted to minimize training costs by using written manuals, videos, or possibly computer interactive programs. A recent survey studied the effectiveness of various compliance training methods and concluded that training programs delivered primarily by means of video, interactive technology, or in game format were ineffective or harmful to a company's compliance environment. Training programs that were delivered in person, interactive, over one contact hour in length, and periodically repeated were found to be effective.[8]

The OIG has publicly favored training programs delivered in person over other methods. Eileen Boyd, former deputy inspector general, stated: "I'm a big believer in hands-on training, where people have a chance to ask questions and get tested on what they were supposed to learn. Putting a manual on a shelf—or herding people into an auditorium to watch a video—doesn't do it for me. If the health care industry is foolish enough to put in compliance programs that aren't viable, they're making a serious mistake."[9]

In selecting the appropriate training methods, healthcare managers should emphasize quality over quantity. Given the OIG's focus on documentation and coding matters, the first step in a compliance program should be to provide focused training, preferably live and in person, on documentation and coding to those personnel with documentation and coding responsibilities, including nonemployed physicians. Training instructors may come from outside or inside the organization; however, for the primary area of documentation and coding, outside experts can provide significant value with their knowledge of the technical requirements. This type of focused training would do far more to prevent the kinds of violations that concern the OIG than distributing to all employees a general written manual or video about compliance.

Over time, the provider should develop a basic compliance seminar, which should be presented to all or nearly all employees and significant contractors, about the existence of the organization's compliance program, business ethics, and basic legal standards relating to healthcare fraud and abuse. Other educational programs for specialty areas such as physician relationships, patient care, marketing practices, labor, and so on, should be developed and implemented by the compliance subcommittees suggested in Section 5.8. Attendance and participation in training programs should be made a condition of continued employment, and failure to comply with training requirements should result in disciplinary action, including possible termination, when such failure is serious. The compliance officer should retain adequate records of compliance training sessions, including attendance logs and material distributed at training sessions. The entire training process should emphasize the positive goals of preventing noncompliant conduct from occurring.

---

### Action Items

1. Provide periodic compliance training focused on documentation and coding issues to all associated professionals, particularly physicians, regardless of whether they are direct employees or independent contractors.
2. Educate to eliminate both overreimbursement and underreimbursement resulting from lack of documentation or evidence of medical necessity.
3. Use effective training methods, such as in-person presentations with an opportunity for questions and answers, to prevent violations from occurring.

---

## Notes

1. Hospital Guidance, 63 Fed. Reg. 8987, 8994 (1998).
2. Ibid., 8995.
3. Ibid.
4. Hospital Guidance, 63 Fed. Reg. 8987, 8990, footnote 10 (1998).
5. Hospital Guidance, 63 Fed. Reg. 8987, 8995, footnote 42 (1998).
6. Ibid., footnotes 43 and 44.
7. U.S. Department of Health and Human Services, Office of Inspector General. *National DRG Validation Study Update: Summary Report*, OEI-12-89-00190. Washington, D.C., August 1992.
8. United States Sentencing Commission, Proceedings of the Second Symposium on Crime and Punishment in the United States. *Corporate Crime in America: Strengthening the "Good Citizen" Corporation.* "A Presentation of Empirical Research on Compliance Practices: What Companies Say They Are Doing—What Employees Hear, A Study of Organizational Practices and Their Effect on Compliance," September 8–9, 1995.
9. *Wall Street Journal*, September 18, 1997, at B1, quoting Eileen Boyd, Deputy Inspector General, U.S. Department of Health and Human Services.

# ELEMENT FOUR: AUDITS AND OTHER EVALUATION TECHNIQUES

## 7.1 What the Audit Should Cover

Although many monitoring techniques are available, both the Sentencing Guidelines and the Hospital Guidance require the use of compliance audits to promote and ensure compliance. Internal or external auditors who have expertise in federal and state healthcare statutes, regulations and federal healthcare program requirements should perform periodic compliance audits. The compliance officer should share the audit findings, including reports of suspected noncompliance, with the provider's senior management on a regular basis.

The OIG declares in its Hospital Guidance that, at a minimum, these audits should be designed to address the hospital's compliance with laws governing the following areas:

- kickback arrangements;
- physician self-referral prohibition;
- CPT and ICD-9 coding;
- claim development and submission;
- cost reporting; and
- marketing.[1]

## 7.2 Is a Financial Audit by an Independent CPA Enough?

Most healthcare providers of any size, particularly hospitals, already obtain financial statement audits from independent certified public accountants (CPAs). The financial statement audit requires more procedures by the CPAs, and results in substantially more expense to the provider, than simpler compilation and review services. Audit reports nevertheless emphasize that the financial statements are the representations of management and the CPAs only perform generally accepted testing procedures to gain a reasonable assurance that the financial statements, taken as a whole, are not materially misstated. Financial statement audits have failed to detect extensive fraud, notably in the savings and loan industry during the late 1980s.

The Private Securities Litigation Reform Act of 1995 added new Section 10A to the Securities Exchange Act of 1934, which requires each public company audit to include procedures designed to provide reasonable assurance of detecting illegal acts that would have a direct and material effect on the determination of financial statement amounts.[2] If, while conducting the audit of the financial statements of a publicly traded company, the auditor becomes aware of information indicating that an illegal act (whether or not material to the financial statements) has or may have occurred, then the auditor must determine the possible consequences of such an act on the company, such as fines, penalties, and damages.[3] The auditor must inform management of the illegal act as soon as practicable. In addition, the auditor must obtain assurance that the board of directors is adequately informed, by management or otherwise, of the illegal act. In the extreme case where the illegal act has a material effect on the financial statements and management has failed to take appropriate remedial actions, the law can obligate the auditor to report the illegal act directly to the Securities and Exchange Commission.[4]

In February 1997, the Auditing Standards Board of the American Institute of Certified Public Accountants (AICPA) issued *Statement of Auditing Standards No. 82* (SAS No. 82), *Consideration of Fraud in a Financial Statement Audit*, which affects all audits of both public and private companies. The new standard describes two types of fraud that are relevant to the auditor's consideration of fraud in a financial statement audit: fraudulent financial reporting and misappropriation of assets. SAS No. 82 requires the auditor to specifically assess the risk of material misstatement resulting from fraud on every audit. An AICPA practice aid specifically suggests that auditors of healthcare organizations should be aware of the intense scrutiny by governmental bodies, watchdog groups, and other interested parties that place unusual pressure on management, particularly in the following areas:

- improper billing of services performed by residents;

- inappropriate transfers or discharges;
- illegal arrangements involving physicians;
- improper referrals; and
- billing for nonapproved medical devices.[5]

## 7.3 Materiality in Healthcare Compliance

The major difficulty in relying exclusively on financial accounting audits for legal compliance purposes is the definition of materiality that is an integral part of generally accepted auditing and accounting principles. Even after the issuance of SAS No. 82, auditors still use testing procedures designed to identify instances of material misstatements. Materiality is not quantified in the auditing standards and can vary as a matter of opinion. One rule of thumb is that cumulative audit adjustments exceeding 5 percent of net income for the period under audit would be material. In applying this notion of materiality to a company like Columbia/HCA, which in 1997 owned more than 300 hospitals around the world, the external auditors would inspect only a sampling of the individual hospitals and even then inspect only a sampling of the transactions at such hospitals. Even if some of the sampled transactions required adjustment for financial statement purposes, such adjustments would be made only if they are material to the financial statements taken as a whole. Auditors often do not make possible audit adjustments because the impact on the financial statements taken as a whole is immaterial.

The notion of materiality is different with respect to legal compliance in the area of healthcare. The OIG has declared a zero tolerance policy toward fraud and abuse in its Model Lab Compliance Program.[6] Immaterial violations quickly become material when the financial penalties can be triple the amount of the claim plus $10,000 per claim, and can also include the death penalty of exclusion from federal health benefit programs. For example, the monetary penalty for a false claim of $10 can be as much as $10,030 per claim.

Furthermore, the OIG's Hospital Guidance states that "even when a hospital is owned by a larger corporate entity, the regular auditing and monitoring of the compliance activities of an individual hospital must be a key feature in any annual review."[7] Columbia/HCA must perform regular compliance audits at each of its more than 300 hospitals to satisfy the OIG, something it would not be required to do for its financial statement audit.

Providers must face financial reality in designing compliance audits. Just as the OIG cannot afford to review each and every claim for federal reimbursement, providers likewise cannot afford to audit each and every claim or transaction that involves compliance issues. Providers must employ reasonable testing procedures to perform compliance audits on an economical basis. It may be possible to perform compliance audits at each individual hospital or location of large provider systems in a cost-efficient manner by using the providers' independent CPAs and rotating the compliance audits over a three- to five-year period, similar to accreditation reviews. The provider should ask the CPA to issue a separate report to the compliance officer to document the compliance audits.

## 7.4 Snapshots and Benchmarking

The introductory section of the OIG's Hospital Guidance boldly states: "The existence of benchmarks that demonstrate implementation and achievements are essential to any effective compliance program."[8] The Hospital Guidance later expands on the benchmarking idea:

> The OIG recommends that when a compliance program is established in a hospital, the compliance officer, with the assistance of department managers, should take a "snapshot" of their operations from a compliance perspective. This assessment can be undertaken by outside consultants, law or accounting firms, or internal staff, with authoritative knowledge of health care compliance requirements. This "snapshot," often used as part of benchmarking analyses, becomes a baseline for the compliance officer and other managers to judge the hospital's progress in reducing or eliminating potential areas of vulnerability. For example, it has been suggested that a baseline level include the frequency and percentile levels of various diagnosis codes and the increased billing of complications and co-morbidities.[9]

Once the snapshot is taken, monitoring techniques may include sampling protocols that permit the compliance officer to identify and review variations from an established baseline. Significant variations from the baseline should trigger an inquiry to determine the cause of the deviation. If the inquiry determines that the deviation occurred for legitimate, explainable reasons, the compliance officer may limit any corrective action or take no action, with appropriate documentation of such a decision. If improper procedures or misunderstanding of rules caused the deviation, the compliance officer should take prompt steps to correct the problem.[10]

The provider should promptly return to the affected payor any overpayments discovered as a result of such deviations, with appropriate documentation and a thorough explanation of the reason for the refund.[11] In addition, if the compliance officer has reason to believe that such deviations violate criminal, civil, or administrative law, then the Hospital Guidance demands that the provider report to the appropriate governmental authority within a reasonable period not to exceed 60 days after determining there is credible evidence of a violation.[12]

## 7.5 Dangers of the Snapshot

The OIG offers no amnesty for voluntarily reporting violations that might be discovered in the process of taking the snapshot. Indeed, federal regulations declare that, absent extraordinary mitigating circumstances, the aggregate penalty should never be less than double the amount of the claim.[13] In the government's healthcare enforcement projects, the government offers the following deal: the provider can extrapolate the reported violations over the entire six-year limitations period and pay up to double the extrapolated amount, or the government may prosecute and seek triple the extrapolated amount plus $10,000 per claim.[14] Thus, the process of taking the snapshot puts the provider at extreme risk, particularly for innocent violations that might be prevented on a going-forward basis by an effective compliance program.

Furthermore, the snapshot process recommended by the Hospital Guidance is not really benchmarking. Benchmarking is an effort to find what policies and practices work the best. The individual provider's practices, or the average or most prevalent practices in the industry, might not be the best or even satisfactory in the current regulatory environment.

## 7.6 Prospective Benchmarking

From the provider standpoint, it is far too dangerous to take a shapshot that might result in sanctions up to double an extrapolated amount over six years. The benchmark is already clear without a historical snapshot: zero instances of fraud and abuse. The provider should act on a prospective, not retrospective, basis. The provider should first educate all employees, contractors, and agents to fairly understand their compliance obligations and the applicable legal and ethical requirements, and only then should the provider begin using auditing and other monitoring techniques to assess compliance with the fairly articulated standards.

## 7.7 Other Monitoring Techniques

In addition to the substantive compliance audits, an effective compliance program should also incorporate periodic (at least annual) reviews of whether the provider is effectively implementing and maintaining the compliance program. For example, such review would confirm that the program's written standards have been appropriately disseminated, ongoing educational programs have been furnished, and discipline has been imposed as necessary. Such reviews could support the creation and maintenance of appropriate records to document the implementation of an effective compliance program. If monitoring discloses that the provider did not detect deviations in a timely manner because of program deficiencies, the provider must modify the compliance program appropriately.

The Hospital Guidance recommends that providers consider the following techniques as part of the review process:

- on-site visits;
- interviews with personnel involved in management, operations, coding, claim development and submission, patient care, and other related activities;
- questionnaires to solicit impressions of a broad cross section of the hospital's employees and staff;
- reviews of medical and financial records and other source documents that support claims for reimbursement and Medicare cost reports;
- reviews of written materials and documentation prepared by the different divisions of a hospital; and
- trend analyses, or longitudinal studies, that seek deviations, positive or negative, in specific areas over a given period.[15]

The reviewers should:

- be independent of physicians and line management;
- have access to existing audit and healthcare resources, relevant personnel, and all relevant areas of operation;
- present written evaluative reports on compliance activities to the compliance officer, CEO, and governing body on a regular basis, but no less than annually; and
- specifically identify areas that need corrective actions.

Management should coordinate the scope of these compliance reviews with the financial statement audits to avoid duplication of effort and expense. For example, CPAs would likely perform the reviews of financial records for general billing compliance while clinical teams may be formed to review medical records for documentation and coding compliance. The review process should include creating a written report to document the provider's efforts to comply with applicable statutes, regulations, and federal healthcare program requirements. Form 7.1 presents a basic compliance audit checklist, which should be tailored to cover the specific risk areas applicable to the healthcare provider.

### FORM 7.1   Compliance Audit Checklist

(To be completed for each compliance audit performed)

The following checklist includes only the basic procedures recommended for a compliance audit. Additional procedures should be developed by compliance officials as appropriate to address particular areas of concern.

1. _____   Conduct interviews with hospital personnel involved in management, operations, and other related activities concerning adherence to the compliance policy.

2. _____   Conduct at least one random review of hospital records, giving special attention to procedures relating to document-ation, coding, and billing.

3. _____   Conduct at least one random review of hospital records, giving special attention to procedures relating to the giving and receiving of remuneration to induce referrals.

4. _____   Conduct at least one random review of hospital records, giving special attention to procedures relating to engagement in certain business affiliations or pricing arrangements that may affect competition.

5. _____   Review new written materials and documentation procedures used by the hospital to identify any compliance issues and incorporate solutions into the compliance policy, if necessary.

6. _____   Review compliance hotline log to determine current compli-ance issues or problems, evaluate the impact of any corrective action taken in response to hotline reports, and establish appropriate guidelines for preventive action.

7. _____   Review employee evaluations and sanction records to determine if disciplinary procedures are followed and if further actions and/or sanctions are warranted.

8. _____   Prepare report to board of directors (or other governing body) concerning compliance activities and actions undertaken during the preceding year, the proposed compliance program/ education for the next year, and any recommendations for changes in the compliance program.

---

### Action Items

1. Coordinate with the provider's independent CPAs to design an audit program for compliance purposes, including fraud detection measures.
2. Avoid retrospective shapshots; use benchmarking on a prospective basis only after furnishing initial education for affected employees and agents.
3. Develop procedures for periodic (at least annual) reviews of the compliance program's implementation and maintenance.

---

# Notes

1. Hospital Guidance, 63 Fed. Reg. 8987, 8996 (1998).
2. Public Law 104-67, December 22, 1995, adding 15 U.S.C. § 78j-1.
3. 15 U.S.C.A. § 78j-1(b) (West 1997).
4. Ibid.
5. American Institute of Certified Public Accountants, *Considering Fraud in a Financial Statement Audit: Practical Guidance for Applying SAS No. 82,* pp. 101–2 (1997).
6. U.S. Department of Health and Human Services, Office of Inspector General, *Model Compliance Plan for Clinical Laboratories,* February 1997, p. 1.
7. Hospital Guidance, 63 Fed. Reg. 8987, 8996, footnote 50 (1998).
8. Ibid., 8988.
9. Ibid., 8996, footnote 51.
10. Ibid., 8996.
11. Ibid.
12. Ibid., footnote 52.
13. 42 C.F.R. § 1003.106(c)(3) (1997).
14. United States General Accounting Office, Report to Congressional Requesters. *Medicare— Application of the False Claims Act to Hospital Billing Practices.* GAO/HEHS-98-195. July 1998, p.9.
15. Hospital Guidance, 63 Fed. Reg. 8987, 8997 (1998).

# ELEMENT FIVE: INTERNAL REPORTING PROCESSES

## 8.1 Open Lines of Communication

The primary reporting process in an effective compliance program should be open lines of communication between the compliance officer and provider personnel. The compliance officer should have an open-door policy to encourage communications. The compliance officer should make an effort to be visible and known to employees and provide opportunities for communications beyond an official meeting.

The compliance officer should also develop several independent reporting paths for an employee to report fraud, waste, or abuse so that supervisors or other personnel cannot divert such reports. Ideally, effective personal communications with the compliance officer or others within the organization will avoid the need to resort to impersonal forms of communications such as a hotline or reporting outside the organization to the *qui tam* plaintiffs' bar or the government.

The affirmative obligation of each employee to report compliance issues to the compliance officer is also an important component of the compliance program. The form compliance program requires employees to immediately report to the compliance officer any suspected or actual violations (whether or not based on personal knowledge) of applicable law or regulations by the provider or any of its employees. Once an employee has made a report, the employee is obligated to update the report as the employee discovers new information. Each employee must acknowledge in writing both the existence of the compliance program and, specifically, the employee's reporting obligation under the form compliance program.

The obligation of employees to report misconduct creates a procedure similar to an honor system, which has been adopted at many U.S. universities. In an honor system, persons are trusted to abide by certain regulations without official supervision or surveillance. The honor system provides that both the act of unethical conduct and the failure to report a known act of unethical conduct are equally culpable. While an effective compliance program must still include supervisory elements, the employee reporting obligation contained in the form compliance program deters violations of the provider's compliance policy and has other important ramifications discussed below.

## 8.2 Nonretaliation Policies for Reporting

The Sentencing Guidelines require that compliance policies must ensure that employees can report noncompliant behavior without fear of retribution.[1] Providers should develop written nonretaliation policies and distribute them to all employees to encourage communication and the reporting of incidents of potential fraud. More important, organizations must in fact protect employees from retaliation when they make compliance reports. Some compliance policies require that employees make reports in good faith, attempting to reserve disciplinary actions against employees who make false or fraudulent reports for their own personal purposes. However, "good faith" is subject to wide interpretation in litigation and any arguably retaliatory action may invalidate the entire compliance program. The safer course, as followed by the form compliance program, Section 4.A.1., is to ensure that under no circumstances shall the reporting of any information or possible impropriety serve as a basis for any retaliatory actions.

Going beyond the requirements of the Sentencing Guidelines, the OIG believes that employee–whistle-blowers who sue under the False Claims Act should be protected against retaliation, in addition to employees who report to the compliance officer within the confines of a compliance program.[2] The OIG asserts that in many cases, employees sue their employers under the False Claims Act's *qui tam* provisions out of frustration because of the company's failure to take action when a questionable, fraudulent, or abusive situation was brought to the attention of senior corporate officials.[3] Indeed, the False Claims Act itself protects employee–whistle-blowers from retaliation with all remedial relief necessary to make the employee whole, including reinstatement, double back pay, special damages, and attorney's fees.[4]

## 8.3 Policies for Not Reporting Internally

Consider the situation in which the provider does have effective reporting mechanisms that require the employee to report to the compliance officer and that protect the employee against retaliation for reporting. Can the employee simply ignore his reporting obligations under the compliance program and seek the monetary rewards available to whistle-blowers under the False Claims Act? If so, employee–whistle-blowers would completely undermine the purpose of the compliance program and the provider's ability to obtain reduced sanctions by self-reporting illegal conduct to the government before an official investigation commences.

Courts have not decided this issue definitively yet. However, the equities clearly shift toward the provider if the whistle-blower ignored internal compliance processes, which might have prevented or limited the alleged illegal conduct without government or judicial intervention. While it would still be risky for the provider to retaliate against a whistle-blower, even an employee–whistle-blower who breached an internal reporting obligation, the employee's breach would be a strong mitigating factor in assessing sanctions and may even provide a legal basis for a counterclaim against the whistle-blower to deter *qui tam* actions. Such a counterclaim could not be a retaliatory action for reporting a compliance violation; rather it would be strictly an action for failing to report the violation as required by the terms of the compliance program. Therefore, an internal employee reporting obligation is a critical aspect for achieving the compliance program goal of making government and judicial intervention unnecessary.

## 8.4 Hotlines

Although not mentioned in the Sentencing Guidelines, the OIG specifically encourages the use of a hotline telephone number that employees can use to anonymously report suspected misconduct.[5] Matters reported through the hotline or other communication sources should be documented and investigated promptly to determine their veracity. The compliance officer should maintain a hotline log that records such calls, including the nature of any investigation and its results. Such information should be included in reports to the governing body and the CEO. Form 8.1 presents a basic form for recording each hotline call and its disposition.

The provider may elect to outsource its hotline function to an independent contractor, which would maintain the telephone line, answering service, and recordkeeping. Employees may be more comfortable reporting to an independent

**FORM 8.1 Compliance Hotline Log**

Date (MM/DD/YY): _____ / _____ / _____     Time: _____ a.m./p.m.

Nature of call (circle one):
Report Violation          Question          Complaint          Other (specify below)

_____

Caller's comments: _____

_____

_____

_____

_____

_____

_____

Taken by: _____
                    Name of hotline operator

**For Administrative Use Only:**

Actions Taken: _____

_____

_____

_____

_____

_____

Recommended Corrective Actions/Preventive Measures: _____

_____

_____

_____

_____

_____

Signed: _____
                    Name of compliance coordinator or other administrator filling out report
            [ATTACH ADDITIONAL NOTES OR COMMENTS TO THIS PAGE]

party than they would if hotline calls are answered within the provider. The Hospital Guidance does not require the use of nationwide toll-free numbers, but the use of some sort of toll-free number may encourage reporting to the provider's hotline if employees live outside of a single local calling area.

The Hospital Guidance recommends that the provider make the hotline telephone number readily available to all employees and independent contractors, possibly by conspicuously posting the telephone number in common work areas. The OIG then goes on to declare that "[h]ospitals should also post in a prominent, available area the HHS-OIG Hotline telephone number, 1-800-HHS-TIPS (447-8477), in addition to any company hotline number that may be posted."[6] Providers who take the trouble to implement compliance programs should question the advisability of posting the OIG's hotline number. If employees choose to report directly to the OIG rather than to the compliance officer or the provider's hotline, the organization loses the opportunity to receive reduced sanctions for self-reporting under the Sentencing Guidelines. A primary reason for providers to adopt compliance programs is to reduce the need for governmental and judicial oversight. By asking healthcare providers to advertise the OIG's hotline number, the OIG is actually encouraging continued and possibly increased government involvement in healthcare compliance.

Ironically, the very need for an anonymous hotline suggests that the organization has failed to create an environment in which employees can report noncompliant conduct within the organization without fear of retribution, as required by the Sentencing Guidelines. The hotline may also be used to report employment-related issues that really do not involve serious compliance matters. Nevertheless, hotlines are easy to establish and inexpensive to maintain, so organizations should use their own hotlines (not the OIG's) while keeping in mind the limitations of hotlines as a compliance reporting tool.

## 8.5 Confidentiality

The OIG emphasizes anonymous reporting and the related concept of confidentiality.[7] However, as discussed in Section 5.3, the organization has no Fifth Amendment right against self-incrimination. Other privileges such as attorney-client and attorney work product may not apply, particularly if the compliance officer is not an attorney (as the OIG recommends). The Hospital Guidance recognizes that "while the hospital should always strive to maintain the confidentiality of an employee's identity, it should also explicitly communicate that there may be a point where the individual's identity may become known or may have to be revealed in certain instances when governmental authorities become involved."[8]

The form compliance program adopts the OIG's advice on confidentiality. All information reported to the hotline by any employee in accordance with the form compliance program shall be kept confidential by the provider to the extent that confidentiality is possible throughout any resulting investigation; however, there may be a point at which the provider may have to reveal an employee's identity in certain instances when governmental authorities become involved. The form compliance program provides assurance that under no circumstances shall the reporting of any such information or possible impropriety serve as a basis for any retaliatory actions against any employee, patient, or other person making the report.

---

### Action Items

1. Provide open lines of communication with an accessible compliance officer to make internal reporting a part of the organization's culture.
2. Emphasize the obligation of employees to report internally to the compliance officer, rather than the government or a *qui tam* plaintiffs' attorney.
3. Establish a hotline and associated procedures for documenting each call and its disposition.

---

## Notes

1. Sentencing Guidelines, § 8A1.2., Application Note 3(k) (1997)
2. Hospital Guidance, 63 Fed. Reg. 8987, 8995, footnote 45 (1998).
3. Ibid.
4. 31 U.S.C.A. § 3730(h) (West 1997).
5. Hospital Guidance, 63 Fed. Reg. 8987, 8995 (1998).
6. Ibid., footnote 46.
7. Ibid.
8. Ibid.

# ELEMENT SIX: DISCIPLINARY MECHANISMS

## 9.1 Discipline Under the Compliance Program

The OIG believes the compliance program should include a written policy statement setting forth the degrees of disciplinary actions that may be imposed on corporate officers, managers, employees, physicians, and other healthcare professionals for failing to comply with the provider's standards and policies and applicable statutes and regulations.[1] Such discipline could range from oral warnings to suspension, privilege revocation (subject to any applicable peer review procedures), termination, or financial penalties (such as reduction in pay), as appropriate.[2]

The form compliance program includes this range of sanctions, with the important addition of retraining. Many technical violations in federal healthcare reimbursement may be purely innocent, and the only fair and effective sanction may be to require training or retraining so the employee will not repeat the violation. If the violation recurs, the more serious and punitive sanctions should then be fairly imposed. The provider should also include adherence to the elements of the compliance program as a factor in formal employee evaluations.[3]

## 9.2 Imprisonment Is Possible

The OIG states that intentional or reckless noncompliance should subject transgressors to significant sanctions. Theoretically, the noncompliance must be intentional or at least reckless before the conduct becomes illegal. Once illegal conduct occurs, the sanctions do indeed become more significant. While not stated in the preceding range of disciplinary actions, illegal conduct such as criminal healthcare fraud is punishable by up to ten years' imprisonment and fines of up to a quarter of a million dollars. Organizations cannot go to jail; only individuals can. With the criminal indictments of three Columbia/HCA middle managers in 1997, federal prosecutors announced their intention to seek the most severe disciplinary actions possible against employees of healthcare providers involved in illegal conduct.

The perpetrators are not the only ones exposed to disciplinary action. The OIG believes that corporate officers, managers, supervisors, medical staff, and other healthcare professionals should be held accountable for failing to comply with, or for the foreseeable failure of their subordinates to adhere to, applicable standards, laws, and procedures.[4] The form compliance program adopts this standard by including as a compliance program violation any lack of attention or diligence on the part of supervisory personnel that directly or indirectly leads to a violation of law.

## 9.3 Avoid Overemphasizing the Negative

While disciplinary standards are a necessary element of an effective compliance program, it is important not to dwell on the negative. When people are threatened with discipline, fear and resentment are natural consequences. Fear of investigation may cause employees to overreact, such as refusing to document, code, or bill for unusual or extraordinary services that were actually provided but involved circumstances that might cause the service provider to be scrutinized. Resentment may undercut the provider's attempt to create open communications about compliance issues.

People want to understand and appreciate the positive side of their actions. Providers should emphasize the positive aspects of compliance, such as:

- Accurate documentation and coding can eliminate both overreimbursement and underreimbursement, making the provider more compliant and economically stable.
- By carefully monitoring and recording clinical conditions, providers can improve the appropriateness of patient care.
- More efficient use of resources will make the provider more attractive to cost-conscious payors, both public and private.
- Structuring proper physician incentives can avoid or reduce unnecessary medical services.

## 9.4 New Employee Policy

According to the OIG, the employee application should specifically require the applicant to disclose any criminal conviction or Medicare exclusion action.[5] The provider should prohibit employing individuals who have been recently convicted of a criminal offense related to healthcare or who have been debarred, excluded, or otherwise ineligible for participation in federal healthcare programs. Likewise, healthcare compliance programs should establish standards prohibiting the execution of contracts with companies that have been recently convicted of a criminal offense related to healthcare or that are debarred, excluded, or otherwise ineligible for participation in federal healthcare programs.[6]

The OIG recommends that providers conduct a reasonable and prudent background investigation, including a reference check, for all new employees who have discretionary authority to make decisions that may involve compliance with the law or compliance oversight.[7] The OIG produces a *Cumulative Sanction Report* that reflects the status of healthcare providers who have been excluded from participation in the Medicare and Medicaid programs. The *Cumulative Sanction Report* is updated regularly and is available on the Internet at www.dhhs.gov/progorg/oig. In addition, the General Services Administration maintains a monthly listing of debarred contractors on the Internet at www.arnet.gov/epls. Legislation enacted in 1996 mandated the development of a healthcare fraud and abuse database.[8] When this database becomes operational, providers should also check it as part of its employee screening process.

---

### Action Items

1. Establish disciplinary mechanisms for noncompliant conduct, including retraining for innocent technical violations, but emphasize the positive aspects of compliance more than the sanctions.
2. Update employee evaluation forms to include compliance as a factor, and update new employee and contracting policies to include background checks for criminal records and exclusion from federal health programs.

---

## Notes

1. Hospital Guidance, 63 Fed. Reg. 8987, 8995 (1998).
2. Ibid., 8996.
3. Ibid., 8993.
4. Ibid., 8996.
5. Ibid.
6. Ibid.
7. Ibid.
8. 42 U.S.C.A. § 1320a-7e (West 1997).

# ELEMENT SEVEN: INVESTIGATION AND REMEDIATION

## 10.1 Prompt Investigation

Detected but uncorrected misconduct can seriously endanger the mission, reputation, and legal status of the healthcare provider. Consequently, on reports or reasonable indications of suspected noncompliance, the chief compliance officer or other management officials must initiate prompt steps to investigate the conduct in question to determine whether a material violation of applicable law or the requirements of the compliance program has occurred and, if so, take steps to correct the problem. As appropriate, such steps may include a corrective action plan, the repayment of any overpayments, and a report to criminal and/or civil law enforcement authorities, if applicable.[1]

For most alleged violations, an internal investigation will probably include interviews and a review of relevant documents. The provider should consider engaging outside counsel, auditors, or healthcare experts to assist in the investigation. Records of the investigation should contain documentation of the alleged violation, a description of the investigative process, copies of interview notes and key documents, a log of the witnesses interviewed and the documents reviewed, the results of the investigation (e.g., any disciplinary action taken), and the corrective action implemented. While any action taken as the result of an investigation will necessarily vary depending on the situation, the provider should strive for some consistency by using sound practices and disciplinary protocols. Further, after a reasonable period, the compliance officer should review the circumstances that formed the basis for the investigation to determine whether similar problems have been uncovered on other occasions.[2]

## 10.2 Corrective Action

The provider should take appropriate corrective action, including prompt identification and restitution of any overpayment to the affected payor and the imposition of proper disciplinary action against the responsible parties. HCFA regulations and contractor guidelines already include procedures for returning overpayments to the government as the provider discovers them. For example, HCFA's *Medicare Program Manual for Hospitals* (hospital manual) establishes detailed procedures for identifying and recovering "credit balances" due to Medicare.[3] A credit balance is defined by HCFA as an improper or excess payment made to a provider as a result of patient billing or claims processing errors. When a provider receives an improper or excess payment for a claim, it may be reflected in the provider's accounting records (patient accounts receivable) as a "credit." However, Medicare credit balances as defined by HCFA include monies due to the Medicare program regardless of its classification in a provider's accounting records. Examples of Medicare credit balances include instances in which a provider was:

- paid twice for the same service either by Medicare or by Medicare and another insurer (duplicate billing);
- paid for services planned but not performed or for noncovered services (false claims or upcoding);
- overpaid because of errors made in calculating beneficiary deductible and/or coinsurance amounts; or
- overpaid for outpatient services that were billed separately but should have been included in a beneficiary's inpatient claim (unbundling).[4]

Under HCFA's procedures, the hospital must complete and submit a *Medicare Credit Balance Report* (HCFA-838) to the Medicare intermediary within 30 days after the close of each calendar quarter.[5] The hospital must report all Medicare credit balances shown in its records regardless of when they occurred.[6] Detailed information is required on each credit balance on a claim-by-claim basis.[7] Repayment of all amounts owed to Medicare is due at the time the provider submits the HCFA-838. However, the hospital manual states that if the amount owed Medicare is so large that immediate repayment would cause financial hardship, the hospital should contact the Medicare intermediary regarding an extended repayment schedule.[8]

HCFA-838 provides a mechanism for returning any overpayments to the federal government (through the fiscal intermediary) that might be discovered in the course of the compliance program without directly involving enforcement officials at the OIG (see Section 10.3). Even if the overpayment detection and return process is working, the OIG still believes that the compliance officer needs to be made aware of these overpayments, violations, or deviations and look for trends or patterns that may demonstrate a systemic problem.[9]

## 10.3  Voluntary Disclosure to the Government

The OIG currently maintains a voluntary disclosure program that encourages providers to report suspected fraud. The government knows that it alone cannot protect the integrity of Medicare and other federal healthcare programs. Healthcare providers must be willing to police themselves, correct underlying problems, and work with the government to resolve these matters. The OIG's voluntary self-disclosure program has four prerequisites: (1) the disclosure must be on behalf of an entity and not an individual; (2) the disclosure must be truly voluntary (i.e., no pending proceeding or investigation); (3) the entity must disclose the nature of the wrongdoing and the harm to the federal programs; and (4) the entity must not be the subject of a bankruptcy proceeding before or after the self-disclosure.[10]

## 10.4  Obligation to Report to the Government?

Even when the provider detects, investigates, and corrects noncompliant conduct —for example, by repaying any Medicare overpayment to the intermediary— the provider has not yet satisfied the OIG's demands. In the Hospital Guidance, the OIG makes the following controversial statement concerning the provider's obligation to report the noncompliant conduct to enforcement officials:

> If the compliance officer, compliance committee or management official discovers credible evidence of misconduct from any source and, after a reasonable inquiry, has reason to believe that the misconduct may violate criminal, civil or administrative law, then the hospital promptly should report the existence of misconduct to the appropriate governmental authority within a reasonable period, but not more than sixty (60) days after determining that there is credible evidence of a violation.[11]

In addition to the provider's normal reporting to the Medicare intermediary, the OIG requires separate reporting to federal and/or state law enforcement authorities having jurisdiction over such matter.[12] Appropriate federal and state authorities include, according to the OIG, the criminal and civil divisions of the Department of Justice, the U.S. attorney in the provider's district, and the investigative arms for the agencies administering the affected federal or state healthcare programs, such as the state Medicaid Fraud Control Unit, the Defense Criminal Investigative Service, the Office of Inspector General of the Department of Health and Human Services, and the Department of Veterans Affairs and the Office of Personnel Management (which administers the Federal Employee Health Benefits Program).[13] The need for reporting to, and involvement of, enforcement officials is exactly what effective compliance programs should obviate. Because healthcare providers already are obligated to furnish periodic reports about Medicare overpayments to the Medicare intermediary, an agent of the federal government, further reporting to the OIG is unnecessarily redundant.

The Sentencing Guidelines state that the sentencing reduction does not apply if, after becoming aware of a criminal offense (not civil or administrative), the organization unreasonably delays reporting the criminal offense to appropriate governmental authorities. However, the Sentencing Guidelines specifically allow the organization a reasonable period of time to conduct an internal investigation and no reporting is required if the organization reasonably concludes, based on the information then available, that no criminal offense had been committed.[14] The organization's burden to report under the Sentencing Guidelines is limited to criminal offenses, and crimes must be proved beyond a reasonable doubt.

The OIG demands reporting when, after a reasonable inquiry, the organization has reason to believe that the misconduct may violate criminal, civil, or administrative law. By including civil and administrative violations, which may exist with a much lower burden of proof than criminal violations, the OIG greatly expands the organization's reporting burden over the requirements of the Sentencing Guidelines.

Under the Sentencing Guidelines, a failure to report means that the organization does not receive the proffered reduction in sanctions; the failure to report is not in itself a criminal act. As for healthcare compliance, does the failure to report to appropriate government officials merely mean that the OIG may not recognize the compliance program as effective and worthy of the promised leniency, or is the failure to report actionable in itself?

The OIG cites the criminal provisions of the Social Security Act, which prohibit anyone who knows of any event affecting Medicare reimbursement from concealing or failing to disclose that event, with the intention of fraudulently securing such benefit or payment either in a greater amount or quantity than is due or when no such benefit or payment is authorized.[15] The OIG may interpret any failure to repay overpayments within a reasonable period of time as an intentional attempt to conceal the overpayment from the government, thereby establishing an independent basis for a criminal violation with respect to the provider, as well as any individuals who may have been involved.  For this reason, healthcare compliance programs should emphasize that the provider shall promptly return all overpayments obtained from Medicare or other federal healthcare programs.

The repayment of any overpayments, and the filing of the HCFA-838 in the case of hospitals in accordance with the intermediary's procedures, will discharge the obligation to disclose under the cited statute as well as other federal statutes prohibiting concealment and obstruction of justice,[16] without any duplicative reporting to the various enforcement agencies listed by the OIG. If government authorities ask about the circumstances surrounding the overpayments, the organization and its employees and agents are obligated to respond because the organization has no Fifth Amendment privilege against self-incrimination. Once repayment is made in accordance with the intermediary's procedures, however, the organization has no legal obligation to affirmatively report the circumstances to enforcement authorities.

Where the violations are serious and likely to be investigated even after repayment, the organization may choose to notify enforcement authorities to gain the benefits of sanction reduction under the Sentencing Guidelines and the OIG's less explicit promises of leniency; however, no affirmative legal duty exists. In other cases, particularly in which the violations are unintentional, the organization may conclude after consulting with its legal counsel that repayment in accordance with the intermediary's procedures is sufficient remediation, and duplicative reporting to the various enforcement agencies listed by the OIG is not necessary or advisable under the circumstances. Providers facing this decision should definitely consult with competent legal counsel before acting.

## 10.5 How to Report to Enforcement Officials

If the provider elects to report to enforcement officials, it should do so as soon as possible. The Hospital Guidance allows 60 days after determining that there is credible evidence of the violation, and the Sentencing Guidelines allow a reasonable period after becoming aware of the offense. However, the provider must provide the report to the government within 30 days after the date when the provider first obtained the information to qualify for provisions of the False Claims Act that can reduce sanctions from triple damages plus $10,000 per claim to not less than double damages without the $10,000 per claim.[17]

The OIG believes that some violations may be so serious that they warrant immediate notification to governmental authorities prior to, or simultaneous with, commencing an internal investigation, if, for example, the conduct: (1) is a clear violation of criminal law; (2) has a significant adverse effect on the quality of care provided to program beneficiaries (in addition to any other legal obligations regarding quality of care); or (3) indicates evidence of a systemic failure to comply with applicable laws, an existing corporate integrity agreement, or other standards of conduct, regardless of the financial impact on federal healthcare programs.[18] Prompt reporting will demonstrate the provider's good faith and willingness to work with governmental authorities to correct and remedy the problem. In addition, the OIG will consider the act of reporting such conduct as a mitigating factor in determining administrative sanctions (e.g., penalties, assessments, and exclusion), if the reporting provider becomes the target of an OIG investigation.[19]

When reporting misconduct to the government, the provider should provide all evidence relevant to the alleged violation of applicable federal or state law(s) and potential cost impact. Governmental authorities may request the compliance officer to continue investigating the reported violation. Once the investigation is completed, the compliance officer should notify the appropriate governmental authority of the outcome of the investigation, including the impact of the alleged violation on the operation of the applicable healthcare programs or their beneficiaries.

---

**Action Items**

1. Be prepared to investigate promptly all reports of noncompliant conduct and formulate appropriate corrective action.
2. Follow fiscal intermediary procedures for remitting any overpayments.
3. Consult with legal counsel before notifying federal or state enforcement officials of possible violations.

---

## Notes

1. Hospital Guidance, 63 Fed. Reg. 8987, 8997 (1998).
2. Ibid.
3. Health Care Financing Administration, *Medicare Program Manual for Hospitals*, § 484 (Rev. 663, 1997).
4. Ibid.
5. Ibid. § 484.1.
6. Ibid.
7. Ibid. § 484.2.
8. Ibid. § 484.3.
9. Hospital Guidance, 63 Fed. Reg. 8987, 8997 (1998).
10. Ibid., footnote 55.
11. Hospital Guidance, 63 Fed. Reg. 8987, 8998 (1998).
12. Ibid., footnote 56.
13. Ibid., footnote 60.
14. Sentencing Guidelines, § 8C2.5.(f) (1997) and Official Commentary thereto.
15. Hospital Guidance, 63 Fed. Reg. 8987, 8998, footnote 61 (1998), citing 42 U.S.C. § 1320a-7b(a)(3).
16. See, e.g., 18 U.S.C.A. §§ 1001, 1505, 1510 and 1516 (West 1997).
17. 31 U.S.C.A. § 3729(a) (West 1997).
18. Hospital Guidance, 63 Fed. Reg. 8987, 8998, footnote 58 (1998).
19. Hospital Guidance, 63 Fed. Reg. 8987, 8998, footnote 59 and related text.

# 11

# THE WRITTEN COMPLIANCE PROGRAM

## 11.1 Putting the Elements Together Concisely

While the notion of creating a compliance program with seven elements may sound simple, the preceding discussion demonstrates the potential complexity of these elements. Add to this complexity the broad array of laws and ethical issues affecting modern healthcare, and it becomes clear that providers face a major challenge in developing a concise compliance policy that is coherent and understandable by the intended readers—the provider's employees and contractors. Many written programs declare that all employees should comply with all laws and ethics and go on to list a wide variety of general areas that range from sexual harassment to environmental to foreign corrupt practices, filling 50 pages or more but failing to convey to the ordinary employee exactly what conduct is noncompliant under any specific law or ethical standard. These types of written programs raise more issues than they solve.

The form compliance program (Appendix A) sets forth the basic elements of the compliance program in a concise and understandable fashion. Although it covers compliance with all laws generally, the form compliance program focuses on those particular areas in healthcare over which the OIG has expressed special concern and demonstrated a propensity to bring enforcement actions. The compliance officer or committees can separately develop more specific compliance policies for each operational area.

## 11.2 Written Standards of Conduct

Article I identifies nine legal areas for special mention in the written compliance program and imposes the obligation to report any instance of noncompliant conduct to the compliance coordinator. These highlighted areas correspond to the special areas of concern announced by the OIG, except the written standards are derived directly from the statutory source, rather than described in terms of media bytes such as "upcoding" and "DRG creep."

## 11.3 Compliance Officer

Article II appoints the compliance coordinator, using a title that gives the provider more flexibility as to where this person fits in the organizational chart. Whether the person in charge of compliance has a formal officer title, the important point is that the person should have a direct reporting line to the governing board of the provider, or a subcommittee of the board, as contemplated in Article II.D. Article II.B. lists the specific duties of the compliance coordinator in overseeing and implementing the compliance program and Article II.C. empowers the compliance coordinator to form compliance committees, as suggested in Section 5.8.

## 11.4 Effective Education and Training

Article III formally establishes an educational program, assigning responsibility for its implementation to the compliance coordinator in conjunction with the provider's legal counsel. The subject matter of the educational program specifically includes areas of special concern to the OIG, including the False Claims Act, federal anti-referral laws, anti-kickback laws and the Sherman Antitrust Act. Selection of training methods is left to the discretion of the compliance coordinator.

## 11.5 Audit and Other Evaluation Techniques

Article VI requires regular compliance audits with formal written reports to the compliance coordinator and the governing body of the provider. The compliance audits should include, at a minimum, interviews conducted by legal counsel with management personnel and random reviews of records, giving special attention to documentation and coding procedures. The retrospective review may expose the provider to sanctions if noncompliant conduct is discovered. For this reason, involvement of legal counsel is important not only to gain the benefit of the attorney-client privilege if possible, but also to obtain sound legal advice in crafting corrective action and possible reporting to enforcement officials.

## 11.6 Internal Reporting Processes

Article II.E. encourages employees to communicate directly with the compliance coordinator and establishes a hotline for anonymous reporting. The form compliance program protects all persons who report to the compliance coordinator or the hotline against retaliatory actions for reporting. As suggested in the Hospital Guidance, the form compliance program provides for confidentiality to the extent possible throughout any resulting investigation; however, there may be a point at which the provider may have to reveal an employee's identity. Article IV contains the employee's obligation to report any suspected or actual violations to the compliance coordinator and requires each employee to acknowledge this obligation in writing. This structure sets up the possible counterclaim and equitable arguments against *qui tam* plaintiffs who are motivated by possible financial rewards to file legal actions directly without giving the compliance process a chance to work. The form compliance program does not give the OIG's hotline number as suggested in the Hospital Guidance.

## 11.7 Disciplinary Mechanisms

Article IV.B. sets forth the disciplinary mechanisms for violations of laws, regulations, or any other aspect of the compliance program, including failure to report suspected violations to the compliance coordinator, lack of appropriate supervision leading to a violation of law, and any retaliatory action against a whistle blower. Possible sanctions include termination, suspension, demotion, reduction in pay, reprimand, and/or retraining. The form compliance program also specifies, as suggested by the Hospital Guidance, that employees who engage in intentional or reckless violation of law, regulation, or this compliance program will be subject to more severe sanctions than accidental transgressors. The compliance coordinator will need to impose discipline consistently across the ranks for the government to deem this element satisfied.

## 11.8 Investigation and Remediation

Article V outlines the procedure for investigating allegations of wrongdoing. Like Article VI on audits, the form compliance program recommends the involvement of legal counsel in the process to ensure appropriate investigation, corrective action, and possible reporting to enforcement officials. The form compliance program does not adopt the 60-day reporting rule of the Hospital Guidance for the reasons set forth in Section 10.4, although the provider may elect to report to enforcement officials in appropriate cases after consulting with legal counsel.

## 11.9 Employee and Contractor Acknowledgments

Two forms of acknowledgments, one for employees and one for nonemployed contractors such as physicians, are included at the end of the form compliance program. The acknowledgments contain two simple, but important, points. First, the individual acknowledges the existence of, understanding of, and commitment to the written compliance program. Second, the individual acknowledges the obligation to report compliance concerns to the compliance coordinator.

## 11.10 Customizing for the Provider

The provider should customize the form compliance program to apply to its particular needs. Tailoring may involve simplification for certain providers or expansion for complex integrated providers with other known areas of compliance concern. Nevertheless, the compliance process can and should proceed while the customization is under way. If no written program currently exists, the provider should immediately adopt a basic written program such as the form compliance program with a minimum of customization. The provider can later refine, modify, and expand the written program as necessary as the provider works through the various compliance issues.

---

**Action Items**

1. Ensure that the written compliance program covers the seven basic elements suggested by the OIG.
2. Proceed with the compliance process and customize the written program over time; do not wait to resolve all details before implementing a compliance program.

# Managing the
# Compliance Program

# 12

# IMPLEMENTING A COMPLIANCE PROGRAM

## 12.1  Do We Have an Effective Compliance Program?

Many providers have heard the call for compliance programs and have adopted programs or at least claim to be working on programs. But are these programs going to be deemed effective by the OIG or under the Sentencing Guidelines? Chapters 3 through 10 discuss at length the various elements, demands, and suggestions that have been promulgated for an effective compliance program. Form 12.1 summarizes the crucial components of an effective compliance program in the form of a questionnaire for a healthcare provider, and focuses particularly on documentation and coding. To have an effective compliance program, the provider should be able to answer yes to all of the 14 questions in Form 12.1.

Even if the provider can currently answer yes to all 14 questions, that does not mean the provider will always have an effective compliance program. An effective compliance program is an ongoing process that is not by any means completed by adopting a written program and appointing a compliance officer. As management works through the process of constructing, implementing, and maintaining a compliance program, it will have to focus on particular areas of the compliance program at particular times. At one point, it will be important to write policy statements. At another time, it will be necessary to strengthen auditing and monitoring mechanisms. An unfortunate result is that management may lose sight of its fundamental goal: preventing noncompliant conduct from occurring.

**FORM 12.1   Compliance Program Questionnaire**

To have an effective compliance program, the healthcare provider should be able to answer yes to each of the following questions:

1. *Clinical Documentation Standards.* Do you have written standards concerning the clinical documentation required for the assignment of a diagnosis or procedure code?

   ❐ Yes                    ❐ No

2. *Teaching Hospital Standards.* If a teaching hospital, have you integrated the requirements set forth in IL-372 into the hospital's policies and procedures?

   ❐ Yes                    ❐ No                    ❐ Not applicable

3. *Conduct Standards.* Do you have written standards of legal and ethical conduct for all documentation and coding personnel that clearly delineate policies with regard to fraud, waste and abuse, and adherence to all laws and regulations governing federally funded healthcare programs?

   ❐ Yes                    ❐ No

4. *Compliance Commitment.* Do you have written policies that promote your commitment to compliance with your standards for documentation and conduct and that address specific areas of potential fraud such as documentation and coding?

   ❐ Yes                    ❐ No

5. *Chief Compliance Officer.* Have you designated a chief compliance officer or other appropriate high-level official who is charged with the responsibility of operating the compliance program?

   ❐ Yes                    ❐ No

6. *Education and Training Programs.* Do you offer education and training programs for all documentation and coding personnel with respect to the standards for clinical documentation, legal and ethical conduct in documentation and coding, and the compliance program itself?

   ❐ Yes                    ❐ No

7. *Recent Legal Developments.* Have you offered training programs for all documentation and coding personnel to explain the new laws relating to federal healthcare reimbursement enacted as part of the Health Insurance Portability and Accountability Act of 1996, which became effective on January 1, 1997, and for all personnel to explain the changes to federal healthcare law effected by the Balanced Budget Act of 1997?

   ❐ Yes                    ❐ No

8. *Audits.* Do you use audits and/or other evaluation techniques to monitor documentation and coding compliance and ensure a reduction in identified problem areas?

   ☐ Yes                    ☐ No

9. *Disciplinary Actions.* Do you have written policies for using disciplinary actions against employees who have violated internal compliance policies or applicable laws or who have engaged in wrongdoing?

   ☐ Yes                    ☐ No

10. *Investigation and Remediation.* Do you have written policies for the investigation and remediation of identified systemic and personnel problems?

    ☐ Yes                    ☐ No

11. *Employee Evaluations.* Do you include adherence to compliance as an element in evaluating all documentation and coding personnel?

    ☐ Yes                    ☐ No

12. *Sanctioned Individuals.* Do you have written policies addressing the nonemployment or retention of sanctioned individuals?

    ☐ Yes                    ☐ No

13. *Hotline.* Do you maintain a hotline to receive complaints, and is the anonymity of complainants protected?

    ☐ Yes                    ☐ No

14. *Records.* Do you have written policies and procedures to ensure all records required by federal or state laws or by the compliance plan are created and maintained?

    ☐ Yes                    ☐ No

As discussed in Sections 4.3 and 6.6, the most effective method for preventing violations is education focused on the special areas of concern to the OIG. Audits, hotlines, discipline, and self-reporting are retrospective compliance tools that address violations after they have occurred. In working through the compliance process, management should seek to incorporate the basic elements of an effective compliance program as quickly as possible and use available resources to maximize the preventive benefits of certain individual elements such as education.

Many consultants offer their services to design and implement an overall corporate compliance program. These consulting offerings often involve overall corporate compliance programs that attempt to cover all areas of legal compliance in general but fail to cover the areas of special concern to the OIG in healthcare, particularly documentation and coding. Because of their expansiveness, the overall corporate compliance programs can take a very long time to implement and are very expensive. Providers should not exhaust their resources just setting up the written compliance program and performing expensive, retrospective audits to take a snapshot for benchmarking purposes.

## 12.2 Implementation Steps

Providers would better serve their fundamental goal of preventing noncompliant conduct by working through the compliance process in a series of manageable steps that reduce their exposure to sanctions as quickly as possible. The steps are as follows:

1. *Adopt a written compliance program.* With appropriate board-level action, the provider should adopt a simple, written compliance program focused on the special areas of concern in healthcare, such as those highlighted in the form compliance program. The provider can expand and modify the written program over time to ultimately address overall corporate compliance, but the provider should focus initially on the high exposure areas as identified by the OIG.

2. *Provide initial compliance awareness education.* The written compliance program is useless if nobody knows about it. Therefore, the provider should disseminate the written program to all employees and contractors. Shortly thereafter, the provider should require all employees and contractors to attend a basic presentation regarding the existence and content of the compliance program, introduce the compliance officer, answer any questions, and obtain the employee and contractor acknowledgments.

3. *Provide initial substantive education.* Early in the compliance process, the provider should provide substantive education to affected employees and nonemployed physicians in the special areas of concern as identified by the OIG, probably in the following order:

   a   documentation and coding;

   b.   kickbacks and physician self-referral;

   c.   patient care issues such as freedom of choice and patient dumping; and

   d.   accounting issues, including cost reports and credit balance reports.

4. *Arrange for an audit mechanism.* Once the provider furnishes the basic substantive education, it then becomes important to see whether employees and contractors are adhering to what was taught and whether the education was effective in preventing noncompliant conduct. This feedback will provide information for adjusting the compliance process as necessary. To minimize cost, the audit of compliance issues can be

performed with the assistance of the provider's existing independent accounting firm as part of the financial statement audit.

## 12.3 Maintaining an Effective Compliance Program

Once the provider completes the initial steps of implementation, it will become important to maintain the momentum with formal ongoing procedures to integrate the compliance program into the organizational fabric of the provider. Again, the maintenance process can be broken down into a series of manageable steps to avoid major impediments. The steps continue as follows:

5. *Train, train, train.* Training, which the provider should pursue relentlessly, is the key preventive aspect of the compliance program. The initial wave of training in the areas of special concern to the OIG is only the beginning, and the areas of concern will shift over time, requiring constant updating of the educational process. The provider should educate different groups of employees and contractors in the areas relevant to their duties. Obviously, the janitorial and cafeteria employees in a hospital do not need to receive documentation and coding training. On the other hand, as the compliance education moves to more general areas of application, such as labor matters, a broader approach may become necessary. Various compliance subcommittees may assist the compliance officer in designing and delivering effective training, as suggested in Section 5.8, in areas such as documentation and coding, billing and accounting, utilization review, kickbacks and physician self-referral, marketing, and labor issues.

6. *Monitor compliance activities.* Beyond the annual compliance audit, the compliance officer should undertake other monitoring activities. The compliance officer should be visible and require reports of compliance activities from the compliance subcommittees or the managers of the operating areas, if no subcommittees exist. The compliance officer should carefully monitor the effectiveness of the education programs and promptly make appropriate revisions.

7. *Investigate all reports of suspected violations.* If any compliance issues are reported to the compliance officer, hotline, or otherwise, the organization must carefully investigate the matter and take appropriate corrective action, as necessary. The compliance officer should involve the organization's legal counsel in this step because of the legal sensitivities. The compliance officer should carefully document the investigation and disposition of all reports to provide evidence that this compliance element was satisfied.

8. *Discipline violators.* Early in the compliance process, appropriate discipline may often be limited to retraining until employees have a fair chance to learn the technicalities of compliant conduct and the importance of compliance procedures. As the process proceeds, discipline should become stricter and should be consistently applied without special favors.

## 12.4 Preparedness: The Columbia/HCA Example

Beyond the steps of implementing and maintaining an effective compliance program, healthcare managers should prepare their respective organizations for the worst in the current regulatory atmosphere. As demonstrated by the Columbia/HCA situation, two issues require special attention: government searches and public relations.

In March 1997, federal authorities executed search warrants on various facilities of Columbia/HCA's El Paso, Texas, operations, and the government removed various records and documents. In July 1997, government agents searched various Columbia/HCA-affiliated facilities and offices pursuant to search warrants issued by the U.S. district courts in several states. Media photographs showed government agents removing records by the truckload. In February 1998, federal authorities executed an additional warrant against Columbia/HCA, and a computer was seized.

The execution of a search warrant, in contrast to a subpoena, gives the recipient no time to consult with counsel, make copies of any documents produced, and exclude all documents that are not relevant to the subject of the warrant. The seizing of healthcare billing records, in particular, can seriously damage the provider because the flow of revenue may be disrupted without the records necessary for billing. As such, a government search resembles a natural disaster such as fire, tornado, or earthquake, and the provider should establish plans to deal with all these situations. The provider should include in the provider's data backup procedures all billing records and other crucial records that might be the subject of a government investigation so that it can retrieve copies of the records from off-site, if necessary.

## 12.5 What to Do During a Government Search

The provider should create and distribute to each facility or office written plans and procedures for handling a government search and should identify individuals responsibile for executing the procedures. An example of a simple list of what to do during a government search follows:

1. *Notify legal counsel.* The compliance officer (if not a lawyer) and other responsible parties should have a list of office and home telephone numbers of the provider's primary legal counsel, with alternative attorneys if the primary counsel is unavailable. If possible, counsel should personally go to the site of the search; otherwise, telephone advice will have to suffice.

2. *Do not answer questions until counsel arrives.* There is no obligation to respond to questions asked by government agents during a search. To eliminate the temptation to respond to agent questioning, all nonessential employees should be asked to leave the premises under search.

3. *Review the search warrant.* With the assistance of legal counsel, the person in charge should review the search warrant. If the warrant relates only to certain documents, the organization may object to attempts to search areas beyond the scope of the warrant.

4. *Do not impede the government agents at all.* While objections may be stated orally, no one should attempt to physically impede or otherwise interfere with the agents.

5. *Record what the agents do.* To the extent possible without impeding the agents, accompany the agents and keep a detailed account of what the agents do and what records they inspect or seize.

6. *Remain calm.* With an effective compliance program, the organization supports the government's efforts to eliminate fraud and abuse and should have nothing to hide.

# 12.6  Public Relations

Perhaps the most compelling lesson out of the Columbia/HCA situation is the importance of good public relations in the healthcare industry. In its audited financial statements for the calendar year 1997, Columbia/HCA's management stated that it believed the ongoing investigations and related media coverage were having a negative effect on the results of operations. Columbia/HCA incurred $140 million of costs during 1997 in connection with the government investigations and changes in management and business strategy. These costs included $61 million in severance costs, $44 million in professional fees related to the investigations, $20 million related to certain canceled projects, and $15 million in other costs.[1]

Yet, these costs pale in comparison to the damage done to Columbia/HCA's core business largely as a result of the negative publicity. For the 1997 calendar year, Columbia/HCA's income from continuing operations before income taxes declined by more than $2 billion, or 84.1 percent, from the prior calendar year. Columbia/HCA attributed the decrease in pretax income to the impairment charges on long-lived assets, restructuring and investigation-related costs, a decline in revenue growth rates, and decreases in the operating margin. During 1997, Columbia/HCA's credit ratings were downgraded, limiting access to commercial paper as a financing source and requiring increased borrowings under more expensive credit facilities. These negative consequences ensued merely from commencement of the government's investigation, prior to any conviction, settlement, or imposition of any penalties by the government. The negative publicity is a major financial and business threat that healthcare executives must carefully manage.

## 12.7 Media Counteroffensive

Like disaster and government search preparedness, healthcare providers also should prepare a plan to combat potential negative publicity associated with a government investigation. Timing is critical as reporters have deadlines and will not wait for days while the provider contacts a public relations agency and coaches its executives on what to say. The provider must engage the public relations agency beforehand to be ready when the need arises. The plan should include a media counteroffensive to diffuse some of the negative impact of an investigation. Elements of the public relations plan should include:

1. *Retain experienced public relations professionals.* Providers can improve media relationships through the assistance of public relations professionals who know the media business.

2. *Identify executive-level spokespersons.* The public relations firms cannot do the live media interviews because the reporters will want to talk to senior executives. The provider should identify spokespersons and rehearse their responses to media questioning.

3. *Alert staff to direct media inquiries to spokespersons.* It is important that the identified spokespersons control and handle all media communications. The provider should notify its staff to promptly refer all media inquiries to the spokespersons so that media calls can be timely returned.

4. *Be professional, truthful, and helpful.* Use the media opportunity to provide professional and accurate information about the provider. The spokesperson should attempt to be helpful, but no matter how friendly things may seem, the discussion should stay formal and on the record.

5. *Do not be defensive.* The provider can explain that it supports the government's efforts to combat fraud with its compliance program. Also, the provider may explain that innocent mistakes are possible because of the complexity of healthcare reimbursement systems, and such mistakes do not constitute fraud or abuse.

## 12.8 Focus on High-Exposure Areas

Compliance with all laws, not to mention ethical principles, is an overwhelming task. Providers cannot expect to instantly implement full-blown compliance programs in all substantive areas of possible legal exposure faced in healthcare today. Again, the provider must break down the compliance effort into manageable steps so that the entire process does not become paralyzed.

As noted in Section 6.2, the area of highest regulatory exposure in healthcare today is billing, particularly documentation and coding issues, which account for the vast majority of improper Medicare payments identified by OIG in its audits of HCFA (see Table 6.1). The OIG's Hospital Guidance and Home Health Guidance emphasize documentation and coding issues as special areas of concern (see Tables 4.1 and 4.2). Because of increased government enforcement funding, severe criminal penalties, and civil sanctions including triple damages plus $10,000 per claim and possible Medicare exclusion, newly implemented compliance programs should focus on documentation and coding issues.

Once the compliance program has addressed documentation and coding issues, the related areas of anti-kickback and self-referral issues should receive prompt attention because of their high risk to providers. Sanctions under both statutes are severe: triple damages plus $50,000 per violation under the anti-kickback statute and $15,000 per violation under the self-referral statute. Although the anti-kickback statute requires proof of intent to induce referrals, providers can innocently violate the federal self-referral statute by the existence of any prohibited remuneration, which the statute defines very broadly.

Antitrust is another area of high exposure and frequent application in healthcare. Despite a seemingly fragmented healthcare market with hundreds of thousands of physicians and roughly 5,100 acute care, nongovernment hospitals, federal regulators narrowly define each relevant geographic market, thereby creating monopolistic concerns in virtually every small to medium-sized community in the country. The government spends an inordinate amount of resources attempting to enforce antitrust principles in healthcare relative to other industries. Antitrust sanctions include the original "treble," or triple, damages and private parties can bring antitrust actions without government participation.

The following chapters of this book focus on billing (including documentation and coding issues), anti-kickback and self-referral, and antitrust to provide the reader with a sound background in these high-exposure areas. Other areas of legal exposure may also require immediate or prioritized attention while implementing a compliance program for a particular provider. The provider should customize the implementation approach to be appropriate for its particular needs.

---

### Action Items

1. Work through the initial compliance implementation in a series of manageable steps: (1) adopt a written compliance program, (2) provide initial compliance awareness education, (3) provide initial substantive education, and (4) arrange for an audit mechanism.
2. After initial implementation is completed, maintain the compliance program with a continuing series of manageable steps: (5) train, train, train, (6) monitor compliance activities, (7) investigate all reports of suspected violations, and (8) discipline violators.
3. Adopt and disseminate written procedures in preparation for government searches, including backup of billing records.
4. Develop plans for a media counteroffensive to respond to negative publicity.

---

## Note

1. Columbia/HCA's Form 10-K for the year ended December 31, 1997, as filed with the Securities and Exchange Commission.

# BILLING COMPLIANCE

## 13.1  Main Sources of Law Affecting Billing

When the government brings an enforcement action against a healthcare provider for billing violations, it may allege violations involving a plethora of federal statutes, including general fraud, conspiracy, mail and wire fraud, and the Racketeer Influenced Corrupt Organizations Act (RICO). However, the main sources of federal law for allegations of healthcare billing violations are as follows:

- Social Security Act
  A. Criminal provisions
  B. Civil provisions
- False Claims Act
- Healthcare fraud (new crime)

## 13.2  Criminal Provisions of the Social Security Act

The criminal provisions of the Social Security Act are extensive and legalistic. After some reduction and simplification, these provisions prohibit *knowingly and willfully* making or causing to be made any *false statement or representation of a material fact* in connection with an *application for or determination of rights to benefits or payment* under Medicare, Medicaid, or a state healthcare program.[1] Each of the italicized phrases will be further explained below.

*Knowingly and willfully* is the heightened intent-based standard that must be present before culpability is sufficient to justify criminal sanctions such as incarceration. Furthermore, all the elements of the crime, including the wrongful intent of the violator, must be proved beyond a reasonable doubt. The O. J. Simpson case provides an excellent example of the difficulty in satisfying this criminal burden of proof. O. J. Simpson was found not guilty of the criminal charges of murder, which required proof beyond a reasonable doubt, but was found liable in the civil action for wrongful death, which required proof by a simple preponderance of the evidence.

The criminal statute applies to *false statements or representations of material fact.* The falsity must involve a material fact, and even intentionally false statements are not actionable under this statute if they relate only to immaterial facts. With the language "application for or determination of rights to benefits or payment," the criminal statute applies both to providers seeking reimbursement from the government and to beneficiaries seeking government health benefits. For example, a 54-year-old who claims Medicare benefits by falsely representing his age as 67 years old would be committing a crime covered by this statute.

Providers who violate the criminal provisions of the Social Security Act can be imprisoned for up to five years and assessed monetary fines of up to $25,000 for individuals. Nonproviders are subject to up to one year imprisonment plus monetary fines of up to $10,000 for individuals. An amendment added by the Balanced Budget Act of 1997 automatically excludes criminal violators from participation in federal health programs.[2]

## 13.3 What Is False in Healthcare?

The word "false" has two distinct and well-recognized meanings in the law: (1) intentionally or knowingly or negligently untrue and (2) untrue mistake or accident.[3] In the criminal provisions of the Social Security Act and under the separate statute for healthcare fraud, the respective statutes explicitly require the untruth to be knowing and willful. In contrast (as more fully discussed below), the civil provisions of the Social Security Act and the False Claims Act apply to a broader concept of what is "false," including untruth that is made in deliberate ignorance or reckless disregard of the truth or falsity of the information. Falsity resulting from mistake or accident is not actionable under federal statutes if it was not made intentionally, in deliberate ignorance, or in reckless disregard of the truth, at least in theory.

In reality, the fine distinctions surrounding the general notion of falsity are very difficult to apply in the context of healthcare billing. Often the issue is not whether the services were truly provided, but whether the documentation and coding were appropriate for those services. With the complex and voluminous requirements associated with documentation and coding for purposes of billing federal health programs, mistakes and accidents are bound to occur. The line between an innocent or even negligent billing mistake (which would not be actionable) and a mistake made in deliberate ignorance or reckless disregard of the truth is impossible to clearly identify. Consequently, civil actions against providers for false billing claims are extremely dangerous to healthcare providers because of the risk that innocent billing errors may be characterized as unlawful because of deliberate ignorance or reckless disregard of the truth.

The criminal provisions of the Social Security Act require falsity that is knowing, willful, and proved beyond a reasonable doubt. While this is a significant burden of proof, federal prosecutors have demonstrated their ability to bear this burden of proof in egregious cases of healthcare fraud. Perhaps the classic example of false billing violating the criminal standards under the Social Security Act is the case of the Mississippi physician who continued billing Medicare for services supposedly rendered to patients well after their dates of death. The physician could hardly argue that he did not know that the patients were dead.

Another example is the Missouri-based company that furnished a simple foam-cushioned seat for nursing home patients but billed Medicare for $1,000 custom-fitted body jackets. In another case, a Maryland hospital contracted with a company to transport patients to a radiation clinic located on hospital grounds. The patients were actually transported by gurney from the hospital emergency room to the clinic, a distance of 47 feet, but the company billed Medicare $210 for each "ambulance" round-trip. These examples demonstrate the kind of blatant misconduct that the government rightfully prosecutes under the criminal provisions of the Social Security Act.

## 13.4 Civil Provisions of the Social Security Act

Like the criminal provisions of the Social Security Act, the civil provisions are extensive and legalistic. Detailed study of this legalese is worthwhile for a good understanding of the civil standards that apply to federal healthcare claims. The Health Insurance Portability and Accountability Act of 1996 (HIPAA) amended the civil provisions of the Social Security Act by adding language specifically directed at documentation and coding issues. The amended statute prohibits knowingly presenting or causing to be presented to the U.S. government, any state agency, or any agent thereof a claim that the secretary of Health and Human Services determines

> is for a medical or other item or service that the person knows or should know was not provided as claimed, including a *pattern* or practice of presenting or causing to be presented a claim for an item or service that is based on a *code* that such person *knows or should know* will result in *a greater payment* to the claimant than the code such person *knows or should know* is applicable to the item or service actually provided.[4]

## 13.5 What Is a Pattern?

The term "pattern" is designed to limit the application of the statute to wide-spread instances of miscoding and excuse the occasional errors that are bound to occur in the complex Medicare system. What is a pattern? HIPAA did not further define "pattern," and its meaning has not yet been litigated under the new language in the Social Security Act. However, similar language appears in RICO,[5] and the meaning of the term "pattern" in RICO has been litigated extensively over the last 25 years. To summarize, the term "pattern" has been held to mean more than one instance but can mean as few as two instances under RICO.[6]

In its DRG 72-hour window project (see Section 13.11), the OIG allowed up to ten errors per hospital before imposing additional sanctions.[7] Given that 853 million Medicare claims were made during the 1997 fiscal year, prosecutors will often be able to show a sufficient number of errors by any provider so as to constitute a pattern, at least as interpreted under the RICO statute and by the OIG. Thus, if courts similarly construe the pattern requirement of the Social Security Act, the addition of the pattern language hardly limits this new focus on miscoding.

## 13.6 What Is the Code?

In 1983, Congress changed the Medicare inpatient hospital reimbursement system from a reasonable cost-basis approach, which arguably inspired overutilization of products and services, to a prospective payment system (PPS), whereby the hospital generally receives a fixed monetary payment per patient discharge, depending on the patient's diseases and procedures. Providers must describe various diseases, procedures, complications, and comorbidities using the approximately 10,000 numerical codes that constitute the International Classification of Diseases, Ninth Revision, Clinical Modification (ICD-9-CM). ICD-9-CM is based on the international classification system developed by the World Health Organization, a specialized agency of the United Nations based in Geneva, Switzerland. However, application of ICD-9-CM in the United States is governed by *Coding Clinic for ICD-9-CM*, a quarterly newsletter published by the American Hospital Association's Central Office on ICD-9-CM and produced in cooperation with the American Hospital Association, American Health Information Management Association, National Center of Health Statistics, and HCFA.

Under PPS, the patient's diseases and procedures as described in ICD-9-CM codes are grouped into approximately 500 diagnosis-related groups (DRGs). The federal government annually assigns to each DRG a fixed dollar payment, which represents the average reasonable cost of care for each DRG. The hospital generally receives the fixed payment regardless of the actual duration of hospitalization and expenditure of resources during the stay. By reimbursing the average cost of care for each DRG, PPS provides an incentive for efficient delivery of healthcare. The Balanced Budget Act of 1997 includes provisions to phase in PPS to the areas of hospital outpatient services, home health services, and skilled nursing facilities.

Physicians must describe their services for federal billing purposes in a set of five-digit numerical codes known as the Current Procedural Terminology (CPT), developed and copyrighted by the American Medical Association. CPT codes are totally different than ICD-9-CM codes and DRG codes, yet all are relevant to defining the code referred to in the HIPAA amendment to the Social Security Act. The term "code" means any code used in a claim for reimbursement, including ICD-9-CM, DRG, and CPT. Thus, the Social Security Act now charges all providers with the responsibility for properly coding under all these systems.

## 13.7 Knows or Should Know

As amended by HIPAA, the Social Security Act now defines "knows or should know" to mean that "a person, with respect to information:

- acts in deliberate ignorance of the truth or falsity of the information; or
- acts in reckless disregard of the truth or falsity of the information,

and no proof of specific intent is required."[8] This definition significantly broadens the scope of the civil provisions of the Social Security Act over the criminal provisions, which require knowing and willful conduct. This broader standard is particularly dangerous to providers in the area of coding, in which thousands of numerical codes are possible and coding standards are established by disparate groups without ordinary legislative or regulatory procedure. For example, providers could be accused of deliberate ignorance if they do not thoroughly know and accurately apply the 50 volumes of interpretations of ICD-9-CM contained in the cumulative editions of *Coding Clinic for ICD-9-CM*. Both the coding interpretations and the codes themselves (e.g., ICD-10) are constantly changing, requiring continuous education for those employees with documentation and coding responsibilities.

## 13.8 Greater Payment

The language added by HIPAA deals with instances in which the claim results in the provider receiving a greater payment for the item or service than is applicable to the item or service actually provided. The statute only covers claims in which the provider received greater payment, and the provider receives no credit for claims in which the provider received lesser payment than it was due. As noted in Section 6.4, physicians often underdocument medical records, resulting in the hospitals receiving less reimbursement than they are due. Providers may also be tempted to code conservatively to avoid attention in the current environment of heightened concern over coding issues. Nevertheless, a provider may violate the statute if it has a few instances (a pattern) of receiving greater payments, even if there are hundreds or thousands of instances in which the provider received lesser payment. The statute is entirely one-sided in favor of the government.

While imprisonment is not a possible sanction under the civil provisions of the Social Security Act, HIPAA amended the statute to significantly increase the possible monetary penalties. Effective January 1, 1997, the amount of the civil monetary penalty increased from $2,000 to $10,000 for each item or service involved, and the additional assessment that a person may be subject to increased from "not more than twice the amount" to "not more than three times the amount" claimed. For example, a $10 claim that does not satisfy the new requirements of the Social Security Act may subject the provider to a fine of $10,030 ($10,000 per claim plus triple the amount of the claim). In addition to the monetary fines, the provider may be excluded from participation in the Medicare program entirely. The imposition of such sanctions could be devastating to the provider.

## 13.9 Expanded Notion of Falsity

The civil provisions of the Social Security Act also prohibit presenting a claim if "the person *knows or should know* the claim is false or fraudulent."[9] While the term "false" is the same term used in the criminal portion of the Social Security Act, the "knows or should know" language significantly changes the meaning of the term "false." Under the civil provision, false includes not only what is intentionally untrue, but also what is untrue because of deliberate ignorance or reckless disregard of the truth or falsity of the information. This distinction enables prosecutors to apply the civil provisions of the Social Security Act to circumstances in which they could not prove intentional false billing. Examples of the application of the expanded civil provisions of the Social Security Act (together with the False Claims Act) include the government's project involving physicians at teaching hospitals (PATH), the DRG 72-hour window project, and the laboratory unbundling project.

## 13.10 PATH

The OIG has undertaken a nationwide initiative focusing on reimbursements to physicians at teaching hospitals (PATH). The specific objectives of the PATH audit initiative are to verify compliance with the Medicare rules governing payment for physician services provided by residents and to ensure that the claims accurately reflect the level of service provided to the patient. Medicare pays the costs of training residents and interns through the graduate medical education (GME) program. Medicare also pays an additional amount per DRG in recognition of the additional costs associated with training residents and interns. The Medicare payments described above include payments to teaching physicians for their role in supervising residents and interns.

The fundamental tenet of the PATH initiative is that to receive reimbursement from Medicare Part B for a service rendered to a patient, the teaching physician must have personally provided that service or have been present when the intern or resident furnished the care.[10] This fundamental tenet, however, was not clearly promulgated until December 1995 in a final regulation, which became effective as of July 1, 1996.[11] Prior to that time, the standards for teaching physician participation were vague, ambiguous, and not vigorously enforced, as admitted by HCFA in the preamble to the final regulation. The OIG has nevertheless claimed in its PATH initiative that the requirement for teaching physician presence was clearly set forth in *Intermediary Letter 372* (IL-372), issued by HCFA's predecessor in 1969 without out public notice and comment.

The PATH initiative focuses on cases in which the intern or resident performed services without the teaching physician being physically present. The OIG considers any claim for reimbursement under Part B by a teaching physician who was not physically present to be improper because it is a duplicate claim—one that has already been paid for under Part A through the graduate medical education program.[12] The OIG has also refused to accept countersignatures by teaching physicians as sufficient evidence of teaching physician involvement, despite references in IL-372 itself and a subsequent *Intermediary Letter,* IL-70-2, indicating that countersignatures are sufficient. The OIG has required additional evidence of the teaching physician's involvement in the medical record, either completed by the resident or the teaching physician.

Several institutions have entered into settlements with the federal government to resolve their civil liability for overpayments related to improper claims submitted in the teaching setting and to charging for a higher level of service than actually delivered. These settlements have resulted in the government's recovery of up to $30 million in overpayments and penalties per institution. The OIG reportedly identified significant instances of noncompliance with the physician presence standard, including physicians who billed Medicare for services on days when they were on leave or out of town.[13] As a condition of settlement, these institutions have also implemented corporate integrity programs to prevent and detect future erroneous claims. To manage this risk area, teaching hospitals need to educate their physicians about the need to properly document their physical presence while supervising residents.

## 13.11 DRG 72-Hour Window Project

In 1995, the OIG, in conjunction with the Department of Justice, launched a national project to recover overpayments made to hospitals as a result of claims submitted for nonphysician outpatient services (usually diagnostic services) that were performed within 72 hours of admission and should be included in the hospital's inpatient payment under PPS. Hospitals that submit claims for the outpatient service in addition to the inpatient admission are, in effect, submitting duplicate claims for the outpatient services. In addition, the project seeks to recover for those services rendered to beneficiaries during the inpatient admission that should be included in the DRG but are separately charged.[14]

This national project identified 4,660 hospitals that submitted improper billings for outpatient services, out of the roughly 5,100 acute care, nongovernment hospitals in the United States. These hospitals may receive notification from the U.S. Attorney's Office (Department of Justice) concerning the OIG's identification of erroneous claims and the facility's potential exposure under the civil provisions of the Social Security Act and the Federal Civil False Claims Act. The OIG and Department of Justice give the hospitals the opportunity to enter into a settlement with the government under which the improper billings by the institution are estimated for the entire six-year limitations period (time allowed by the statute for bringing litigation). Any institution with more than a nominal number of errors must then pay up to double damages, which the government advertises as being substantially less than the triple damages plus $10,000 per claim that could be assessed if the matter were litigated. The terms of the settlement also require compliance measures to prevent and detect erroneous billing. As of April 1998, the Department of Justice had executed settlements with approximately 2,400 hospitals and recovered about $58 million.[15] Providers typically manage this risk area with billing software that flags for further evaluation all outpatient billings within 72 hours of the admission of the same patient.

## 13.12 Project Bad Bundle

Project Bad Bundle seeks to recover improper claims plus penalties related to erroneous or excessive claims submitted for hematology and automated blood chemistry tests by hospital outpatient laboratories. The OIG believes that laboratory services are particularly vulnerable to excessive claims because of the multiple number of tests ordered at one time and the capability of automated equipment to run several tests from one sample. The reimbursement for tests bundled into a panel is less than that for each test run separately, and hospitals are required to bill certain groupings of blood tests using a "bundled" code.

Project Bad Bundle targets hospital outpatient laboratories, using an ongoing computer-based audit of claims submitted for outpatient laboratory services. The U.S. Attorney's Office sends a letter to each hospital identifying the scope of the abusive practice at that facility and its potential exposure under the civil provisions of the Social Security Act and the Federal Civil False Claims Act. In many jurisdictions, the hospitals are invited to participate in a self-audit program, the results of which are separately verified. In recognition of their participation in this self-audit process, the hospitals generally receive the so-called "benefit" of damages equal to 1.6 to 1.8 times the overpayments rather than triple damages for settlement purposes. The terms of all of the settlements require implementation of compliance measures to correct the identified misconduct and to prevent future similar misconduct. As of May 1998, the Department of Justice has recorded settlements with 80 hospitals as a result of Project Bad Bundle and its predecessor pilot and recovered more than $22 million.[16] Billing software can be used to minimize the provider's exposure to improper unbundling.

## 13.13 Medically Unnecessary Services

HIPAA added two practices to the list of prohibited practices for which civil money penalties may be assessed. The first, discussed above, occurs when a person engages in a pattern or practice of presenting a claim for an item or service based on a code that the person knows or should know will result in greater payments than appropriate. The second is the practice whereby a person submits a claim or claims that the person knows or should know is for a medical item or service that is not medically necessary. Specifically, the statute prohibits claims "for a *pattern* of medical or other items or services that a person *knows or should know* are *not medically necessary.*"[17]

The discussions in Section 13.5 about the term "pattern" and in Section 13.7 about the phrase "knows or should know" also apply in interpreting this portion of the statute. However, a full discussion about what is *not medically necessary* is far beyond the scope of this book. Definition of medical necessity requires clinical expertise and is subject to wide variations of opinion. The conference report to HIPAA provides assurance that the amended standard is not intended to penalize providers simply because of a professional difference of opinion regarding diagnosis or treatment. The legislators did not intend to penalize the exercise of medical judgment of healthcare treatment choices made in good faith and that are supported by significant evidence or held by a respectable minority of those providers who customarily provide similar methods of treatment.[18] Even with these assurances, the inclusion of the vague notion of medical necessity together with the broader "know or should know" standard greatly increases the risk that violations could unknowingly occur for which severe civil monetary penalties may be assessed. Designing mechanisms to ensure compliance with the vague notion of medical necessity is also very difficult.

Medicare and other government and private healthcare plans will pay only for those services that meet appropriate reimbursement standards. For example, no payment may be made under Medicare for any expenses that are not reasonable and necessary for the diagnosis or treatment of illness or injury or to improve the functioning of the malformed body.[19] The government's definition of what it will reimburse does not always comport with the clinical opinion of what is medically necessary; nevertheless, the government's definition controls for billing purposes. Providers should train their physicians and clinicians to document in medical records, when appropriate, the elements of medical necessity as defined by the government and its agents.

As discussed in Section 6.2, the OIG is focusing on lack of medical necessity as a primary cause for improper Medicare payments. Consistent with its 1996 HCFA audit report, the OIG estimated that lack of medical necessity was the cause of 37 percent of the improper payments for all of Medicare in fiscal year 1997, and accounted for 63 percent and 53 percent of improper payments in the areas of hospital inpatient and home health agency claims, respectively.[20] The OIG gives the following examples of medically unnecessary services:

- A beneficiary who had been hospitalized five years earlier was admitted to a hospital to increase her strength. Rehabilitation therapies included occupational, physical, and speech therapies, as well as continuation of routine medications. Based on a review of the medical records, the Peer Review Organization concluded that the documentation did not support the medical necessity for 37 days ($38,672) of inpatient hospital care.
- A $2,915 home health agency claim for home care visits, including skilled nursing services, was denied because the skilled services were medically unnecessary. The OIG's interview with the beneficiary determined that he left home daily and therefore did not meet the definition of "homebound" necessary for Medicare coverage of home health services.
- Although an ambulance service billed $7,844 for transporting a beneficiary from a nursing home to a dialysis center, the OIG determined that the beneficiary could have traveled safely by far less expensive means.

The foregoing examples demonstrate the kind of second guessing to which all providers may be subjected under the amended civil legal standards.[21] The OIG may also raise questions where the services truly were medically necessary, but the documentation in the medical records does not fully explain the clinical rationale for ordering the services. Even full clinical documentation may not be sufficient to explain medical necessity to government attorneys and auditors who lack a clinical background.

## 13.14 Involvement of Physicians

With the recent amendments to the Social Security Act focusing on issues of coding and medical necessity, now more than ever providers must involve all physicians and clinical professionals in the compliance process, whether or not they are directly employed by the provider. In many jurisdictions, providers such as hospitals and home health agencies do not directly employ the physicians who direct patient care. Yet Medicare payment to hospitals and other providers is based in part on each patient's principal and secondary diagnoses and the major procedures performed on the patient, as attested to by the patient's attending physician in the medical record.[22] The Hospital Guidance recognizes that accurate coding depends on the quality and completeness of the physician's documentation. Likewise, issues of medical necessity are determined by the physician. The Hospital Guidance expressly states that the OIG believes that active staff physicians should participate in educational programs focusing on coding and documentation.[23]

As discussed in Sections 6.5 and 14.15, legal considerations exist about involving nonemployed physicians in the compliance process, including anti-kickback, self-referral, and private inurement for tax-exempt entities. In light of the government's fight against fraud and abuse and its explicit encouragement of involving physicians in the compliance process as stated in the Hospital Guidance, inclusion of physicians in documentation and coding training must now take precedence over other legal considerations. Furnishing such documentation and coding training to physicians means discharging the provider's compliance duties and not providing illegal remuneration or operating outside of the provider's tax-exempt purpose.

## 13.15 False Claims Act

The Federal Civil False Claims Act (False Claims Act) was originally adopted in 1863 during the Civil War to discourage suppliers of the Union army from overcharging the federal government.[24] The crux of the False Claims Act is to punish any person who *knowingly* presents, causes to be presented, or conspires to present a *false claim* for payment or a related false record or statement to any agent of the U.S. government. Until 1986, the term "knowingly" meant what it said and the notion of falsity incorporated in the statute was the narrow interpretation of only what was intentionally untrue. In response to concerns about overcharging in the defense industry, Congress amended the False Claims Act in 1986 to redefine the term "knowingly" to include acts in deliberate ignorance or reckless disregard of the truth or falsity of the information, with no proof of specific intent to defraud required.[25] This 1986 amendment serves as the genesis of the 1996 amendment to the Social Security Act with respect to the "know or should know" language discussed in Section 13.7.

Penalties under the False Claims Act were also significantly increased in 1986 to triple damages plus not less than $5,000 and not more than $10,000 per claim. The act further provides that if the court finds that the person committing the violation disclosed all known facts about the violation to officials of the United States within 30 days of discovery and prior to commencement of any government enforcement action, and the person fully cooperated with the government investigation, the court may assess not less than double damages in lieu of the higher statutory sanctions. This language provides the basis for the government's settlement offers in the various civil enforcement projects discussed in Sections 13.10, 13.11, and 13.12.

Prior to January 1, 1997, the now similar civil provisions of the Social Security Act did not contain the "know or should know" standard of falsity and the statutory penalties were merely double damages plus $2,000 per claim. Thus, the federal government prosecutes conduct that occurred prior to January 1, 1997, under the False Claims Act because of its stiffer penalties for false healthcare billings without having to prove intentional untruth. With an applicable six-year limitations period, such use of the False Claims Act will continue through January 1, 2003, absent further statutory amendments.

## 13.16  Provider Objections

Providers have strongly objected to the OIG's heavy-handed tactics in these civil enforcement projects. Providers argue that the technical rules being enforced were unknown or unclear to them during some or all of the six-year limitations period. In some cases, providers were following procedures specifically set forth by their fiscal intermediaries, which conflicted with the positions asserted by the government in the projects. While providers claim that they did not know and were not acting in deliberate ignorance or reckless disregard, they generally choose to settle with the government rather than litigate over the civil legal standards because of threat of disastrous civil sanctions, including triple damages plus $10,000 per claim plus exclusion from participation in federal health programs. Various provider associations, including the American, Ohio, New Jersey, and Greater New York Hospital Associations, have commenced litigation seeking to stop the government from using such threatening tactics. Lobbying efforts by providers led to the bipartisan introduction in March 1998 of federal legislation that would have limited the use of the False Claims Act against healthcare providers.[26] By June 1, 1998, support for the proposed amendments to the False Claims Act grew to 201 cosponsors in the U.S. House of Representatives.

On June 3, 1998, the OIG and Department of Justice took action to address some provider objections about their tactics by issuing memoranda to their respective employees that provided guidance on the use of the False Claims Act in national enforcement projects.[27] The introduction to the Department of Justice memorandum acknowledges that the national enforcement initiatives have caused significant and understandable concerns in the provider community. "For example, there is a widespread perception that we are using the False Claims Act to 'punish' honest billing mistakes, and threatening rural and other small hospitals with costly legal action and thereby forcing them into settlements that are not justified by the evidence."[28] The Department of Justice memorandum instructs U.S. attorneys to:

- investigate before concluding the provider "knowingly" submitted false claims;
- substitute "contact" letters for demand letters in national initiatives to allow discussion with the provider before any demands for settlement are made; and
- consider ability to pay issues in determining fair settlements.

By issuing the memoranda, the OIG and Department of Justice successfully blunted efforts to amend the provisions of the False Claims Act. Congress, however, did add language to the appropriations act for fiscal year 1999 requiring the General Accounting Office to report to specified congressional committees on the compliance by U.S. attorneys with the Department of Justice memorandum on the use of the False Claims Act in civil healthcare matters.[29] Compliance has now come full circle: just as providers must have programs to document their efforts to comply with all laws, the government must now document its compliance in enforcing the laws.

## 13.17 *Qui Tam* Actions

Private parties can also bring actions under the False Claims Act on behalf of the government and share in any recovery. Such actions, known as *qui tam* actions (abbreviated Latin phrase meaning "he who sues on behalf of the king as well as for himself"), are initially filed under seal or secretly with the court. The legal complaint is furnished only to the government, which then has a period of time to review the allegations and decide whether to take over the prosecution or decline to participate. Only after the government makes this decision does the provider receive official notice that the matter is pending.

Plaintiffs' attorneys generally handle *qui tam* actions on a contingent-fee basis and may assist the plaintiff in funding some expenses of the litigation. By statute, the *qui tam* plaintiff receives up to 30 percent of any recovery depending on the level of involvement of the plaintiff.[30] For example, when SmithKline Beecham was assessed $325 million for clinical laboratory over-billing as a result of a *qui tam* action that the government did join, the *qui tam* plaintiffs and their attorneys shared more than $52 million of the recovery.

Sections 8.3 and 11.9 suggest using employee acknowledgments in the course of compliance program implementation to discourage *qui tam* actions and possibly provide a counterclaim against the *qui tam* plaintiff for breach of his employment duties if he brings the action without first notifying the compliance officer of the problem. *Qui tam* plaintiffs have a huge financial incentive to go to the court first with any damaging information, rather than report through normal compliance channels. Without helpful legislative changes, the *qui tam* risk will be one of the most difficult and costly issues for healthcare providers to manage during the coming years.

## 13.18 Healthcare Fraud

In addition to the foregoing criminal and civil sanctions, HIPAA created the new crime of healthcare fraud.[31] The statute prohibits *knowingly and willfully* executing, or attempting to execute, a scheme or artifice:

- to defraud *any healthcare benefit program*; or
- to obtain, by means of *false or fraudulent pretenses, representations, or promises*, any of the money or property owned by, or under the custody or control of, *any health benefit program*.

This criminal statute requires knowing and willful conduct, which must be proved beyond a reasonable doubt. The notion of falsity under this statute is similar to the criminal provisions of the Social Security Act: intentional untruth. The crime of healthcare fraud adds two major elements to the legal analysis. First, the crime is punishable by up to ten years' imprisonment, double the maximum sentence under the criminal provisions of the Social Security Act. Second, the crime is committed by false statements to *any healthcare benefit program*, whether public or private.

## 13.19 The Threat of Private Payors

Both the Social Security Act and the False Claims Act apply only to government-funded programs. Prior to the addition of the crime of healthcare fraud, private payors relied on common-law fraud and, in some cases, RICO to punish healthcare fraud. With the new crime of healthcare fraud, private payors have a powerful deterrent to fraud with the threat of ten years' imprisonment. Furthermore, private insurers will have the opportunity to ride the government's coattails in civil fraud cases. Once the government achieves a judgment or settlement, private payors will follow with their own litigation. For example, after Caremark settled fraudulent billing allegations with federal and state governments and certain insurers for $250 million, another group of private payors sued Caremark seeking damages of $2 billion.

The threat posed by private payors complicates the design of compliance programs. Private payors often have their own technical rules for provider reimbursement, which may vary from the government's rules and may differ with each individual payor. While compliance policies and education should immediately focus on the applicable government standards, a thorough compliance program should also eventually cover the rules for private reimbursement. The provider will need to implement the compliance program in a series of manageable steps, and while variations among private payors may not be at the top of the priority list, such variations should not be overlooked.

## 13.20 Common Billing Frauds

The following list summarizes some of the general types of billing frauds that the government is prosecuting using these legal standards.

1. *Billing for services not rendered.* The easy cases, such as billing for services after the date of death, are known as the "prosecutor's dream." The more egregious of these cases warrant criminal prosecution.

2. *Misrepresenting service/product actually provided.* Typically, the government prosecutes these cases in civil actions using the expanded notion of falsity. The provider rendered some service, but perhaps not the level of service claimed. For example, a psychiatrist takes ten minutes to review the patient file and prepare for a 30-minute counseling session and bills Medicare for a 40-minute session, although under Medicare rules preparation time is incorporated into payment for a 30-minute session. Another example is the OIG's new pneumonia upcoding project, which specifically focuses on the relative frequencies, documentation requirements, and coding conventions for simple pneumonia (DRG 89) and complex pneumonia (DRG 79).[32]

3. *Unbundling and separately charging for services.* The government claims that unbundling is prevalent in surgery. This practice is the subject of Project Bad Bundle, discussed in Section 13.12.

4. *Medically unnecessary services.* To date, this category has been the least prosecuted because of varying opinions of medical necessity. In light of the 1996 and 1997 HCFA audits by the OIG that identified lack of medical necessity as a leading cause of improper Medicare payments, providers should expect the government to bring significant enforcement efforts on the issue of medical necessity in the near future.

5. *Duplicate billings.* Duplicate billing includes any separate billing for a service that should be incorporated in a fixed payment under PPS.

6. *False cost reports.* Cost reporting involves complex accounting issues. Given the possible legal ramifications of erroneous cost accounting, providers should obtain expert review and advice before filing all cost reports.

7. *Billing for discharge instead of transfer.* Another OIG nationwide initiative focuses on improper payments to hospitals for patient transfers between two PPS hospitals.[33] Under Medicare reimbursement rules, the hospital transferring a patient is to receive a per diem payment based on the length of stay, and the hospital receiving the transferred patient is to be paid a diagnosis-related payment based on the final discharge code.

8. *Teaching hospital issues.* The controversial PATH project, discussed in Section 13.10, disallows reimbursement for the teaching physician unless he is physically present in the room.

## 13.21 Conclusion—Billing Compliance

The best defense to billing prosecutions is accurate and complete clinical documentation and coding. To ensure documentation and coding compliance, training is necessary because coding requirements are voluminous and complex, and the lack of actual knowledge is not a defense to severe civil penalties. Physicians, whether employed by the provider or not, must be involved in the training, because accurate coding depends on the quality and completeness of the physician's documentation. Medical documentation also must plainly support the medical necessity of all procedures and services.

---

**Action Items**

1. Educate all billing and clinical personnel, including physicians, about the recent legal changes, focusing on coding and medical necessity.
2. Provide extensive training to all clinical personnel to improve clinical documentation, including evidence in the patient record of medical necessity.
3. Use targeted education and billing software to minimize the provider's exposure to announced enforcement projects such as PATH audits, 72-hour DRG window project, Project Bad Bundle, and the pneumonia upcoding project, if applicable.
4. Develop compliance procedures for billings to private payors, to the extent that such requirements differ from federal health reimbursement.

---

## Notes

1. 42 U.S.C.A. § 1320a-7b(a) and (d) (West 1997) (emphasis added).
2. 42 U.S.C.A. § 1320a-7(a) (West 1997). In addition, conduct that violates the criminal provisions of the Social Security Act will also likely constitute federal crimes outside of the Social Security Act that carry even more severe sanctions. For example, the crime of false

statements relating to healthcare matters carries fines of up to $250,000 for both providers and nonproviders. 18 U.S.C.A. §§ 1035, 3571(b)(3) (West 1997).

3. *Black's Law Dictionary 5th Ed.*, p. 540 (1979).

4. 42 U.S.C.A. § 1320a-7a(a)(1)(A) (West 1997) (emphasis supplied).

5. 18 U.S.C.A. § 1961 *et seq.* (West 1997).

6. See e.g. *Sedima, S.P.R.L. v. Imrex Co., Inc.*, 473 U.S. 479 (1985); *H.J., Inc. v. Northwestern Bell Tel. Co.*, 492 U.S. 229 (1989). The RICO statute defines "pattern of racketeering activity" to require at least two acts of racketeering activity. 18 U.S.C.A. § 1961(5) (West 1997). In contrast, the Social Security Act does not further define "pattern" for purposes of assessing civil monetary penalties.

7. United States General Accounting Office, Report to Congressional Requesters, *Medicare—Application of the False Claims Act to Hospital Billing Practices*, GAO/HEHS-98-195, July 1998, pp. 8-9.

8. 42 U.S.C.A. § 1320a-7a(i)(7) (West 1997).

9. 42 U.S.C.A. § 1320a-7a(a)(1)(B) (West 1997).

10. 42 C.F.R. § 415.170 and 415.172 (West 1997).

11. 60 Fed. Reg. 63178 (1995).

12. U.S. Department of Health and Human Services, Office of Inspector General, *Semi-Annual Report*, April 1, 1997–September 30, 1997, p. 7.

13. United States General Accounting Office, Report to Chairman, Subcommittee on Health, Committee on Ways and Means, House of Representatives, *Medicare—Concerns With Physicians at Teaching Hospitals (PATH) Audits*, GAO/HEHS-98-174, July 1998, p. 21. This report also states: "The OIG's workpapers for Penn and Jefferson do not contain convincing evidence that teaching physicians were not working on days they billed Medicare. Rather, the workpapers show that teaching physicians did not always document their presence when services were rendered by a resident. While this lack of documentation may be insufficient to obtain Medicare reimbursement, it does not necessarily mean that the teaching physicians were not at work when the services were rendered."

14. U.S. Department of Health and Human Services, Office of Inspector General, *Semi-Annual Report*, April 1, 1997–September 30, 1997, p. 8.

15. United States General Accounting Office, Report to Congressional Requesters, *Medicare—Application of the False Claims Act to Hospital Billing Practices*, GAO/HEHS-98-195, July 1998, p. 9.

16. United States General Accounting Office, Report to Congressional Requesters, *Medicare—Application of the False Claims Act to Hospital Billing Practices*, GAO/HEHS-98-195, July 1998, p. 13; see also U.S. Department of Health and Human Services, Office of Inspector General, *Semi-Annual Report*, April 1, 1997–September 30, 1997, p. 9.

17. 42 U.S.C.A. § 1320a-7a(a)(1)(E) (West 1997).

18. 1996 Cong. Rec. H9473, H9537 (1996).

19. Home Health Guidance, 63 Fed. Reg. 42410, 42414, footnote 21 (1998) (citing 42 U.S.C. § 1395y(a)(1)(A)).

20. Committee on Commerce, Subcommittee on Health and Environment, the Subcommittee on Oversight and Investigations, and the Subcommittee on Government Management, Information and Technology of the Committee on Government Reform and Oversight, testimony of June Gibbs Brown, inspector general of Health and Human Services, before a joint hearing, April 24, 1998.

21. See also Home Health Guidance, 63 Fed. Reg. 42410, 42416-7, footnote 55 (1998) (suggesting that a home health agency has a duty to investigate the appropriateness of physician certifications on the issue of medical necessity).

22. 42 C.F.R. § 412.46 (1997).

23. Hospital Guidance, 63 Fed. Reg. 8987, 8995, footnote 43 (1998).

24. 31 U.S.C.A. § 3729 *et seq.* (West 1997).

25. Ibid. (b).

26. H.R. 3523, introduced in the U.S. House of Representatives in March 1998.

27. Memorandum dated June 3, 1998, from Eric H. Holder, Jr., deputy attorney general, to all United States Attorneys re: Guidance on the Use of the False Claims Act in Civil Health Care Matters; Memorandum dated June 3, 1998, from June Gibbs Brown, inspector general, to Deputy and Assistant Inspectors General re: National Project Protocols—Best Practice Guidelines.

28. Memorandum dated June 3, 1998, from Eric H. Holder, Jr., deputy attorney general, to all United States Attorneys re: Guidance on the Use of the False Claims Act in Civil Health Care Matters, Introduction.

29. Public Law 105-277 (1998), Omnibus Consolidated and Emergency Supplemental Appropriations Act of 1999, enacted October 21, 1998.

30. 31 U.S.C.A. § 3730(d) (West 1997).

31. 18 U.S.C.A. § 1347 (West 1997).

32. U.S. Department of Health and Human Services, Office of Inspector General, *Semi-Annual Report*, October 1, 1997–March 31, 1997, pp. 8-9.

33. Ibid., p. 8.

# ANTI-KICKBACK AND
# SELF-REFERRAL COMPLIANCE

## 14.1 Strategic Importance

On August 7, 1997, in an effort to address some areas of concern that may have led to investigations by certain government agencies, the management of Columbia/HCA announced several significant steps it plans to take to redefine the company's approach to a number of business practices. Some of these steps include elimination of annual cash incentive compensation for the company's employees, divestiture of the home health care business, discontinuing sales of interests in hospitals to physicians, and the unwinding of existing physician interests in hospitals.

Even these steps, if successfully implemented, will not insulate Columbia/HCA from the expansive scope of the federal anti-kickback statute[1] (anti-kickback) and the federal self-referral statute, commonly known as "Stark."[2] Anti-kickback and Stark laws will continue to affect a wide variety of ownership, compensation, and other financial relationships that are common in the healthcare industry. All providers are at risk of anti-kickback and/or Stark attacks by the federal government. Today's challenge for healthcare executives and individual providers alike is to successfully navigate through Stark-infested waters. This chapter charts the course for avoiding the implication of these extremely vague laws when possible and, when necessary, defending against their application.

## 14.2 Overview of the Federal Anti-Kickback Statute

The federal anti-kickback statute makes it a crime to knowingly and willfully offer, pay, solicit, or receive *any remuneration* to induce a person

(A) to refer an individual to a person for the furnishing of any item or service covered under a federal healthcare program; or

(B) to purchase, lease, order, arrange for, or recommend any good, facility, service, or item covered under a federal healthcare program.[3]

The term "any remuneration" encompasses:

- any kickback, bribe, or rebate;
- direct or indirect;
- overt or covert;
- cash or in kind; and
- any ownership interest or compensation interest.[4]

Knowing and willful conduct is a necessary element of this criminal offense.[5] The burden of proving intent beyond a reasonable doubt makes criminal prosecution difficult but not impossible, and the government has demonstrated some willingness to bear the criminal burden of proof.[6] Pursuant to a 1987 congressional mandate,[7] safe harbor regulations have been promulgated in 14 general areas to give healthcare providers some protection from an extremely vague statute.[8]

Criminal penalties for violations of the anti-kickback statute include up to five years imprisonment plus fines up to $25,000 for each violation. In addition, all claims for reimbursement made while an illegal kickback arrangement exists may constitute false claims under the False Claims Act because the provider would have falsely certified that it is in compliance with all Medicare billing requirements by submitting claims and filing cost reports, whether or not the related services were induced by the illegal remuneration.[9] Thus, providers are exposed to *qui tam* actions for anti-kickback and Stark violations because private plaintiffs can use the Medicare certification of compliance procedures to bootstrap claims that are actionable under the False Claims Act.

## 14.3 New Civil Monetary Penalty

The Balanced Budget Act of 1997[10] created a civil monetary penalty for anti-kickback violations in addition to the criminal penalties and the sanction of exclusion.[11] The civil penalty is treble damages (three times the illegal remuneration) plus $50,000 per violation plus possible exclusion from Medicare.[12] The government can now impose exorbitant fines for anti-kickback violations that it proves with a simple preponderance of the evidence, a standard much easier to satisfy than the criminal standard of beyond a reasonable doubt. The government will be much more likely to pursue anti-kickback prosecutions now that a lower civil burden of proof applies.

## 14.4  Requisite Intent

As with the criminal and civil provisions of the Social Security Act and the False Claims Act, a determination of requisite intent is critical to the application of the anti-kickback statute. In the context of this statute, knowing and willful conduct means providing remuneration with some sort of intent to induce referrals. The exact nature of the required intent has been the subject of extensive litigation.

The government's position, based on a 1985 Third Circuit Court of Appeals decision,[13] is that a violation exists if a purpose of the remuneration is to induce referrals, even if it is not the only purpose (e.g., some services were rendered in consideration for the services). In 1995, the Ninth Circuit Court of Appeals stated the intent requirement in a way much more favorable to providers. It held that the government must prove actual knowledge that remuneration is unlawful and must prove specific intent to disobey law.[14] Since then, the Eighth and Eleventh Circuit Courts of Appeals have adopted a middle ground on the issue, holding that the government must prove actual knowledge that the remuneration is wrongful, rather than prove intent to violate a known legal duty.[15] Regardless of the particular standard, a provider can defend against the anti-kickback statute by asserting that the provider lacked the requisite intent.

Examples of illegal remuneration that have been prosecuted under the anti-kickback statute include:

- 40 percent of the Medicare payment for cardiac monitoring paid to the referring physician;
- limited partnership interest of a physician in a clinical lab;
- $1,000 per month from a hospital to a physician for unspecified marketing duties; and
- alcoholic beverages worth $400 per month received by a nursing home administrator from a drug supplier.

## 14.5  Overview of Stark

In contrast to the federal anti-kickback statute, Stark is only a civil prohibition, not a crime. The good news is that jail is not a potential punishment; the bad news is that the government does not need to prove any intent to induce referrals. As originally adopted in 1989, Stark applied only to physician referrals to clinical laboratories in which the physician had a financial interest.[16]

Congress significantly expanded the scope of Stark in 1993 to referrals for "designated health services," which include clinical laboratory, physical therapy, occupational therapy, radiology, radiation therapy, durable medical equipment and supplies, home health, outpatient prescription drugs, and (as if the foregoing list was not enough) all inpatient and outpatient hospital services.[17] In addition, a number of states (including California, New York, Florida, and Georgia) have enacted their own versions of self-referral laws that should be examined carefully, if applicable, but are beyond the scope of this book.

Stark simply prohibits all referrals for the provision of designated health services[18] and all claims for federal reimbursement for such services furnished pursuant to a referral,[19] if a physician has a *financial relationship* (either an ownership or a compensation arrangement)[20] with the entity. Intent is irrelevant. If the financial relationship exists, all referrals and associated claims are illegal unless specifically excepted by statute. Unlike anti-kickback, which is still defensible based on lack of intent even if no safe harbor applies, any and all referrals of designated health services will violate Stark unless a general statutory exception applies. Table 14.1 contains a brief comparison of anti-kickback and Stark laws.

Under Stark, a *financial relationship* with an entity means both an ownership or investment interest and a compensation arrangement. An ownership or investment interest in the entity includes equity, debt, or indirect ownership through controlling entities. A compensation arrangement means any arrangement involving any remuneration between a physician (or an immediate family member of such physician) and the entity.[21] Stark defines "remuneration" broadly to include any remuneration received by a physician directly or indirectly, overtly or covertly, in cash or in kind, excluding only:

- forgiveness of amounts owed for inaccurate or mistakenly performed tests or procedures, or the correction of minor billing errors;
- provision of items, devices, or supplies that are used solely to collect specimens or order procedures for the entity; and
- certain payments from insurers to physicians on a fee-for-service basis.[22]

**Table 14.1**  Comparison of Anti-Kickback and Stark Laws

| Anti-Kickback | Stark |
| --- | --- |
| Prohibits any remuneration to induce referrals | Prohibits referrals if financial relationship exists |
| Regulatory safe harbors | Statutory general exceptions |
| Criminal and civil penalties—may also trigger false claims | Civil penalties only—may also trigger false claims |
| Requires proof of intent | Intent is irrelevant |

Providers should take extreme care in managing Stark because of the ease with which technical violations can occur. Penalties for violating Stark are severe, including fines of up to $15,000 per service (these fines quickly become exorbitant in an extended financial relationship), and exclusion from participation in federal healthcare programs.[23]

Examples of common remuneration arrangements that will implicate Stark unless a statutory exception applies are as follows:

- investment partnerships for referring physicians;
- interest-free loans;
- free and below-market office space;
- consultation fees without corresponding services;
- reimbursement for malpractice insurance; and
- income guarantees for physicians.

## 14.6  General Exceptions to Stark

Stark contains a total of 16 statutory exceptions. Eight exceptions relate only to compensation arrangements,[24] four exceptions relate only to ownership arrangements,[25] and four exceptions relate to both ownership and compensation arrangements.[26] Some of the eight exceptions relating to compensation arrangements overlap with areas covered by the anti-kickback safe harbors as will be more fully explored below. The four exceptions relating only to ownership deal with very specific arrangements: certain publicly traded securities,[27] hospitals in Puerto Rico,[28] rural providers,[29] and direct hospital ownership.[30] Three of the four exceptions relating to both ownership and compensation arrangements deal with specific situations: physicians' services provided personally by or under the supervision of the physician,[31] in-office ancillary services,[32] and prepaid plans.[33] The fourth statutory exception to Stark relating to both ownership and compensation arrangements ("Other Permissible Exceptions")[34] deserves special consideration for its defensive potential.

## 14.7  Other Permissible Exceptions

The Stark statute provides as follows:

> (4) Other permissible exceptions. In the case of any other financial relationship which the Secretary determines, and specifies in regulations, does not pose a risk of program or patient abuse.[35]

Thus the statute contains two simple elements for "Other Permissible Exceptions" to apply: (1) the financial relationship must be specified in regulations, and (2) the secretary of the Department of Health and Human Services must determine that the financial relationship does not pose a risk of program or patient abuse.

Regulations have been issued to implement Stark as it existed before the 1993 amendments (commonly known as Stark I regulations)[36] and new regulations were proposed in 1998 to reflect the 1993 amendments to Stark (commonly known as Stark II regulations).[37] As the Stark II regulations have not been finalized and are the subject of considerable industry comment, this book will only discuss the Stark I regulations as officially adopted. The general exceptions in the Stark I regulations largely mirror the exceptions in the statute itself, except for one additional exception for certain services included in composite rates for an ambulatory surgical center, end-stage renal disease facility, or hospice.[38]

The regulations establishing safe harbors from the anti-kickback statute also specify financial relationships that do not pose a risk of program or patient abuse.[39] What is the interplay between the Stark regulations and the anti-kickback regulations? The 1989 legislative history of Stark contains the following:

> The conferees wish to clarify that any prohibition, exemption, or exception authorized under this provision [Stark] in no way alters (or reflects on) the scope and application of the anti-kickback provisions in [42 U.S.C. §1320-7b(b)]. The conferees do not intend that this provision [Stark] should be construed as affecting, or in any way interfering, with the efforts of the Inspector General to enforce current law [anti-kickback statute], such as cases described in the recent Fraud Alert issued by the Inspector General. In particular, entities that would be eligible for a specific exemption would be subject to all of the provisions of current law [anti-kickback statute].[40]

The legislative intent was that general exceptions to Stark would not constitute an exception to the anti-kickback statute. But what about vice versa? The quoted material does not address the possibility that anti-kickback safe harbors could apply to Stark. The 1989 legislative history of Stark also contained the following comments about anti-kickback law:

> The Medicare and Medicaid Patient and Program Protection Act of 1987 (P.L. 100-93) provided authority to the Inspector General of the Department of Health and Human Services to exclude a person or entity from participation in Medicare and State health care programs if it is determined that the party is engaged in a prohibited remuneration scheme. The Act required the promulgation of regulations specifying those payment practices that will not be subject to criminal prosecution and that will not provide a basis for exclusion from the Medicare and State health care programs. These are sometimes referred to as "safe harbors." On January 23, 1989, the Secretary published a proposed rule to provide such "safe harbors." The rule has not yet been issued in final form.[41]

Thus, just two years prior to the enactment of Stark, Congress had mandated that the secretary issue safe harbor regulations to clarify which business ventures would not subject a provider to the severe sanction of exclusion. The

1989 legislative history of Stark repeats Congress' concern that clear safe harbors should be established so that providers could fairly avoid exclusion. Significantly, Stark itself includes the sanction of exclusion.[42]

## 14.8 Financial Relationship Specified in Regulations

When Congress adopted Stark in 1989, it knew that the secretary of the Department of Health and Human Services (secretary) had not yet finalized the regulations that Congress had directed the secretary to issue to provide safe harbors from Medicare exclusion. Following the adoption of Stark, the secretary implemented two sets of regulations: (1) the anti-kickback regulations, finalized in 1991,[43] and (2) the Stark I regulations, first proposed in 1992 and finalized in 1995.[44] Both sets of regulations describe various financial relationships, some that are quite similar and some that are different. For example, both sets of regulations describe a financial relationship in certain publicly traded entities,[45] but only the anti-kickback regulations contain the exception for small investments in nonpublicly traded entities, otherwise known as the "60-40 rule."[46]

The financial relationships described in both sets of regulations satisfy the first element of the "Other Permissible Exceptions" to Stark, namely that the financial relationships are specified in regulations. Congress expressed no intention, either in the Stark statute itself or in the related legislative history, to exclude the then-pending anti-kickback regulations (which Congress specifically directed in 1987 and acknowledged again in 1989 in the legislative history to Stark) from the "Other Permissible Exceptions" to Stark.

## 14.9 Risk of Program or Patient Abuse

For a financial relationship described in the safe harbor regulations under the anti-kickback statute to meet the second element of "Other Permissible Exceptions" to Stark, the financial relationship must be one that the secretary determines does not pose a risk of program or patient abuse. When the anti-kickback regulations were originally proposed in 1989, the 60-40 rule was not part of the proposed regulations.[47] However, the notice of rule making issued when the anti-kickback regulations were first proposed in January 1989 solicited comments on expanding the proposed investment interest safe harbor for certain publicly traded securities. The purpose was to protect payments from investments in small entities.[48] In light of an enormous response in favor of the safe harbor for small entities, the secretary adopted the 60-40 rule in 1991 with the following explanation:

Because of the significant business investment activity in these small entities—typically joint ventures—and the advantages of permitting them in certain situations, we believe that safe harbor protection is warranted. However, we have also observed widespread abuses in many of these joint ventures. Therefore, any safe harbor protection must include significant safeguards to minimize any corrupting influence the investment interest may have on the physician-investor's decision where to refer a patient.[49]

Eight standards were specified in the 60-40 safe harbor to minimize any corrupting influence the investment interest may have on the physician-investor's decision of where to refer a patient:

1. Referring persons can own no more than 40 percent of the investment interests;[50]

2. The terms of investment must be the same as those offered to passive investors;[51]

3. The terms of investment must not be related to the volume of referrals;[52]

4. The terms of investment must not be tied to any requirement to make referrals;[53]

5. The entity and all investors must not market or furnish the entity's items or services to passive investors differently than to noninvestors;[54]

6. No more than 40 percent of the gross revenue of the entity may come from referrals from investors;[55]

7. The entity must not lend funds to, or guarantee a loan for, a referring investor;[56] and

8. Payments to investors must be directly proportional to the amount of capital investment.[57]

The 60-40 safe harbor applies only if all eight of these standards are satisfied. The secretary went to great lengths to ensure that the financial relationship described in the 60-40 safe harbor does not pose a risk of program or patient abuse.

Separately, Richard P. Kusserow, the inspector general of the Department of Health and Human Services at the time the anti-kickback safe harbor regulations were drafted and adopted in 1991, authored a 1992 article published in *Health Matrix* which provides the following explanation behind the regulations:

In drafting the safe harbor regulations, OIG attempted to balance two competing concerns. First, we tried to draft the regulations to accommodate as many non-abusive arrangements as possible. Second, we tried to minimize the risks of allowing abusive arrangements within the safe harbor. We believe each of the eleven [later expanded] safe harbors contained in the final rule contains criteria which offer reasonable assurance that abusive activities will not receive the comfort of being in a safe harbor.[58]

The 60-40 safe harbor contained in the anti-kickback regulations satisfies both the first and second elements of the "Other Permissible Exceptions" to

Stark, namely that the 60-40 safe harbor is a financial relationship specified in regulations and the secretary has determined that the financial relationship does not pose a risk of program or patient abuse. The "Other Permissible Exceptions" exemption from Stark requires nothing more. Therefore, the 60-40 safe harbor in the anti-kickback regulations satisfies the "Other Permissible Exceptions" to Stark and affords providers with a possible defense to a Stark attack.

A similar case can be made for all of the other anti-kickback safe harbors. In fact, in the preamble to the 1998 proposed Stark II regulations, HCFA solicited comments on whether meeting an anti-kickback safe harbor would qualify the arrangement as one that involves no risk of program or patient abuse.[59] Each anti-kickback safe harbor specifies a financial relationship in regulations as required by the first element of Stark's "Other Permissible Exceptions." Each safe harbor contains criteria to provide reasonable assurance that the financial relationship does not pose a risk of program or patient abuse as required by the second element of Stark's "Other Permissible Exceptions." In short, all anti-kickback safe harbors provide protection against exposure related to Stark provisions.

## 14.10 Comparison of Anti-Kickback Safe Harbors and Stark Exceptions

Because anti-kickback safe harbors may satisfy one of the statutory exceptions to Stark, it is useful to compare the anti-kickback safe harbors with the Stark exceptions to determine when it may be advantageous to use an anti-kickback safe harbor as a statutory exception to Stark. Remember that the legislative history is clear that the converse does not apply—Stark exceptions cannot be used as safe harbors from anti-kickback laws.[60]

At the end of Chapter 14, Appendixes 14.1, 14.2, and 14.3 analyze the interplay between anti-kickback safe harbors and Stark general exceptions by grouping the various safe harbors and exceptions into the following three classes:

1. Appendix 14.1—Overlapping Anti-Kickback Safe Harbors and Stark General Exceptions;
2. Appendix 14.2—Anti-Kickback Safe Harbors Without Similar Stark General Exceptions; and
3. Appendix 14.3—Stark General Exceptions Without Similar Anti-Kickback Safe Harbors.

Healthcare executives and individual providers would enhance their abilities to manage the vagaries of anti-kickback and Stark by studying these tables and appreciating the interplay between the two statutes. Without rehashing the information set forth in the tables, some observations will be made about the groupings in general and some particular safe harbors/exceptions.

## 14.11 Areas of Overlap

Appendix 14.1 identifies eight areas where the anti-kickback safe harbors and the Stark exceptions overlap. In general, the technical requirements of the Stark exceptions are more difficult to satisfy than the comparable anti-kickback safe harbor. For example, the public securities exception to Stark applies only to public corporations having more than $75 million in stockholder equity,[61] while the anti-kickback safe harbor applies to all entities (both corporate and noncorporate) having more than $50 million in net tangible assets (without reduction for liabilities).[62]

Anti-kickback and Stark laws also overlap in the area of risk-sharing arrangements, but with vastly different technical requirements. The anti-kickback statute was amended in 1996 to exclude all risk-sharing arrangements from the definition of illegal remuneration.[63] On the other hand, Stark contains no general exception for risk sharing but rather a series of specific exceptions where risk is shared: group practice,[64] in-office ancillary services,[65] certain services included in composite rates,[66] certain physician incentive plans,[67] and certain group practice services billed by the hospital.[68] Each specific exception entails a number of technical requirements to avoid a Stark violation. Providers should exercise extreme care to ensure risk-sharing arrangements comply with Stark.

Providers may use the financial relationships specified in the anti-kickback safe harbor regulations to defend a situation in which the technical requirements of Stark are not met, but the anti-kickback safe harbor is satisfied. This defense will not presently work for risk-sharing arrangements, because the arrangements are excluded by the anti-kickback statute itself, and safe harbor regulations have not yet been issued. The lack of a clear Stark exception may impede the development of innovative risk-sharing arrangements that otherwise would be permitted under the anti-kickback statute.

## 14.12 Anti-Kickback Safe Harbors Without Similar Stark Exceptions

Appendix 14.2 identifies seven areas in which an anti-kickback safe harbor exists without a similar Stark exception. This is the grouping where an anti-kickback safe harbor may save an otherwise blatant Stark violation. In the areas of warranties, discounts, and waivers of coinsurance or deductibles, large volumes of transactions may implicate Stark even though an anti-kickback safe harbor exists.[69] The government has not yet used Stark frequently as its primary grounds for an attack, but that may change in the current political and regulatory climate.

Providers may use the safe harbor for small entities (60-40 rule) under anti-kickback[70] defensively to save those residual financial arrangements that

Stark implicated when Congress expanded it from just clinical laboratories to all designated health services, effective in 1995. The use of anti-kickback safe harbors against Stark attacks has not yet been thoroughly litigated, and as a result providers should not use the 60-40 anti-kickback safe harbor offensively to structure new arrangements without separately complying with a Stark exception.

## 14.13 Stark Exceptions Without Similar Anti-Kickback Safe Harbors

Appendix 14.3 identifies five areas in which a Stark exception exists without a similar anti-kickback safe harbor. Because the legislative history makes it clear that Stark exceptions do not apply to anti-kickback, a trap exists for anyone relying on the Stark exceptions for specific providers. While Stark has specific exceptions for hospitals in Puerto Rico,[71] rural providers,[72] and hospital ownership,[73] anti-kickback has no similar safe harbors in these situations. A provider probably would have to look to the safe harbors for small entities (60-40 rule)[74] or public securities[75] to find an anti-kickback safe harbor. Unlike Stark, anti-kickback always has the backup defense that no intent to induce referrals existed.

The Stark exception for isolated transactions[76] is the best chance under Stark for saving an innocent arrangement that fails the technical requirements of the other Stark exceptions. Even this exception has a technical requirement that no additional transactions occur between the parties for six months, which significantly limits the usefulness of the exception.[77]

## 14.14 Columbia/HCA's Abandoned Strategies

The decisions by Columbia/HCA to eliminate annual cash incentive compensation for the company's employees, divest its home health care business, discontinue sales of interests in hospitals to physicians, and unwind existing physician interests in hospitals go beyond what the law requires under anti-kickback and Stark. Both the anti-kickback safe harbors and the Stark exceptions permit cash incentive compensation to employees.[78] Columbia/HCAs ownership of home health agencies is a permitted risk-sharing arrangement under anti-kickback.[79] Stark only applies to physician (not hospital) financial relationships,[80] and any indirect ownership by physicians in home health agencies by virtue of stock ownership in Columbia/HCA is permitted under the public corporation exception to Stark.[81] Stark expressly permits investments by physicians directly in hospitals.[82] Anti-kickback also permits certain physician investments in hospitals at the public holding company level under the public securities safe harbor[83] or at the subsidiary level as long as the requirements of the 60-40 rule are satisfied.[84]

The business strategies that Columbia/HCA abandoned can be defended under existing safe harbors to anti-kickback and exceptions to Stark. The decision to abandon those strategies may be understandable in light of the intense regulatory and media pressure faced by Columbia/HCA. However, before other healthcare providers abandon their similar strategies, they should carefully analyze two issues:

1. Is the strategy well supported under current laws and regulations, including anti-kickback, Stark, and any applicable state laws?
2. Is the strategy still appropriate from an economic and business standpoint?

Several strategies that have developed in healthcare during the last decade may still be appropriate even after this analysis. For example, the notion of integrated healthcare systems remains the trend and can be accommodated within anti-kickback and Stark laws. Incentive-based compensation works well in business generally and should also work in healthcare, if properly structured and monitored.

## 14.15 Compliance Training of Physicians

In May 1992, the OIG issued a *Special Fraud Alert* suggesting that certain economic incentives provided by hospitals to physicians may be for the purpose of inducing referrals in violation of the anti-kickback statute. To help identify suspect incentive arrangements, the OIG provided examples of practices that are "often questionable." One of the "questionable" examples was "[f]ree training for a physician's office staff in such areas as management techniques, CPT coding and laboratory techniques."[85] There are no reported cases in which free training served as the basis for an anti-kickback prosecution.

Since the issuance of that *Special Fraud Alert,* the OIG has specifically recommended that healthcare providers participate in a nationwide effort to reduce fraud and abuse by adopting compliance programs. In connection with these initiatives to combat fraud and abuse, the OIG has provided written guidance advising hospitals and clinical laboratories to provide training to all personnel (including physicians) involved in documentation, coding, and billing for healthcare services. The Home Health Guidance specifically states that compliance training should include "[p]roper documentation of services rendered, including the correct application of official ICD and CPT coding rules and guidelines."[86]

In addition to the focus on training in the OIG's compliance guidance, the OIG has required hospitals to agree to adopt compliance programs providing for physician training as part of settling federal investigations of Medicare fraud. For example, one stipulation of the OIG's $12,000,000 settlement with the teaching hospital at Thomas Jefferson University in Philadelphia, Pennsylvania, was the implementation of and adherence to a compliance program, which contained the following provisions:

> TJU/JeFF shall institute and maintain an information and education program designed to ensure that each officer, director, contractor, and employee is aware of all applicable health care laws, regulations, and standards of business conduct that such individual is expected to follow and the consequences both to the individual and Hospital that will ensue from any violation of such requirements. Each officer, director and employee shall receive and review the TJU/JeFF Corporate Integrity Program.
>
> TJU/JeFF shall also implement a training program for all JeFF physicians and billing staff employees involved in preparing or submitting Medicare bills through TJU/JeFF or its subsidiaries. This program shall provide for formal training in the submission of accurate bills for services rendered to Medicare or Medicaid patients and the personal obligation of each individual involved in the billings process to ensure that such billings are accurate. The legal sanctions for improper billings, and examples of improper billing practices must also be covered. TJU/JeFF shall certify that such training has been provided, and set forth generally the format, dates, and materials provided in its annual report to HHS/OIG. [87]

Compliance training in the area of documentation and coding will necessarily include discussion of matters that relate to CPT coding. If the hospital provides such education without charge to the physicians, the *Special Fraud Alert* suggests that such training may be an illegal remuneration under the anti-kickback statute. In light of the OIG's more recent encouragement of such compliance training, the *Special Fraud Alert* should not be read so broadly as to preclude furnishing the necessary compliance training by providers to physicians. Such training is not remuneration; rather, it is discharging providers' compliance duties. In the current environment, providers who offer compliance training to physicians as recommended by the OIG are certainly not offering such training with the intent of inducing referrals or violating the law. To confirm the provider's altruistic intent, providers should offer compliance training to all affiliated physicians without regard to the level of referrals.

The suggestion that free compliance training is remuneration may also implicate Stark, for which lack of intent is no defense. Nevertheless, compliance training can be easily fit into statutory exceptions to Stark and safe harbors to anti-kickback. Both Stark and anti-kickback offer exceptions for arrangements with employees and independent contractors that would cover compliance training if provided pursuant to a written agreement and if certain other technical requirements are met.[88] The physician acknowledgment form attached to the form compliance program includes the written agreement and technical requirements so that compliance training would fit within the applicable Stark and anti-kickback exceptions and safe harbors. In addition, the isolated transactions exception to Stark may also apply if the training is offered no more frequently than every six months.[89] The proposed Stark II regulations also offer a new *de minimis* exception for incidental benefits up to $300 per year and further explanation of the statutory exception for remuneration unrelated to the provision of designated health services that, if adopted, would also appear to exempt compliance training.[90] For all these reasons, compliance training can and should involve physicians while at the same time complying with Stark and anti-kickback.

## 14.16 Implications for Tax-Exempt Organizations

Anti-kickback compliance is also critical for maintaining the federal income tax exemption for charitable organizations such as hospitals. An organization does not qualify for the federal tax exemption if its net earnings inure in whole or in part to the benefit of private shareholders or individuals.[91] Violations of this prohibition are commonly referred to as private inurement.

The proscription against private inurement applies to "insiders" or persons who have an opportunity to control or influence the activities of the organization. Physicians with substantial influence over the affairs of a hospital are insiders and cannot receive private inurement. Even though physicians may be subject to the private inurement proscription, they may still have economic dealings with the hospital, such as reasonable compensation to the physician for providing the hospital with needed services as an employee or contractor. The private inurement proscription is aimed at preventing dividend-like distributions of charitable assets or expenditures to benefit a private interest.[92]

In addition, a tax-exempt entity must serve a public rather than private interest. The organization must establish that it is not organized or operated for the benefit of private interests such as designated individuals.[93] This private benefit prohibition applies to all kinds of persons and groups, not only to the "insiders" subject to the private inurement proscription.

The IRS concedes that some private benefit is present in all typical hospital-physician relationships. Physicians generally use hospital facilities at no cost to themselves while providing services to private patients for which they earn a fee. The private benefit accruing to the physicians is incidental to the public benefit resulting from having the combined resources of the hospital and its professional staff available to serve the public.[94]

The IRS applied these tax-exempt concepts in a revenue ruling involving physician recruitment incentives. It found that physician signing bonuses, malpractice insurance reimbursement, office rental subsidies, home mortgage guarantees, and income guarantees were permissible physician recruitment incentives having a public benefit consistent with the hospital's exempt purpose, with only incidental private benefits to the physician. The IRS held, however, that if the incentives were judged to be illegal under the anti-kick-back statute, such unlawful activities would disqualify the hospital from maintaining tax-exempt status.[95] Compliance with the anti-kickback statute and regulatory safe harbors is therefore essential to maintaining a provider's federal income tax exemption.

While the IRS has not provided specific guidance on the tax implications of an exempt hospital providing free compliance training to its medical staff (see Section 14.15), its position on physician recruiting incentives suggests that such training would not endanger the hospital's exempt status. Free compliance training would not constitute the dividend-like distribution that is the intent of the private inurement proscription. Any private benefit from compliance training would be incidental to the overall public benefit achieved by promoting compliance, curbing fraud and abuse, and reducing improper Medicare payments, which the OIG estimated at $20 billion for fiscal year 1997.

# 14.17 Conclusion—Anti-Kickback and Stark Compliance

Anti-kickback safe harbors and Stark exceptions overlap in many respects. Healthcare executives, individual providers, and their counsel should use extreme care in structuring ownership, compensation, and other financial relationships, particularly with respect to Stark, because any failure to satisfy the many technical requirements of the statutory exceptions to Stark will result in violating the statute. While Stark exceptions may not be used to shelter a financial relationship from anti-kickback, anti-kickback safe harbors may provide protection against Stark attacks.

---

### Action Items

1. Educate all managers and physicians about the intricacies of anti-kickback and Stark laws.
2. Fit all remuneration and financial relationships involving physicians (including the provision of compliance training) into applicable anti-kickback safe harbors and Stark general exceptions.
3. Analyze all business strategies involving integration with physicians to ensure continuing appropriateness and compliance with anti-kickback and Stark laws, and any applicable state-level self-referral laws.
4. Consider the "Other Permissible Exceptions" to Stark as a defense to an arrangement that has an anti-kickback safe harbor but no Stark general exception.

# Notes

1. 42 U.S.C.A. § 1320a-7b(b) (West 1997). For a discussion regarding, and further analysis of, the anti-kickback law and regulations, see Andrea Tuwiner Vavonese, *The Medicare Anti-Kickback Provision of the Social Security Act—Is Ignorance of the Law an Excuse for Fraudulent and Abusive Use of the System?*, 45 Catholic Univ. L. Rev. 943 (1996).

2. 42 U.S.C.A. § 1395nn (West 1997). U.S. Representative Fortney ("Pete") Stark, a Democrat from California, was the primary proponent of this law.

3. 42 U.S.C.A. § 1320a-7b(b)(1) (West 1997); 42 U.S.C.A. § 1320a-7b(b)(2) (West 1997) (emphasis added).

4. 42 U.S.C.A. § 1320a-7b(b)(1) (West 1997).

5. Ibid.

6. See *The Hanlester Network v. Shalala*, 51 F.3d 1390 (9th Cir. 1995); *U.S. v. Jain*, 93 F.3d 436 (8th Cir. 1996), *cert. den.* 117 S. Ct. 2452 (1997).

7. Medicare and Medicaid Patient Program Protection Act of 1987, Public Law 100-93, § 14, 101 Stat. 680, 697 (1987).

8. 42 C.F.R. § 1001.952 (1996).

9. *U.S. ex rel. Thompson v. Columbia/HCA Healthcare Corporation*,125 F.3d 899 (5th Cir. 1997).

10. Public Law 105-33 (1997).

11. 42 U.S.C.A. § 1320a-7a(a)(7) (West 1997).

12. Ibid.

13. *U.S. v. Greber*, 760 F.2d 68 (3rd Cir. 1985), *cert. den.* 474 U.S. 988 (1985).

14. *The Hanlester Network v. Shalala*, 51 F.3rd 1390 (9th Cir. 1995).

15. *U.S. v. Jain*, 93 F.3d 436 (8th Cir. 1996), *cert. den.* 117 S.Ct. 2452 (1997); *U.S. v. Starks*, 157 F.3d 833 (11th Cir. 1998).

16. See 42 U.S.C.A. § 1395nn (West 1997).

17. 42 U.S.C.A. § 1395nn(h)(6) (West 1997).

18. 42 U.S.C.A. § 1395nn(a)(1)(A) (West 1997).

19. 42 U.S.C.A. § 1395nn(a)(1)(B) (West 1997).

20. 42 U.S.C.A. § 1395nn(a)(2) (West 1997).

21. 42 U.S.C.A. § 1395nn(h)(1)(A) (West 1997).

22. 42 U.S.C.A. § 1395nn(h)(1)(B) and (C) (West 1997).

23. 42 U.S.C.A. § 1395nn(g) (West 1997).

24. 42 U.S.C.A. § 1395nn(e) (West 1997).

25. 42 U.S.C.A. § 1395nn(c) and (d) (West 1997).

26. 42 U.S.C.A. § 1395nn(b) (West 1997)

27. 42 U.S.C.A. § 1395nn(c) (West 1997); See Appendix 14.1, Item 1—Public Securities.

28. 42 U.S.C.A. § 1395nn(d)(1) (West 1997); See Appendix 14.3, Item 1—Specific Providers.

29. 42 U.S.C.A. § 1395nn(d)(2) (West 1997); See Appendix 14.3, Item 1—Specific Providers.

30. 42 U.S.C.A. § 1395nn(d)(3) (West 1997); See Appendix 14.3, Item 1—Specific Providers.

31. 42 U.S.C.A. § 1395nn(b)(1) (West 1997); See Appendix 14.1, Item 8—Risk-Sharing Arrangements.

32. 42 U.S.C.A. § 1395nn(b)(2) (West 1997); See Appendix 14.1, Item 8—Risk-Sharing Arrangements.

33. 42 U.S.C.A. § 1395nn(b)(3) (West 1997); See Appendix 14.1, Item 7—Price Reductions Offered to Health Plans.

34. 42 U.S.C.A. § 1395nn(b)(4) (West 1997).

35. Ibid.

36. 42 C.F.R. § 411.350 *et seq.* (1996).

37. 63 Fed. Reg. 1659 (1998).

38. 42 C.F.R. § 411.355(d) (1996).

39. 42 C.F.R. § 1001.952 (1996).

40. 135 Cong. Rec. H9333, H9570 (1989) (bracketed material added).

41. 135 Cong. Rec. H9333, H9566 (1989).

42. See 42 U.S.C.A. § 1395nn(g) (West 1997).

43. 42 C.F.R. § 1001.952 (1996).

44. 42 C.F.R. § 411.350 *et seq.* (1996).

45. 42 C.F.R. § 411.356(a) and 42 C.F.R. § 1001.952(a)(1) (1996); See Appendix 14.1, Item 1—Public Securities.

46. 42 C.F.R. § 1001.952(a)(2) (1996); See Appendix 14.2, Item 1—Small [Private] Entities.

47. See 42 U.S.C.A. § 1395nn (West 1997).

48. 54 Fed. Reg. 3088 (1989).

49. 56 Fed. Reg. 35966 (1991).

50. 42 C.F.R. § 1001.952(a)(2)(i) (1996); See Appendix 14.2, Item 1—Small [Private] Entities.

51. 42 C.F.R. § 1001.952(a)(2)(ii) (1996); See Appendix 14.2, Item 1—Small [Private] Entities.

52. 42 C.F.R. § 1001.952(a)(2)(iii) (1996); See Appendix 14.2, Item 1—Small [Private] Entities.

53. 42 C.F.R. § 1001.952(a)(2)(iv) (1996); See Appendix 14.2, Item 1—Small [Private] Entities.

54. 42 C.F.R. § 1001.952(a)(2)(v) (1996); See Appendix 14.2, Item 1—Small [Private] Entities.

55. 42 C.F.R. § 1001.952(a)(2)(vi) (1996); See Appendix 14.2, Item 1—Small [Private] Entities.

56. 42 C.F.R. § 1001.952(a)(2)(vii) (1996); See Appendix 14.2, Item 1—Small [Private] Entities.

57. 42 C.F.R. § 1001.952(a)(2)(viii) (1996); See Appendix 14.2, Item 1—Small [Private] Entities.

58. Richard P. Kusserow, *The Medicare & Medicaid Anti-Kickback Statute and the Safe Harbor Regulation—What's Next?*, 2 Health Matrix 49, 53 (1992).

59. 63 Fed. Reg. 1659, 1712-13 (1998).

60. 135 Cong. Rec. H9333, H9570 (1989).

61. 42 U.S.C.A. § 1395nn(c)(1)(B) (West 1997); 42 C.F.R. § 411.356(a) (1996); See Appendix 14.1, Item 1—Public Securities.

62. 42 C.F.R. § 1001.952(a)(1) (1996); See Appendix 14.1, Item 1—Public Securities.

63. See 42 U.S.C.A. § 1320a-7b(b)(3)(F) (West 1997); See Appendix 14.1, Item 8—Risk-Sharing Arrangements.

64. 42 U.S.C.A. § 1395nn(b)(1) (West 1997); 42 C.F.R. § 411.355(a) (1996); See Appendix 14.1, Item 8—Risk-Sharing Arrangements.

65. 42 U.S.C.A. § 1395nn(b)(2) (West 1997); 42 C.F.R. § 411.355(b) (1996); See Appendix 14.1, Item 8—Risk-Sharing Arrangements.

66. 42 C.F.R. § 411.355(d) (1996); See Appendix 14.1, Item 8—Risk-Sharing Arrangements.

67. 42 U.S.C.A. § 1395nn(e)(3)(B) (West 1997); 42 C.F.R. § 411.357(d)(2) (1996); See Appendix 14.1, Item 8—Risk-Sharing Arrangements.

68. 42 U.S.C.A. § 1395nn(e)(7) (West 1997); 42 C.F.R. § 411.357(h) (1996); See Appendix 14.1, Item 8—Risk-Sharing Arrangements.

69. See 42 U.S.C.A. § 1320a-7b(b)(3)(A), (B), (C), and (D) (West 1997); See 42 C.F.R. § 1001.952(g), (h), and (k) (1996); See Appendix 14.2, Items 3, 4, and 6.

70. 42 C.F.R. § 1001.952(a)(2) (1996); See Appendix 14.2, Item 1—Small [Private] Entities.
71. 42 U.S.C.A. § 1395nn(d)(1) (West 1997); 42 C.F.R. § 411.355(c)(2) (1996); See Appendix 14.3, Item 1—Specific Providers.
72. 42 U.S.C.A. § 1395nn(d)(2) (West 1997); 42 C.F.R. § 411.355(c)(1) (1996); See Appendix 14.3, Item 1—Specific Providers.
73. 42 U.S.C.A. § 1395nn(d)(3) (West 1997); 42 C.F.R. § 411.355(c)(3) (1996); See Appendix 14.3, Item 1—Specific Providers.
74. 42 C.F.R. § 1001.952(a)(2) (1996); See Appendix 14.2, Item 1—Small [Private] Entities.
75. 42 C.F.R. § 1001.952(a)(1) (1996); See Appendix 14.1, Item 1—Public Securities.
76. 42 U.S.C.A. § 1395nn(e)(6) (West 1997); 42 C.F.R. § 411.357(f) (1996); See Appendix 14.3, Item 4—Isolated Transactions.
77. 42 U.S.C.A. § 1395nn(e)(6) (West 1997); 42 C.F.R. § 411.357(f) (1996); See Appendix 14.3, Item 4—Isolated Transactions.
78. 42 C.F.R. § 411.357(c) and 42 C.F.R. § 1001.952(i) (1996); See Appendix 14.1, Item 6—Employees.
79. 42 U.S.C.A. § 1320a-7b(b)(3)(F) (West 1997); See Appendix 14.1, Item 8—Risk-Sharing Arrangements.
80. See 42 U.S.C.A. § 1395nn(a)(1) (West 1997), providing that Stark prohibits only certain referrals to, and claims by, an entity with which a *physician* (or an immediate family member of a physician) has a financial relationship.
81. 42 U.S.C.A. § 1395nn(c)(1) (West 1997); 42 C.F.R. § 411.356(a) (1996); See Appendix 14.1, Item 1—Public Securities.
82. 42 U.S.C.A. § 1395nn(d)(3) (West 1997); See Appendix 14.3, Item 1—Specific Providers.
83. 42 C.F.R. § 1001.952(a)(1) (1996); See Appendix 14.1, Item 1—Public Securities.
84. 42 C.F.R. § 1001.952(a)(2) (1996); See Appendix 14.2, Item 1—Small Entities.
85. U.S. Department of Health and Human Services, Office of Inspector General, *Special Fraud Alert: Hospital Incentives to Physicians,* May 1992, reprinted at 59 Fed. Reg. 65372 (1994).
86. Home Health Guidance, 63 Fed. Reg. 42410, 42421 (1998).
87. Copy of Settlement Agreement was included in seminar materials of Healthcare Financial Management Association Annual National Institute, June 29–July 3, 1997, as Attachment 5 to "Health Care Fraud/Abuse Recent Developments," presented on July 2, 1997 by Joseph J. Russo and James Florio of Cabot Marsh Corporation.
88. 42 C.F.R. § 411.357(c) and (d); 42 C.F.R. § 1001.952(d) and (i) (1996); See Appendix 14.1, Item 4—Personal Services and Management Contracts and Item 6—Employees.
89. 42 U.S.C.A. § 1395nn(e)(6) (West 1997); 42 C.F.R. § 411.357(f) (1996); See Appendix 14.3, Item 4—Isolated Transactions.
90. 63 Fed. Reg. 1659, 1725 (1998).
91. Treas. Reg. § 1.501(c)(3)-1(c)(1) (1997).
92. IRS General Counsel Memorandum 39,862 (Dec. 2, 1991).
93. Treas. Reg. § 1.501(c)(3)-1(d)(1) (1997).
94. IRS General Counsel Memorandum 39,862 (Dec. 2, 1991).
95. Rev. Rul. 97-21, 1997-18 I.R.B. 8 (May 5, 1997).

**Appendix 14.1**    Overlapping Anti-Kickback Safe Harbors and Stark General Exceptions

| Description of Safe Harbor/General Exception | Anti-Kickback Safe Harbor<br>*Sources:* 42 U.S.C. § 1320a-7b(b) and 42 C.F.R. § 1001.952 | Stark General Exception<br>*Sources:* 42 U.S.C. § 1395nn and 42 C.F.R. § 411.350 *et seq.* |
|---|---|---|
| 1. Public Securities | Entity's net tangible assets > $50 million and all of the following:<br>  i. Entity (both corporate and noncorporate) must be registered with SEC.<br>  ii. Investment terms must be equally available to public.<br>  iii. Entity and referring investors cannot favor passive investors over noninvestors.<br>  iv. No loans/guarantees can be made by entity to referring investors.<br>  v. Returns must be directly proportional to capital investment.[1] | Corporation [ONLY] traded on recognized foreign, national, or regional exchange and having > $75 million in stockholder equity[2]; and<br><br>Mutual fund with total assets > $75 million.[3] |
| 2. Space Rental | All of the following five standards:<br>  i. Lease must be in writing.<br>  ii. Premises must be specified.<br>  iii. Terms for any periodic intervals must be specified.<br>  iv. Term of lease cannot be for less than one year.<br>  v. Rent must be set in advance, consistent with fair market value and not tied to referrals.[4] | Same five standards as anti-kickback plus both of the following:<br>  vi. Space does not exceed that which is reasonable and necessary.<br>  vii. Lease would be commercially reasonable even if no referrals.[5] |
| 3. Equipment Rental | Five standards corresponding to those for Space Rental above.[6] | Same five standards as Anti-Kickback plus both of the following:<br>  vi. Equipment does not exceed that which is reasonable and necessary.<br>  vii. Lease would be commercially reasonable even if no referrals.[7] |

*Continued*

## Appendix 14.1 Continued

| Description of Safe Harbor/General Exception | Anti-Kickback Safe Harbor<br>*Sources:* 42 U.S.C. § 1320a-7b(b) and 42 C.F.R. § 1001.952 | Stark General Exception<br>*Sources:* 42 U.S.C. § 1395nn and 42 C.F.R. § 411.350 *et seq.* |
|---|---|---|
| 4. Personal Services and Management Contracts | Five standards corresponding to those for Space Rental above, and<br>vi. Services do not violate state or federal law.[8] | Same six standards as anti-kickback plus:<br>vii. Arrangement covers all of the services to be furnished by physician to entity.[9] |
| 5. Sale of Practice | Both of the following standards:<br>i. Period from agreement to completion of sale does not exceed one year.<br>ii. Seller will not be in professional position to refer to purchaser after one year from date of first agreement to sell.[10] | All of the following three standards:<br>i. Remuneration is not related to referrals by seller to purchaser, except for productivity bonus for services personally performed by seller.<br>ii. Remuneration would be commercially reasonable even if no referrals.<br>iii. No additional transactions between seller and purchaser are allowed for six months after sale except for other transactions excepted from Stark.[11] |
| 6. Employees | Any amount paid to an employee who has a bona fide employment relationship, for employment in the furnishing of any item or service.[12] | Same as anti-kickback plus all of the following:<br>i. Employment is for identifiable services.<br>ii. Remuneration is consistent with fair market value of services.<br>iii. Remuneration is not related to referrals by employee to purchaser, except for productivity bonus for services personally performed by employee.[13] |
| 7. Price Reductions Offered to Health Plans | All of the following six standards:<br>i. Term is not less than one year.<br>ii. Items and services are specified.<br>iii. Fee schedule must remain in effect throughout term.<br>iv. There are no claims to Medicare or Medicaid in excess of fee schedule. | All prepaid health plans and HMOs qualified under the Social Security Act.[15] |

*Continued*

## Appendix 14.1   Continued

| Description of Safe Harbor/General Exception | Anti-Kickback Safe Harbor<br>*Sources:* 42 U.S.C. § 1320a-7b(b) and 42 C.F.R. § 1001.952 | Stark General Exception<br>*Sources:* 42 U.S.C. § 1395nn and 42 C.F.R. § 411.350 *et seq.* |
|---|---|---|
| | v. Price reductions must be reported on cost report.<br>vi. No claims to Medicare or Medicaid by contract health providers under health plan.[14] | |
| 8. Risk-Sharing Arrangements | Any remuneration pursuant to written agreement where the individual or entity is at a substantial financial risk for the cost or use of the items or services provided.[16] | Remuneration for:<br>A. Physicians' services that are furnished personally or by another physician in the same group practice if:<br>  i. each physician furnishes full range of care through joint facilities;<br>  ii. at least 75% of patient services are furnished through group; and<br>  iii. practice expenses and income are distributed in accordance with previously determined methods.[17]<br>B. In-office ancillary services if:<br>  i. furnished by referring physician, member of group practice, or supervised person;<br>  ii. furnished in physician's or group's offices or building used by group for clinical laboratory services; and<br>  iii. billed by physician or group or wholly owned entity.[18]<br>C. Services included in composite rates for:<br>  i. ambulatory surgical center;<br>  ii. end-stage renal disease; or<br>  iii. hospice.[19]<br>D. Physician incentive plan (withhold, capitation, bonus, or otherwise) that does take into account volume of referrals if: |

*Continued*

## Appendix 14.1  Continued

| Description of Safe Harbor/General Exception | Anti-Kickback Safe Harbor<br>*Sources:* 42 U.S.C. § 1320a-7b(b) and 42 C.F.R. § 1001.952 | Stark General Exception<br>*Sources:* 42 U.S.C. § 1395nn and 42 C.F.R. § 411.350 *et seq.* |
|---|---|---|
| | | i. no payment induces reducing or limiting medically necessary services;<br>ii. physician is at financial risk; and<br>iii. disclosure to secretary on request.[20]<br>E. Group practice provides services, but the hospital does billing pursuant to certain arrangements in effect without interruption since December 19, 1989.[21] |

## Notes

1. 42 C.F.R. § 1001.952(a)(1) (1996).
2. 42 U.S.C.A. § 1395nn(c)(1) (West 1997); 42 C.F.R. § 411.356(a) (1996).
3. 42 U.S.C.A. § 1395nn(c)(2) (West 1997); 42 C.F.R. § 411.356(b) (1996).
4. 42 C.F.R. § 1001.952(b) (1996).
5. 42 U.S.C.A. § 1395nn(e)(1)(A) (West 1997); 42 C.F.R. § 411.357(a) (1996).
6. 42 C.F.R. § 1001.952(c) (1996).
7. 42 U.S.C.A. § 1395nn(e)(1)(B) (West 1997); 42 C.F.R. § 411.357(b) (1996).
8. 42 C.F.R. § 1001.952(d) (1996).
9. 42 U.S.C.A. § 1395nn(e)(3) (West 1997); 42 C.F.R. § 411.357(d) (1996).
10. 42 C.F.R. § 1001.952(e) (1996).
11. 42 U.S.C.A. § 1395nn(e)(6) (West 1997); 42 C.F.R. § 411.357(f) (1996).
12. 42 U.S.C.A. § 1230a-7b(b)(3)(B) (West 1997); 42 C.F.R. § 1001.952(i) (1996).
13. 42 U.S.C.A. § 1395nn(e)(2) (West 1997); 42 C.F.R. § 411.357(c) (1996).
14. 42 C.F.R. § 1001.952(m) (1996).
15. 42 U.S.C.A. § 1395nn(b)(3) (West 1997); 42 C.F.R. § 411.355(c) (1996).
16. 42 U.S.C.A. § 1320a-7b(b)(3)(F) (West 1997).
17. 42 U.S.C.A. § 1395nn(b)(1) (West 1997); 42 C.F.R. § 411.355(a) (1996).
18. 42 U.S.C.A. § 1395nn(b)(2) (West 1997); 42 C.F.R. § 411.355(b) (1996).
19. 42 C.F.R. § 411.355(d) (1996).
20. 42 U.S.C.A. § 1395nn(e)(3)(B) (West 1997); 42 C.F.R. § 411.357(d)(2) (1996).
21. 42 U.S.C.A. § 1395nn(e)(7) (West 1997); 42 C.F.R. § 411.357(h) (1996).

**Appendix 14.2**  Anti-Kickback Safe Harbors Without Similar Stark Exceptions

| Description of Safe Harbor/General Exception | Anti-Kickback Safe Harbor *Sources:* 42 U.S.C. § 1320a-7b(b) and 42 C.F.R. § 1001.952 | Stark General Exception *Sources:* 42 U.S.C. § 1395nn and 42 C.F.R. § 411.350 *et seq.* |
|---|---|---|
| 1. Small [Private] Entities | All of the following eight standards:<br>i. < 40% of investment interests are held by referring investors.<br>ii. Investment terms are same as offered to nonreferring investors.<br>iii. Terms are not related to expected referrals.<br>iv. No requirement exists to make referrals.<br>v. Entity and referring investors cannot favor passive investors.<br>vi. < 40% of entity's gross revenues come from referring investors.<br>vii. There are no loans/guarantees by entity to referring investors.<br>viii. Returns must be directly proportional to capital investment.[1] | No general exception. |
| 2. Referral Services | All of the following four standards:<br>i. Referral service is non-exclusive if provider is qualified.<br>ii. Any fees from participants are assessed equally, are based only on operating costs of service, and are not tied to referrals by participant to referring service.<br>iii. There are no requirements on manner in which the participant provides services.<br>iv. Referral service must maintain written records showing disclosures to persons seeking referrals as specified in regulations.[2] | No general exception, but Stark only prohibits referrals by physicians, not referrals by nonphysician referral services. |

*Continued*

## Appendix 14.2 Continued

| Description of Safe Harbor/General Exception | Anti-Kickback Safe Harbor<br>*Sources:* 42 U.S.C. § 1320a-7b(b) and 42 C.F.R. § 1001.952 | Stark General Exception<br>*Sources:* 42 U.S.C. § 1395nn and 42 C.F.R. § 411.350 *et seq.* |
|---|---|---|
| 3. Warranties | All of the following four standards:<br>i. Buyer must report price reduction from warranty on cost report.<br>ii. Buyer must provide invoices evidencing warranties on request.<br>iii. Manufacturer must report warranty on invoice and advise buyer of obligations under (i) and (ii).<br>iv. Manufacturer may not pay remuneration beyond cost of warranted item.[3] | No general exception. Warranties may implicate Stark because the definition of "designated health services" includes durable medical equipment and supplies.[4] |
| 4. Discounts | All of the following five standards:<br>i. Discounts must be based on purchases within a single fiscal year of buyer.<br>ii. Buyer must claim discount in fiscal year earned or following year.<br>iii. Buyer must report discount in cost report.<br>iv. Buyer must provide invoices showing discounts on request.<br>v. Seller must report discount on invoice and advise buyer of obligations under (iii) and (iv).[5] | No general exception. Discounts may implicate Stark because they may comprise a financial relationship between the physician and the entity giving the discount.[6] |
| 5. Group Purchasing Organization (GPO) | Both of the following standards:<br>i. There is a written agreement with GPO fees fixed or capped at 3%.<br>ii. GPO must disclose in writing at least annually the amount received from each vendor.[7] | No general exception. Payments to GPOs may implicate Stark because they may comprise a financial relationship between the physician and the entity paying the GPO.[8] |

*Continued*

## Appendix 14.2   Continued

| Description of Safe Harbor/General Exception | Anti-Kickback Safe Harbor<br>*Sources:* 42 U.S.C. § 1320a-7b(b)<br>and 42 C.F.R. § 1001.952 | Stark General Exception<br>*Sources:* 42 U.S.C. § 1395nn and<br>42 C.F.R. § 411.350 *et seq.* |
|---|---|---|
| 6. Waiver of Coinsurance or Deductibles | All of the following three standards:<br>i. Hospital must not claim waiver as bad debt on cost report.<br>ii. Hospital must offer to waive without regard to reason for admission, length of stay, or DRG.<br>iii. Waiver must not be part of price reduction agreement with third-party payor, unless part of a Medicare supplemental policy.[9] | No general exception. Waivers of coinsurance or deductibles may implicate Stark because they may comprise a financial relationship between the physician and the entity granting the waivers.[10] |

## Notes

1.  42 C.F.R. § 1001.952(a)(2) (1996).
2.  42 C.F.R. § 1001.952(f) (1996).
3.  42 C.F.R. § 1001.952(g) (1996).
4.  See 42 U.S.C.A. § 1395nn(h)(6)(F) (West 1997).
5.  42 U.S.C.A. § 1320a-7b(b)(3)(A) (West 1997); 42 C.F.R. § 1001.952(h) (1996).
6.  See 42 U.S.C.A. § 1395nn(h)(1) (West 1997).
7.  42 U.S.C.A. § 1320a-7b(b)(3)(C) (West 1997); 42 C.F.R. § 1001.952(j) (1996).
8.  See 42 U.S.C.A. § 1395nn(h)(1) (West 1997).
9.  42 U.S.C.A. § 1320a-7b(b)(3)(D) (West 1997); 42 C.F.R. § 1001.952(k) (1996).
10.  See 42 U.S.C.A. § 1395nn(h)(1) (West 1997).

## Appendix 14.3 Stark General Exceptions Without Similar Anti-Kickback Safe Harbors

| Description of Safe Harbor/General Exception | Anti-Kickback Safe Harbor<br>*Sources:* 42 U.S.C. § 1320a-7b(b) and 42 C.F.R. § 1001.952 | Stark General Exception<br>*Sources:* 42 U.S.C. § 1395nn and 42 C.F.R. § 411.350 *et seq.* |
|---|---|---|
| 1. Specific Providers | No specific safe harbor, but see safe harbor for Small [Private] Entities (Item 1 in Appendix 14.2.)[1] | A. Hospitals in Puerto Rico;[2]<br>B. Rural provider (as defined under the Social Security Act);[3]<br>C. Hospital ownership if:<br>  i. referring physician is authorized to perform services at hospital; and<br>  ii. investment interest is in hospital itself and not subdivision.[4] |
| 2. Remuneration Unrelated to Provision of Designated Health Services | No safe harbor but still defensible if remuneration was not willfully paid or received to induce referrals. | Not defined by regulations and vague.[5] |
| 3. Physician Recruitment | No safe harbor but there may be no willful intent to induce referrals if requirements of Stark general exception are met. | Remuneration provided by hospital physician to induce relocation if all four items apply:<br>  i. Written agreement is signed by each party.<br>  ii. Physician is not required to refer to hospital.<br>  iii. Remuneration is not determined by referrals.<br>  iv. Physician is not precluded from establishing privileges at another hospital or referring business to another entity.[6] |
| 4. Isolated Transactions | No safe harbor except for sale of practice but still defensible if remuneration was not willfully paid or received to induce referrals. | All of the following three standards:<br>  i. Remuneration is not related to referrals, except for productivity bonus for services personally performed.<br>  ii. Remuneration would be commercially reasonable even if no referrals.<br>  iii. There are no additional transactions between parties for six months except for other transactions excepted from Stark.[7] |

*Continued*

## Appendix 14.3   Continued

| Description of Safe Harbor/General Exception | Anti-Kickback Safe Harbor<br>*Sources:* 42 U.S.C. § 1320a-7b(b) and 42 C.F.R. § 1001.952 | Stark General Exception<br>*Sources:* 42 U.S.C. § 1395nn and 42 C.F.R. § 411.350 *et seq.* |
|---|---|---|
| 5. Payments by Physician | No safe harbor but still defensible if remuneration was not willfully paid or received to induce referrals. | Either:<br>i. to laboratory for clinical laboratory services; or<br>ii. to entity as compensation for other items or services furnished at price consistent with fair market value.[8] |

### Notes

1. 42 C.F.R. § 1001.952(a)(2) (1996).
2. 42 U.S.C.A. § 1395nn(d)(1) (West 1997); 42 C.F.R. § 411.355(c)(2) (1996).
3. 42 U.S.C.A. § 1395nn(d)(2) (West 1997); See 42 C.F.R. § 411.355(c)(1) (1996).
4. 42 U.S.C.A. § 1395nn(d)(3) (West 1997); 42 C.F.R. § 411.355(c)(3) (1996).
5. 42 U.S.C.A. § 1395nn(e)(4) (West 1997).
6. 42 U.S.C.A. § 1395nn(e)(5) (West 1997); 42 C.F.R. § 411.357(e) (1996).
7. 42 U.S.C.A. § 1395nn(e)(6) (West 1997); 42 C.F.R. § 411.357(f) (1996).
8. 42 U.S.C.A. § 1395nn(e)(8) (West 1997); 42 C.F.R. § 411.357(i) (1996).

# 15

# ANTITRUST COMPLIANCE

## 15.1 Main Sources of Antitrust Law

The three main sources of antitrust law have a long history in American jurisprudence. The Sherman Act, which prohibits monopolies and other unreasonable restraints of trade, was first adopted in 1890. The Clayton Act, which prohibits certain kinds of anticompetitive conduct, was adopted in 1914. The Federal Trade Commission Act, which established a separate federal agency to police unfair methods of competition, was also adopted in 1914.

Notwithstanding this long history, antitrust law had virtually no application to the healthcare industry before 1975 because of the doctrine that antitrust laws were inapplicable to the "learned professions," including the practice of medicine. Since the U.S. Supreme Court rejected the "learned professions" doctrine in 1975,[1] the healthcare industry has become a frequent target of antitrust litigation from regulators and private parties.

The Antitrust Division of the Department of Justice and the Federal Trade Commission jointly enforce federal antitrust laws. The primary antitrust statutes that have been applied against healthcare providers in recent years are:

- Sections 1 and 2 of the Sherman Act,[2] which prohibit restraining or monopolizing trade; and

- Section 7 of the Clayton Act,[3] which prohibits acquisitions that substantially lessen competition or tend to create a monopoly.

## 15.2 Restraint of Trade

Section 1 of the Sherman Act provides that "[e]very contract, combination in the form of trust or otherwise, or conspiracy, *in restraint of trade* or commerce among the several States, or with foreign nations," is illegal.[4] Courts interpreting this statute quickly realized that all contracts restrain trade to some extent, and in 1911 the U.S. Supreme Court held that the antitrust laws prohibit only "unreasonable" restraints of trade.[5] The courts then developed two standards for analyzing the unreasonableness of trade restraints: the *per se* standard and the rule of reason standard.

*Per se* means "by itself" in Latin. Under the *per se* standard, certain types of business arrangements are considered inherently anticompetitive and injurious to the public without any need to prove that the agreement actually damaged market competition. Moreover, any procompetitive benefits are not considered in the analysis. The classic example of *per se* illegal conduct is price-fixing; however, other conduct such as agreements among competitors to divide markets, group boycotts, and refusals to deal can also be *per se* violations. Group boycott claims have arisen from various types of arrangements common in healthcare, including:

- staff privilege decisions of hospitals;
- providers collectively refusing to deal with government and managed care programs; and
- joint provider negotiations with private payors.

Business arrangements that are not *per se* illegal are judged under the rule of reason, which determines the legality of restraints of trade by weighing the procompetitive benefits against the anticompetitive effects. All factors of the case may be considered, including the history of the restraint, the evil believed to exist, the reason for adopting the particular remedy, and the purpose or end sought.[6]

While the difference between a *per se* violation and the rule of reason is easy to describe in theory, this distinction is not easy to apply in practice. Providers should carefully review any conduct that might be characterized as price-fixing or another *per se* violation, because once the conduct is determined to be *per se* illegal, the provider cannot justify the conduct based on procompetitive factors.

## 15.3 Monopolization

Section 2 of the Sherman Act states that "[e]very person who shall *monopolize*, or attempt to monopolize, or combine or conspire with any person or persons, to monopolize any part of the trade or commerce among the several States, or with foreign nations, shall be deemed guilty of a felony."[7] As interpreted by the courts, monopolization has two main elements: possession of monopoly power in the relevant market and willful acquisition or maintenance of that power, as distinguished from growth or development as a consequence of a superior product, business acumen, or historic accident. An excellent example of the difficulty in making distinctions between monopolistic intent and successful business acumen is Microsoft Corporation, which is the subject of extensive antitrust litigation resulting from its 20-year rise from a start-up to a dominant company in the international computer industry.

In contrast to the large market share enjoyed by Microsoft worldwide, the healthcare industry remains fragmented with thousands of hospitals, tens of thousands of home health providers, and hundreds of thousands of physicians. Even Columbia/HCA at its zenith owned less than 350 hospitals, only 7 percent of the roughly 5,100 nongovernment, acute care hospitals in the United States. Yet, the federal government vigorously enforces antitrust law in healthcare.

## 15.4 Relevant Market

The key antitrust concept in healthcare is the relevant market. Antitrust enforcers view the relevant market in healthcare as very localized, resulting in actual or potential monopolies in most small and many medium-sized cities and towns throughout the country. For example, in a recent case involving the proposed merger of the only two hospitals in Dubuque, Iowa, the government argued that the relevant market was only Dubuque County, Iowa (1993 population of 86,403), plus a 15-mile radius from Dubuque across the Mississippi River into neighboring Wisconsin and Illinois.[8] The merging hospitals argued that the relevant market included the regional hospitals located in Cedar Rapids, Waterloo, Iowa City, and Davenport, Iowa, and in Madison, Wisconsin, all 70 to 100 miles distant. Under the government's definition of the relevant market, the merging hospitals' market share was 86 percent; under the broader definition of the relevant market, market share was 10 percent. Definition of the relevant market was critical to the disposition of the antitrust case. Although the merging hospitals prevailed in this particular case, providers must be prepared for the government's extremely narrow view of the relevant geographic market.

If a community will support only a single hospital, then there can be no monopolistic intent at the hospital level. The government, however, also segments the market by type of provider and by specialty. So, if physicians in a single-hospital town want to form groups with the hospital or among themselves to negotiate managed care arrangements with payors, the government may view the physicians as having monopolistic intent. When physician specialties are included, the market segmentation for purposes of antitrust analysis becomes microscopic.

## 15.5 Lessening Competition

Section 7 of the Clayton Act provides that "[n]o person engaged in commerce or in any activity affecting commerce shall acquire, directly or indirectly, the whole or any part of the stock" or assets of another person, where "the effect of such acquisition may be *substantially to lessen competition*, or to tend to create a monopoly."[9] With its focus on acquisitions, this statute is the source for most of the merger analysis under federal antitrust law. The Clayton Act prohibits acquisitions that *may* substantially lessen competition or *tend* to create a monopoly, both somewhat lesser burdens of proof compared to Sections 1 and 2 of the Sherman Act.

## 15.6 Antitrust Penalties

Violations of either Section 1 or 2 of the Sherman Act are felonies punishable by up to three years' imprisonment. In addition, the government may fine corporations up to $10 million per violation, and individuals up to $350,000 per violation. Only the Antitrust Division of the Department of Justice is empowered to institute criminal actions for violations of Sections 1 and 2 of the Sherman Act.

In contrast, Clayton Act violations may also be prosecuted by the Federal Trade Commission, state attorneys general, and private parties. Potential recourse includes injunctive relief and treble, or triple, damages.[10] The combination of criminal penalties, treble damages, and exposure to private plaintiffs makes antitrust a high-priority item in healthcare compliance.

## 15.7 Antitrust Policy Statements

Since the demise of the "learned profession" doctrine in 1975, the healthcare industry has faced a significant amount of antitrust litigation and enforcement action. As the evolution of the healthcare industry accelerated during the 1990s, providers expressed concern that the vague antitrust standards were hindering innovations in healthcare delivery systems. In response to this concern, the Antitrust Division of the Department of Justice and the Federal Trade Commission (the agencies) issued joint statements of their antitrust enforcement policies regarding mergers and various joint activities in the healthcare area. The agencies issued their first joint statements in 1993, which they revised in 1994 and revised and expanded in 1996 into a set of nine statements of antitrust policy in healthcare. The agencies also committed to issuing expedited Department of Justice business reviews and Federal Trade Commission advisory opinions in response to requests for antitrust guidance on specific proposed conduct involving the healthcare industry.

The agencies designed the policy statements and expedited specific agency guidance to advise the healthcare community in a time of tremendous change and to address, as completely as possible, the problem of uncertainty concerning the agencies' enforcement policy that might deter mergers, joint ventures, or other activities that could lower healthcare costs.[11] The agencies emphasized that their intent is not to treat healthcare networks either more strictly or more leniently than joint ventures in other industries or to favor any particular pro-competitive organization or structure of healthcare delivery over other forms that consumers may desire. Rather, their goal is to ensure a competitive marketplace in which consumers will have the benefit of high-quality, cost-effective healthcare and a wide range of choices, including new provider-controlled networks that expand consumer choice and increase competition.

Seven of the nine policy statements create "antitrust safety zones" for certain arrangements common in the healthcare industry that the agencies will not challenge, absent extraordinary circumstances. The policy statements also offer assurance that rule of reason analysis will apply for certain arrangements falling outside the safety zones but satisfying other criteria. Providers may ask either of the agencies to review a proposed transaction and declare its enforcement intentions on an expedited basis. The agencies have committed to respond to requests for such reviews from the healthcare community within a 90-day or 120-day period after they receive all necessary information regarding any matter addressed in the statements. Unfortunately, the determination about when all necessary information has been received is solely within the discretion of the agencies. As a result, the time period from initial request for review to receipt of the regulatory intention has been up to nine months, a delay that greatly diminishes the usefulness of the review process.

Table 15.1 summaries the antitrust safety zones and other information contained in the nine policy statements. Further discussion about each of the nine areas is provided below.

## 15.8 Hospital Mergers

Policy Statement 1 creates an antitrust safety zone for any merger between two general acute care hospitals where one of the hospitals has the following characteristics:

- fewer than 100 licensed beds;
- average daily census fewer than 40 patients; and
- more than five years old.

**TABLE 15.1** Summary of DOJ/FTC Statements of Antitrust Enforcement Policy in Healthcare

| Antitrust Enforcement Policy Statement | Antitrust Safety Zone | Outside Safety Zone |
|---|---|---|
| 1. Hospital Mergers | • One hospital has fewer than 100 licensed beds<br>• Average daily census fewer than 40 patients<br>• More than five years old | Antitrust analysis:<br>• Market definition, measurement, and concentration<br>• Potential adverse competitive effects<br>• Entry analysis<br>• Efficiencies<br>• Possible failure and exiting without merger<br>*Butterworth Health* (6th Cir. 1997): High concentration cannot be presumed to result in anticompetitive effects, particularly for nonprofits |
| 2. High-Tech and Equipment Ventures | • Joint venture includes only the number of hospitals needed to recover costs over the useful life of technology | Rule of reason analysis:<br>• Market definition, measurement, and concentration<br>• Potential adverse competitive effects<br>• Efficiencies<br>• Collateral agreements restricting competition |
| 3. Specialized Clinical or Other Expensive Services | • No safety zone; DOJ/FTC seeking more expertise in evaluating cost of, demand for, and benefits from such joint ventures | Rule of reason analysis:<br>• Market definition, measurement, and concentration<br>• Potential adverse competitive effects<br>• Efficiencies<br>• Collateral agreements restricting competition |
| 4. Providing Non-Fee Information to Purchasers of Healthcare Services | • Medical society's collection of outcome data and provision to purchasers<br>• Suggested practice parameters for clinical decision making | Safety zone excludes collective boycott or other behavior to coerce purchaser's decision making |

| Antitrust Enforcement Policy Statement | Antitrust Safety Zone | Outside Safety Zone |
|---|---|---|
| 5. Providing Fee Information to Purchasers of Healthcare Services | • Collection of current or historical fee information is managed by third party (purchaser, government agency, consultant, academic institution, or trade association)<br>• Any information shared with other providers must be more than three months old and include at least five providers for each statistic with no one representing > 25% of any statistic<br>• Information must be sufficiently aggregated | Safety zone excludes:<br>• Collective negotiations between nonintegrated providers and purchasers<br>• Boycott or other behavior to coerce purchaser's decision making<br>• Prospective fee information |
| 6. Exchanging Price and Cost Information Among Providers | Provider participation in written surveys of prices for services or wages, salaries, or benefits of health-care personnel if:<br>• Collection of current price and cost information is managed by third party (purchaser, government agency, consultant, academic institution, or trade association)<br>• Any information must be more than three months old and include at least five providers for each statistic with no one representing > 25% of any statistic<br>• Aggregated results cannot identify anyone | • Weighing of anticompetitive and procompetitive effects<br>• Exchanging future prices or future compensation of employees will likely be anticompetitive |
| 7. Joint Purchasing Arrangements | • Purchases are < 35% of total sales of purchased product or service in relevant market; and<br>• Cost of products and services purchased jointly is < 20% of total revenues of each competing participant | Safeguards to mitigate antitrust concerns:<br>• Optional use of arrangement (voluntary commitments are okay)<br>• Purchasing agent is independent from all participants<br>• Confidential communications |

*Continued*

**TABLE 15.1** Continued

| Antitrust Enforcement Policy Statement | Antitrust Safety Zone | Outside Safety Zone |
|---|---|---|
| 8. Physician Network Joint Ventures | • Limited concentrations of physicians in each specialty in relevant geographic market:<br>  Exclusive: ≤20%<br>  Nonexclusive: ≤30%<br>• For either, participants must share substantial financial risk, such as:<br>  1. capitation;<br>  2. predetermined percentage of premium or revenue of health plan;<br>  3. significant financial incentives to achieve cost-containment goals, such as 20% risk withhold; and/or<br>  4. complex or extended course of treatment requiring coordination of care by different types of providers. | Rule of reason analysis (see Policy 2 above) if:<br>• Share substantial financial risk, or<br>• Integration is likely to produce significant efficiencies (e.g., UR/QA, capital investment)<br>• Seven examples in Policy Statement 8, plus business review letters |
| 9. Multiprovider Networks | No safety zone because DOJ/FTC believe such networks are relatively new and can vary substantially. | Rule of reason analysis if:<br>• Share substantial financial risk, or<br>• Integration is likely to produce significant efficiencies and use messenger model to avoid *per se* price fixing:<br>  1. Agent obtains minimum acceptable fee schedule from each participant.<br>  2. Agent can have authority to contract on participant's behalf at that level or above.<br>  3. Agent cannot negotiate with payors or share pricing information with competing participants.<br>  4. Price offers below minimum must be conveyed to each participant for decision.<br>• Four examples in Policy Statement 9, plus business review letters |

*Source:* U.S. Department of Justice and Federal Trade Commission. *Statements of Antitrust Enforcement Policy in Health Care.* August 1996.

The safety zone will have very limited use in medium to large metropolitan areas where hospitals are typically larger than 100 licensed beds. Hospital mergers that fall outside the antitrust safety zone are not necessarily anticompetitive and may be procompetitive. The agencies analyze five aspects of the proposed merger:

1. market definition, measurement, and concentration;
2. potential adverse competitive effects;
3. ease of entry to the market;
4. efficiencies from the merger; and
5. possible failure and exiting without the merger.

Policy Statement 1 asserts that antitrust challenges to hospital mergers are relatively rare. However in recent years, the agencies have challenged (albeit unsuccessfully) proposed hospital mergers in Joplin, Missouri,[12] Grand Rapids, Michigan,[13] and Long Island, New York,[14] in addition to the Dubuque, Iowa, case discussed in Section 15.4 above. Notwithstanding the recent success by hospitals in overcoming government enforcement action against hospital mergers, antitrust regulators have publicly disagreed with the analysis used by the courts in recent merger cases and reiterated their intention to vigorously enforce antitrust laws in the context of hospital mergers.

In the Grand Rapids case, the two largest acute care hospitals in the city proposed to merge. After the merger, the government's economic expert estimated the surviving entity would control 65 to 70 percent of the market for primary care inpatient hospital services in the relevant geographic area. The court nevertheless decided that the hospitals successfully rebutted the government's case by showing that increased market share in the case of nonprofit hospitals does not automatically convert into higher prices and profits and that it was not likely to do so in that case in light of the past history of community responsibility and the hospitals' commitment to freeze prices. The merging hospitals agreed to a price freeze for three years and capped price increases for years four through seven by reference to the increase in the Consumer Price Index. With roughly 85 percent of the acute care hospitals operating on a nonprofit basis, this case provides a significant road map for justifying mergers among nonprofit hospitals that will not qualify for the antitrust safety zone.

## 15.9 High-Technology and Equipment Ventures

Policy Statement 2 declares that the agencies have never challenged a joint venture among hospitals to purchase or otherwise share the ownership cost of, operate, and market high-technology or other expensive healthcare equipment and related services. It goes on to set forth an antitrust safety zone that describes hospital high-technology or other equipment joint ventures that the agencies will not challenge, absent extraordinary circumstances. The safety zone applies to any joint venture among hospitals to purchase or otherwise share the ownership cost of, operate, and market the related services of high-technology or other expensive healthcare equipment if the joint venture includes only the number of hospitals whose participation is needed to support the equipment.

This safety zone is of minimal importance because the agencies have never challenged such ventures in the first place. Policy Statement 2 also promises rule of reason analysis for ventures that do not fall within the safety zone. Examples of such ventures include sharing a helicopter to provide emergency transportation for patients or sharing a magnetic resonance imaging device among providers.

## 15.10 Specialized Clinical or Other Expensive Services

Like Policy Statement 2 on high-technology and equipment ventures, Policy Statement 3 declares that the agencies have never challenged an integrated joint venture among hospitals to provide a specialized clinical or other expensive healthcare service. Unlike Policy Statement 2, Policy Statement 3 offers no safety zone for such ventures because the agencies need more expertise in evaluating the cost of, demand for, and potential benefits from such joint ventures before they can articulate a meaningful safety zone.

The agencies apply a rule of reason analysis in their antitrust review of hospital joint ventures involving specialized clinical or other expensive healthcare services. The sole example of such a venture contained in Policy Statement 3 is the sharing by two hospitals of the revenues and expenses of establishing an open-heart surgery program, to be located at one of the hospitals, and recruiting a cardiac surgery team to run the program. In the example, neither hospital currently offers open-heart surgery services, and the community has demand sufficient to support only one local open-heart surgery unit.

## 15.11 Providers' Collective Provision of Information to Healthcare Purchasers

Providers' collective provision of non–fee-related information to purchasers of healthcare services (Policy Statement 4) likely either will not raise risk of anticompetitive effects or will provide procompetitive benefits. The same is true with respect to providers' collective provision of fee-related information (Policy Statement 5), with the additional stipulation that reasonable safeguards to prevent participating providers from identifying the prices charged by any individual provider. Both Policy Statements 4 and 5 offer antitrust safety zones as summarized in Table 15.1, and both state that the applicable safety zone excludes collective boycott or other behavior to coerce purchaser's decision making.

## 15.12 Provider Participation in Exchanges of Price and Cost Information

Participation by competing providers in surveys of prices for healthcare services, or surveys of salaries, wages, or benefits of personnel, does not necessarily raise antitrust concerns. In fact, such surveys can have significant benefits for healthcare consumers. Providers can use information derived from price and compensation surveys to price their services more competitively and to offer compensation that attracts highly qualified personnel. Purchasers can use price survey information to make more informed decisions when buying healthcare services. Without appropriate safeguards, however, information exchanges among competing providers may facilitate collusion or otherwise reduce competition on prices or compensation, resulting in increased prices or reduced quality and availability of healthcare services. A collusive restriction on the compensation paid to healthcare employees, for example, could adversely affect the availability of healthcare personnel.

An antitrust safety zone exists under Policy Statement 6 for provider participation in written surveys of (1) prices for healthcare services or (2) wages, salaries, or benefits of healthcare personnel, if all of the following conditions are satisfied:

- The survey is managed by a third party (e.g., a purchaser, government agency, healthcare consultant, academic institution, or trade association).
- The information provided by survey participants is based on data more than three months old.
- There are at least five providers reporting data on which each disseminated statistic is based; no individual provider's data represents more than 25 percent on a weighted basis of that statistic; and any information disseminated is sufficiently aggregated such that it would not allow recipients to identify the prices charged or compensation paid by any particular provider.

The agencies will generally evaluate exchanges of price and cost information that fall outside the antitrust safety zone to determine whether the information exchange may have an anticompetitive effect that outweighs any procompetitive justification for the exchange. However, exchanges of future prices for provider services or future compensation of employees are very likely to be considered anticompetitive. If an exchange among competing providers of price or cost information results in an agreement among competitors as to the prices for healthcare services or the wages to be paid to healthcare employees, the agencies will consider that agreement unlawful *per se*.

## 15.13 Joint Purchasing Arrangements

Joint purchasing arrangements involve the purchase of a product or service used in providing the ultimate package of healthcare services or products sold by the participants. Examples include the purchase of laundry or food services by hospitals, the purchase of computer or data processing services by hospitals or other groups of providers, and the purchase of prescription drugs and other pharmaceutical products. Through such joint purchasing arrangements, the participants frequently can obtain volume discounts, reduce transaction costs, and have access to consulting advice that may not be available to each participant on its own. Some providers are using joint purchasing arrangements to obtain compliance consulting services on a cost-effective basis.

Joint purchasing arrangements are unlikely to raise antitrust concerns unless (1) the arrangement accounts for so large a portion of the purchases of a product or service that it can effectively exercise market power in the purchase of the product or service, or (2) the joint purchases account for so large a proportion of the total cost of the services being sold by the participants that the joint purchasing arrangement may facilitate price fixing or otherwise reduce competition. If neither factor is present, the joint purchasing arrangement will not present competitive concerns.

Policy Statement 7 establishes an antitrust safety zone for any joint purchasing arrangement among healthcare providers where two conditions are present:

1. The joint purchases account for less than 35 percent of the total sales of the purchased product or service in the relevant market, and
2. The joint purchases account for less than 20 percent of the total revenues from all products or services sold by each competing participant in the joint purchasing arrangement.

For arrangements falling outside of the safety zone, Policy 7 suggests the adoption of safeguards to help demonstrate that the participants intend the joint purchasing arrangement to achieve economic efficiencies rather than to serve an anticompetitive purpose. First, the joint purchasing arrangement should be nonexclusive, although it can ask for minimum purchase commitments from members to negotiate a volume discount or other favorable contract. Second, an independent employee or agent who is not also an employee of a participant should conduct the negotiations on behalf of the joint purchasing arrangement. Third, communications between the purchasing group and each individual participant should be kept confidential, and not discussed with or disseminated to, other participants.

## 15.14 Physician Network Joint Ventures

Many physicians and physician groups have recently organized physician network joint ventures such as individual practice associations (IPAs) and preferred provider organizations (PPOs), as well as other arrangements to market their services to managed care plans. Typically, such networks provide physician services to plan subscribers at predetermined prices, and the physician participants in the networks agree to controls aimed at containing costs and ensuring the appropriate and efficient provision of high-quality physician services. By developing and implementing mechanisms that encourage physicians to collaborate in practicing efficiently as part of the network, many physician network joint ventures promise significant procompetitive benefits for consumers of healthcare services. Such physician networks also pose the risk of anticompetitive conduct, however, because of the possibility of collusive pricing behavior, a risk that increases as the market share of the network increases.

Policy Statement 8 establishes antitrust safety zones, which allow limited concentrations of physicians in each specialty in the relevant geographic market provided that the physicians share substantial financial risk. The maximum concentrations are 20 percent for exclusive networks and 30 percent for nonexclusive networks. In an exclusive venture, the network's physician participants are restricted in their ability to individually contract or affiliate with other network joint ventures or health plans. In a nonexclusive venture, the physician participants may affiliate with other networks or contract individually with health plans. Because the safety zones stratify the market by both geography and medical specialty, the practical application of the safety zones is limited to networks in heavily populated areas with sufficient pools of each specialty so the maximum concentrations are not exceeded.

Outside the safety zones, rule of reason analysis will apply if the physicians share substantial financial risk, or integration is likely to produce significant efficiencies such as improved quality of care or enhanced services. Sharing substantial financial risk means:

- capitation;
- predetermined percentage of premium or revenue of health plan;
- significant financial incentives to achieve specified cost-containment goals, such as a 20 percent risk withhold; or
- complex or extended course of treatment requiring coordination of care by different types of providers.

Policy Statement 8 contains seven examples of how the agencies would apply antitrust principles to different fact patterns involving physician network joint ventures. If the physician network is not likely to produce significant procompetitive efficiencies (including one of the examples in Policy Statement 8), the agencies will treat the arrangement as an unlawful conspiracy or cartel whose price agreements are *per se* illegal. For example, antitrust regulators commenced enforcement action in 1997 against an IPA located in Grand Junction, Colorado, which allegedly controlled more than 90 percent of the relevant market. The possibility of *per se* antitrust analysis makes physician networks a very dangerous area deserving special compliance attention.

## 15.15 Multiprovider Networks

If the healthcare network involves any providers other than just physicians (e.g., physician-hospital organizations [PHOs] or networks involving both physician and nonphysician professionals), the antitrust analysis becomes even more difficult. Because multiprovider networks are new and involve a large variety of structures and relationships, Policy Statement 9 offers no antitrust safety zones. Like physician networks, multiprovider networks may obtain rule of reason analysis if the providers share substantial risk. If the providers do not share substantial risk, a concentrated multiprovider network will constitute *per se* price fixing unless the network employs the so-called messenger model.

The messenger model, as described in Policy Statement 9, refers to a system whereby the providers appoint an agent, or messenger, to convey to purchasers information obtained individually from the providers about the prices or price-related terms that the providers are willing to accept. The key issue in any messenger model arrangement is whether the arrangement creates or facilitates an agreement among competitors on prices or price-related terms. Determining whether there is such a pricing agreement is a question of fact in each case. In particular, the agencies will examine whether the agent coordinates the providers' responses to a particular proposal, disseminates to network providers the views or intentions of other network providers as to the proposal, expresses an opinion on the terms offered, collectively negotiates for the providers, or decides whether to convey an offer based on the agent's judgment about the attractiveness of the prices or price-related terms. If the agent engages in such activities, the arrangement may amount to a *per se* illegal price-fixing agreement.

The agencies have accommodated some variations on the pure messenger model. For instance, the agent can have authority to contract on each participant's behalf at or above some minimum level so that the agent may not have to canvass every provider for every managed care contract. But the agent cannot negotiate with payors or share pricing information with competing participants, and all price offers below the minimum must be conveyed to each participant for decision.

Even if rule of reason analysis applies to multiprovider networks, the procompetitive benefits must outweigh the anticompetitive effects. Non-exclusivity among providers in the network, both in formal structure and in actual practice, mitigates anticompetitive concerns. Accordingly, the rule of reason analysis is easier to satisfy if the providers in the network are free to contract outside the network at competitive terms.

Policy Statement 9 contains four examples of the application of antitrust principles to multiprovider networks. The agencies have brought enforcement actions against multiprovider networks, including 1995 actions against PHOs located in Danbury, Connecticut, and St. Joseph, Missouri. Because of the lack of applicable safety zones and uncertainty over whether the specific messenger structure will satisfy the agencies' concerns, new multiprovider networks may need to obtain a business review or advisory opinion from the agencies for reasonable assurance before proceeding with operations.[15]

## 15.16 Conclusion—Antitrust Compliance

The healthcare industry is highly exposed to antitrust laws and the associated recourse, which includes imprisonment, exorbitant monetary fines, treble damages, and injunctive relief. The agencies frequently bring enforcement actions against healthcare providers, and lawsuits by private parties against providers are not uncommon. Antitrust principles significantly affect the development of innovative structures for healthcare delivery, creating a need for healthcare executives to know and understand these principles. For these reasons, antitrust should be highlighted in the early stages of compliance program implementation.

---

### Action Items

1. Educate all senior executives about the application of antitrust to healthcare.
2. Structure mergers, joint ventures, and physician networks to fall within the antitrust safety zones, where possible.
3. Consider seeking a business review letter when forming a multiprovider network because of the lack of available safety zones.
4. Highlight nonprofit status and agreements to limit price increases to justify mergers resulting with large market shares in the localized market.

---

## Notes

1. *Goldfarb v. Virginia State Bar*, 421 U.S. 773 (1975).
2. 15 U.S.C.A. § 1 and 2 (West 1997).
3. 15 U.S.C.A. § 18 (West 1997).
4. 15 U.S.C.A. § 1 (West 1997) (emphasis added).
5. *Standard Oil Co. of New Jersey v. United States*, 221 U.S. 1 (1911).
6. *Levine v. Central Florida Medical Affiliates, Inc.*, 72 F.3d 1538 (11th Cir. 1996); *cert. den.* 117 S.Ct. 75 (1996).
7. 15 U.S.C.A. § 2 (West 1997) (emphasis added).

8. *U.S. v. Mercy Health Systems*, 902 F. Supp. 968 (N.D. Iowa 1995); *vacated as moot*, 107 F.3d 632 (8th Cir. 1997)

9. 15 U.S.C.A. § 18 (West 1997) (emphasis added).

10. 15 U.S.C.A. § 15 (West 1997).

11. U.S. Department of Justice and Federal Trade Commission, *Statements of Antitrust Enforcement Policy in Health Care*, August 1996, Introduction.

12. *Federal Trade Commission v. Freeman*, 69 F.3d 260 (8th Cir. 1995).

13. *Federal Trade Commission v. Butterworth Health Corporation*, 946 F.Supp. 1285 (W.D. Mich. 1996); *aff'd* 121 F.3d 708 (6th Cir. 1997).

14. *U.S. v. Long Island Jewish Medical Center*, 983 F. Supp. 121 (1997).

15. See, e.g., Anne K. Bingaman, assistant attorney general, to Scott Withrow, Esq., business review letter dated March 5, 1996, regarding PHO named Southeastern HealthCare Alliance, Inc.

# CONCLUSION

## 16.1 Other Areas of Healthcare Compliance

Chapters 13, 14, and 15 focus on three areas of high exposure in healthcare today: billing (including documentation and coding), anti-kickback and Stark, and antitrust. Once the provider addresses these important areas, it can expand the compliance process into many other areas that implicate legal and ethical compliance, such as the following:

- end-of-life decision making;
- informed consent;
- confidentiality of patient records;
- medical waste;
- handicapped patients;
- emergency room screening and admission;
- hospital transfers;
- patient discharge;
- conflicts of interest;
- illegal/questionable gifts;
- political lobbying;
- trade secret and software piracy;
- human resources;
- equal opportunity;
- affirmative action;
- sexual harassment;

- alcohol and drug use;
- family and medical leave;
- Americans with Disabilities Act; and
- Occupational Safety and Health Administration regulations.

Some of these other areas may also involve large dollar exposure to the provider, particularly with respect to patient care issues that can result in large malpractice verdicts if the provider does not satisfy standards of care. However, a thorough discussion of each of these areas is beyond the scope of this book. Providers should methodically work through the compliance process in a series of manageable steps to address all significant areas of compliance in due course.

## 16.2 Summary

This book has explained how to design a written compliance program, incorporating each of the seven basic elements required for an effective compliance program:

1. written standards of conduct;
2. designating a compliance officer;
3. effective education and training;
4. audits and other evaluation techniques;
5. internal reporting processes (such as a hotline);
6. disciplinary mechanisms; and
7. investigation and remediation.

With the current prosecutorial emphasis on compliance, healthcare managers must design and implement an effective compliance program immediately. Providers should initially focus on training in high-risk areas (such as documentation and coding) to prevent violations from occurring, and proceed to implement the other necessary elements of a compliance program in a series of manageable steps. Form 16.1 summarizes the compliance action items that were presented at the end of Chapters 2 through 15 of this book.

Managing the compliance process and integrating compliance issues into the provider's strategic planning are even more important than the basic design and initial implementation of the compliance program. Compliance is a process that will continue over the long term and will require constant oversight. Areas of special concern may change over time and providers will need to adjust their strategies accordingly.

Providers can no longer claim ignorance of the technical requirements or expect legislative salvation from the enforcement onslaught. Compliance demands a strong commitment from the highest organizational level and the participation of everyone associated with the provider. Providers and executives who successfully manage healthcare compliance not only will preserve their businesses and careers, but also will distinguish themselves in today's competitive healthcare marketplace.

---

### FORM 16.1  Summary of Compliance Action Items

**Chapter 2**

1. Make the decision to adopt and implement a compliance program.
2. Quickly customize and adopt a simple written compliance program such as the form compliance program in Appendix A.
3. Commit substantial time, energy, and resources of senior management to implement and maintain the compliance program appropriately.

**Chapter 3**

4. Emphasize the preventive elements of the compliance program, such as extensive training and concurrent oversight.
5. Include elements necessary for an effective compliance program, such as retrospective audits, reporting mechanisms, and appropriate disciplinary procedures.
6. Critically analyze the OIG's guidance before adopting all of the OIG's demands.

**Chapter 4**

7. Develop written standards of conduct for the compliance program that are straightforward and understandable by all employees.
8. Avoid using media buzzwords such as "upcoding" in a written standard; instead, refer to the applicable legal requirement for a precise statement of the applicable standard.
9. Distill the OIG's areas of "special" concern to a concise number of areas that truly require special compliance attention by the provider.

**Chapter 5**

10. Select a compliance officer who is knowledgeable about technical compliance issues, has good organizational relationships, and can devote the time necessary to implement and maintain the compliance program. A legal background is helpful but not required.
11. Understand the limitations of the attorney-client privilege with respect to compliance communications.
12. Organize compliance committees that are subordinate to the compliance officer to avoid paralysis in implementing the compliance program.

**Chapter 6**

13. Provide periodic compliance training focused on documentation and coding issues to all associated professionals, particularly physicians, regardless of whether they are direct employees or independent contractors.

14. Educate to eliminate both overreimbursement and underreimbursement resulting from lack of documentation or evidence of medical necessity.

15. Use effective training methods, such as in-person presentations with an opportunity for questions and answers, to prevent violations from occurring.

**Chapter 7**

16. Coordinate with the provider's independent CPAs to design an audit program for compliance purposes, including fraud detection measures.

17. Avoid retrospective shapshots; use benchmarking on a prospective basis only after furnishing initial education for affected employees and agents.

18. Develop procedures for periodic (at least annual) reviews of the compliance program's implementation and maintenance.

**Chapter 8**

19. Provide open lines of communication with an accessible compliance officer to make internal reporting a part of the organization's culture.

20. Emphasize the obligation of employees to report internally to the compliance officer, rather than the government or a *qui tam* plaintiffs' attorney.

21. Establish a hotline and associated procedures for documenting each call and its disposition.

**Chapter 9**

22. Establish disciplinary mechanisms for noncompliant conduct, including retraining for innocent technical violations, but emphasize the positive aspects of compliance more than the sanctions.

23. Update employee evaluation forms to include compliance as a factor, and update new employee and contracting policies to include background checks for criminal records and exclusion from federal health programs.

**Chapter 10**

24. Be prepared to investigate promptly all reports of noncompliant conduct and formulate appropriate corrective action.

25. Follow fiscal intermediary procedures for remitting any overpayments.

26. Consult with legal counsel before notifying federal or state enforcement officials of possible violations.

**Chapter 11**

27. Ensure the written compliance program covers the seven basic elements suggested by the OIG.

28. Proceed with the compliance process and customize the written program over time; do not wait to resolve all details before implementing a compliance program.

**Chapter 12**

29. Work through the initial compliance implementation in a series of manageable steps: (1) adopt a written compliance program, (2) provide initial compliance awareness education, (3) provide initial substantive education and (4) arrange for an audit mechanism.

30. After initial implementation is completed, maintain the compliance program with a continuing series of manageable steps: (5) train, train, train, (6) monitor compliance activities, (7) investigate all reports of suspected violations, and (8) discipline violators.

31. Adopt and disseminate written procedures in preparation for government searches, including backup of billing records.

32. Develop plans for a media counteroffensive to respond to negative publicity.

**Chapter 13**

33. Educate all billing and clinical personnel, including physicians, about the recent legal changes, focusing on coding and medical necessity.

34. Provide extensive training to all clinical personnel to improve clinical documentation, including evidence in the patient record of medical necessity.

35. Use targeted education and billing software to minimize the provider's exposure to announced enforcement projects such as PATH audits, 72-hour DRG window project, Project Bad Bundle, and the pneumonia upcoding project, if applicable.

36. Develop compliance procedures for billings to private payors, to the extent that such requirements differ from federal health reimbursement.

**Chapter 14**

37. Educate all managers and physicians about the intricacies of anti-kickback and Stark laws.

38. Fit all remuneration and financial relationships involving physicians (including the provision of compliance training) into applicable anti-kickback safe harbors and Stark general exceptions.

39. Analyze all business strategies involving integration with physicians to ensure continuing appropriateness and compliance with anti-kickback and Stark laws, and any applicable state-level self-referral laws.

40. Consider the "Other Permissible Exceptions" to Stark as a defense to an arrangement that has an anti-kickback safe harbor but no Stark general exception.

### Chapter 15

41. Educate all senior executives about the application of antitrust to healthcare.

42. Structure mergers, joint ventures, and physician networks to fall within the antitrust safety zones, where possible.

43. Consider seeking a business review letter when forming a multiprovider network because of the lack of available safety zones.

44. Highlight nonprofit status and agreements to limit price increases to justify mergers resulting with large market shares in the localized market.

# FORM COMPLIANCE PROGRAM

## (Compliance Program)

## I. STATEMENT OF POLICY ON ETHICAL PRACTICES (Policy)

_____ (the Hospital) has a policy of maintaining the highest level of professional and ethical standards in the conduct of its business. The Hospital places the highest importance on its reputation for honesty, integrity, and high ethical standards. This Policy is a reaffirmation of the importance of the highest level of ethical conduct and standards.

These standards can be achieved and sustained only through the actions and conduct of all personnel of the Hospital. Each and every employee, including management employees, of the Hospital is obligated to conduct himself/herself in a manner to ensure the maintenance of these standards. Such actions and conduct will be important factors in evaluating an employee's judgment and competence, and an important element in the evaluation of an employee for raises and for promotion. Employees who ignore or disregard the principles of this Policy will be subject to appropriate disciplinary actions.

Employees must be cognizant of all applicable federal and state laws and regulations that apply to and affect the Hospital's documentation, coding, billing, and competitive practices, as well as the day-to-day activities of the Hospital and its employees and agents. Each employee who is materially involved in any of the Hospital's documentation, coding, billing or competitive practices has an obligation to familiarize himself or herself with all such applicable laws and regulations and to adhere at all times to the requirements thereof. Where any question or uncertainty regarding these requirements exists, it is incumbent on, and the obligation of, each employee to seek guidance from a knowledgeable officer of, or attorney for, the Hospital.

In particular, and without limitation, this Policy prohibits the Hospital and each of its employees from directly or indirectly engaging or participating in any of the following:

1. *Improper Claims*

   Presenting or causing to be presented to the U.S. government or any other healthcare payor a claim:

   a. *Item or Service Not Provided as Claimed*

      For a medical or other item or service that such person knows or should know[1] was not provided as claimed, including a pattern or practice of presenting or causing to be presented a claim for an item or service that is based on a code that such person knows or should know will result in a greater payment to the claimant than the code such person knows or should know is applicable to the item or service actually provided;

   b. *False Claim*

      For a medical or other item or service and such person knows or should know the claim is false or fraudulent;

   c. *Service by Unlicensed Physician*

      For a physician's service (or an item or service incident to a physician's service) when such person knows or should know the individual who furnished (or supervised the furnishing of) the service:

      i. was not a licensed physician;

      ii. was licensed as a physician, but such license had been obtained through a misrepresentation of material fact (including cheating on an examination required for licensing); or

      iii. represented to the patient at the time the service was furnished that the physician was certified in a medical specialty by a medical specialty board when the individual was not so certified;

   d. *Excluded Provider*

      For a medical or other item or service furnished during a period in which such person knows or should know the claimant was excluded from the program under which the claim was made;

   e. *Not Medically Necessary*

      For a pattern of medical or other items or services that such person knows or should know are not medically necessary;

---

1. For purposes of this Policy, the term "should know" means that a person, with respect to information (1) acts in deliberate disregard of the truth or falsity of the information or (2) acts in reckless disregard of the truth or falsity of the information.

2. *False Statement in Determining Rights to Benefits*

   Making, using, or causing to be made or used any false record, state-ment, or representation of a material fact for use in determining rights to any benefit or payment under any healthcare program;

3. *Conspiracy to Defraud*

   Conspiring to defraud the U.S. government or any other healthcare payor by getting a false claim allowed or paid;

4. *Patient Dumping*

   Refusing to treat, transferring, or discharging any individual who comes to the emergency department, and on whose behalf a request is made for treatment or examination, without first providing for an appropriate medical screening examination to determine whether or not such indi-vidual has an emergency medical condition, *and*, if such individual has such a condition, stabilizing that condition or appropriately transferring such individual to another hospital in compliance with the requirements of 42 U.S.C. § 1395dd;

5. *Provision of Care to Contract HMO Patients*

   Knowingly failing to provide covered services or necessary care to members of a health maintenance organization with which the Hospital has a contract;

6. *Healthcare Fraud/False Statements Relating to Healthcare Matters*

   Executing or attempting to execute a scheme or artifice to defraud any healthcare benefit program or to obtain, by means of false, fictitious, or fraudulent pretenses, representations or promises, any of the money or property owned by, or under the custody or control of, any healthcare benefit program;

7. *Anti-Referral*

   Presenting or causing to be presented a claim for reimbursement to any individual, third-party payor, or other entity for designated health ser-vices[2] that were furnished pursuant to a referral by a physician who has a financial relationship with the Hospital, as such is defined in 42 U.S.C. § 1395nn;

8. *Anti-Kickback*

   Except as otherwise provided in 42 U.S.C. § 1320a-7b(b), knowingly and willfully:

---

2. The term "designated health services" means any of the following items or services: clini-cal laboratory services; physical therapy services; occupational therapy services; radiology ser-vices, including magnetic resonance imaging, computerized axial tomography scans, and ultrasound services; radiation therapy services and supplies; durable medical equipment and supplies; parenteral and enteral nutrients, equipment, and supplies; prosthetics, orthotics, and prosthetic devices and supplies; home health services; outpatient prescription drugs; or inpa-tient and outpatient hospital services.

   a.   soliciting or receiving any remuneration (including any kickback, bribe, or rebate) directly or indirectly, overtly or covertly, in cash or in kind either:

       i.   in return for referring an individual to a person for the furnishing or arranging for the furnishing of any item or service for which payment may be made in whole or in part under a federal healthcare program; or

     ii.   in return for purchasing, leasing, ordering, or arranging for or recommending purchasing, leasing, or ordering any good, facility, service, or item for which payment may be made in whole or in part under a federal healthcare program; or

   b.   offering or paying any remuneration (including any kickback, bribe, or rebate) directly or indirectly, overtly or covertly, in cash or in kind to any person to induce such person either:

       i.   to refer an individual to a person for the furnishing or arranging for the furnishing of any item or service for which payment may be made in whole or in part under a federal healthcare program; or

     ii.   to purchase, lease, order, or arrange for or recommend purchasing, leasing, or ordering any good, facility, service, or item for which payment may be made in whole or in part under a federal healthcare program;

9. *Antitrust*

Engaging in any activity, including without limitation being a member of a multiprovider network or other joint venture or affiliation that is in restraint of trade or that monopolizes, or attempts to monopolize, any part of interstate trade or commerce; or

10. *Failure to Report Violations to Compliance Coordinator*

Failing to promptly report to the Compliance Coordinator (as defined below) any instance of noncompliant conduct, including without limitation violations of the standards described in subparagraphs 1 through 9 above, with respect to the Hospital or any of its employees which is known to such person.

## II. APPOINTMENT OF COMPLIANCE COORDINATOR

### A. Compliance Coordinator

In an effort to ensure compliance with this Policy, [THE GOVERNING BODY] is adopting a formal Compliance Program. To oversee and implement this program, the Hospital has appointed _____ as its Compliance Coordinator. The Hospital has chosen its Compliance Coordinator based on his or her outstanding record of commitment to honesty, integrity, and high ethical standards, and on the officer's knowledge and understanding of the applicable laws and regulations. The Compliance Coordinator will provide for education and training programs for employees, respond to inquiries from any employee regarding appropriate billing, documentation, coding, and business practices and investigate any allegations of possible impropriety.

## B. Duties and Responsibilities of the Compliance Coordinator

The duties and responsibilities of the Compliance Coordinator shall include, but are not limited to, the following:

1. working with [THE GOVERNING BODY], chief executive officer, chief financial officer, chief operating officer, and general counsel in the preparation and development of, and overseeing the implementation of, written guidelines on specific federal and state legal and regulatory issues and matters involving ethical and legal business practices, including, without limitation, documentation, coding, and billing practices with respect to requests for payments and/or reimbursements from Medicare or any other federally funded healthcare program, the giving and receiving of remuneration to induce referrals and engagement in certain business affiliations or pricing arrangements that may affect competition;

2. developing and implementing an educational training program for Hospital personnel to ensure understanding of federal and state laws and regulations involving ethical and legal business practices including, without limitation, documentation, coding, and billing practices with respect to requests for payments and/or reimbursements from Medicare or any other federally funded healthcare program, the giving and receiving of remuneration to induce referrals and engagement in certain business affiliations or pricing arrangements that may affect competition;

3. handling inquiries by employees regarding any aspect of compliance;

4. investigating any information or allegation concerning possible unethical or improper business practices and recommending corrective action when necessary;

5. providing guidance and interpretation to [THE GOVERNING BODY], the chief executive officer and Hospital personnel, in conjunction with the Hospital's legal counsel, on matters related to the Compliance Program;

6. planning and overseeing regular, periodic audits of the Hospital's operations to identify and rectify any possible barriers to the efficacy of the Compliance Program;

7. developing policies and programs that encourage managers and employees to report suspected fraud and other improprieties without fear of retaliation;

8. preparing at least annually a report to [THE GOVERNING BODY] and the chief executive officer concerning the compliance activities and actions undertaken during the preceding year, the proposed compliance program for the next year, and any recommendations for changes in the Compliance Program;

9. coordinating personnel issues with the Hospital's human resources office (or its equivalent) to ensure that the National Practitioner Data Bank and *Cumulative Sanction Report* have been checked with respect to all employees, medical staff and independent contractors;

10. ensuring that independent contractors and agents who furnish medical services to the Hospital are aware of the Hospital's Compliance Program including, without limitation, its policies with respect to the specific areas of documentation, coding, billing, and competitive practices; and

11. performing such other duties and responsibilities as [THE GOVERNING BODY] may request.

## C. Compliance Committees

The Compliance Coordinator may create one or more committees to advise the Compliance Coordinator and assist in the implementation of the Compliance Program. Each committee may have one or more members, who may be Hospital employees, independent contractors, or other interested parties, and such members shall serve at the pleasure of the Compliance Coordinator. The purpose of providing for such committees is to allow the Hospital and the Compliance Coordinator to benefit from the combined perspectives of individuals with varying responsibilities in the Hospital such as, by way of example only and not obligation, operations, finance, audit, human resources, utilization review, social work, discharge planning, medicine, coding, and legal, as well as employees and managers of key operating units.

## D. Reporting by Compliance Coordinator

In general, recommendations from the Compliance Coordinator regarding compliance matters will be directed to the appropriate officer or manager of the Hospital. If the Compliance Coordinator is not satisfied with the action taken in response to his or her recommendations, he or she will report such concern to [THE GOVERNING BODY] and the chief executive officer. In no case will the Hospital endeavor to conceal Hospital or individual wrongdoing.

## E. Establishment of a Hotline

The Compliance Coordinator shall have an open-door policy with respect to receiving reports of violations, or suspected violations, of the law or of the Policy and with respect to answering employee questions concerning adherence to the law and to the Policy. In addition, the Hospital shall establish a hotline to the Compliance Coordinator for such reporting or questions. The telephone number for the hotline is _____. Telephone calls to the hotline may come from Hospital employees, patients of the Hospital or others, whether or not affiliated with the Hospital. All information reported to the hotline by any employee in accordance with the Compliance Program shall be kept confidential by the Hospital to the extent that confidentiality is possible throughout any resulting investigation; however, there may be a point at which an employee's identity may become known or may have to be revealed in certain instances when governmental authorities become involved. Under no circumstances shall the reporting of any such information or possible impropriety serve as a basis for any retaliatory actions to be taken against any employee, patient, or other person making the report to the Compliance Coordinator or the hotline.

The telephone number for the hotline, along with a copy of the Compliance Program, shall be posted in conspicuous locations throughout the Hospital.

## III. EDUCATIONAL PROGRAM

### A. Purpose of Educational Program

The Compliance Program promotes the Hospital's policy of adherence to the highest level of professional and ethical standards, as well as all applicable laws and regulations. The Hospital will make available appropriate educational and training programs and resources to ensure that all employees are throughly familiar with those areas of law that apply to and affect the conduct of their respective duties, including, without limitation, the specific areas of documentation, coding, billing, and competitive practices of the Hospital.

### B. Responsibility for Educational Program

The Compliance Coordinator, in conjunction with the Hospital's legal counsel, is responsible for implementation of the educational program. The program is intended to provide each employee of the Hospital with an appropriate level of information and instruction regarding ethical and legal standards, including, without limitation, standards for documentation, coding, billing, and competitive practices, and with the appropriate procedures to carry out the Policy. Education and training of all employees shall be conducted at least annually. The determination of the level of education needed by particular employees or classes of employees will be made by the Compliance Coordinator. Each educational program presented by the Hospital shall allow for a question and answer period at the end of such program.

### C. Subject Matter of Educational Program

The educational program shall explain the applicability of pertinent laws, including, without limitation, applicable provisions of the False Claims Act

(31 U.S.C. § 3729), the civil and criminal provisions of the Social Security Act (42 U.S.C. § 1320a-7a and § 1320a-7b, respectively), the patient antidumping statute (42 U.S.C. § 1395dd), laws pertaining to the provision of medically necessary items and services that are required to be provided to members of an HMO with whom the Hospital contracts (42 U.S.C. § 1320a-7(b)(6)(D)), criminal offenses concerning false statements relating to healthcare matters (18 U.S.C. § 1035), the criminal offense of healthcare fraud (18 U.S.C. § 1347), the federal anti-referral laws (42 U.S.C. § 1395nn), the anti-kickback laws (42 U.S.C. § 1320a-7b(b)), and the Sherman Antitrust Act (15 U.S.C. §§ 1, 2 and 18). As additional legal issues and matters are identified by the Compliance Coordinator, those areas will be included in the educational program. Each education and/or training program conducted hereunder shall reinforce that strict compliance with the law and with the Hospital's Policy is a condition of employment with the Hospital.

### D. Training Methods

Different methods may be used to communicate information about applicable laws and regulations to Hospital employees, as determined by the Compliance Coordinator. The Hospital may conduct training sessions regarding compliance, which may be mandatory for selected employees. The seminars will be conducted by the Compliance Coordinator, legal counsel for the Hospital, or, where appropriate, by Hospital managers or consultants. The Compliance Coordinator may require that certain employees or representatives of the Hospital attend, at the Hospital's expense, publicly available seminars covering particular areas of law. The Hospital's orientation for new employees will include discussions of the Compliance Program and an employee's obligation to maintain the highest level of ethical and legal conduct and standards.

While the Hospital will make every effort to provide appropriate compliance information to all employees, and to respond to all inquiries, no educational and training program, however comprehensive, can anticipate every situation that may present compliance issues. Responsibility for compliance with this Compliance Program, including the duty to seek guidance when in doubt, rests with each employee of the Hospital.

## IV. EMPLOYEE OBLIGATIONS

The Compliance Program imposes several obligations on Hospital employees, all of which will be enforced by the standard disciplinary measures available to the Hospital as an employer. Adherence to the Compliance Program will be considered in personnel evaluations.

## A. Employee Obligations

1. *Reporting Obligation.* Employees must immediately report to the Compliance Coordinator any suspected or actual violations (whether or not based on personal knowledge) of applicable law or regulations by the Hospital or any of its employees. Any employee making a report may do so anonymously if he or she so chooses. Once an employee has made a report, the employee has a continuing obligation to update the report as new information comes into his or her possession. All information reported to the Compliance Coordinator by any employee in accordance with the Compliance Program shall be kept confidential by the Hospital to the extent that confidentiality is possible throughout any resulting investigation; however, there may be a point where an employee's identity may become known or may have to be revealed in certain instances when governmental authorities become involved. Under no circumstances shall the reporting of any such information or possible impropriety serve as a basis for any retaliatory actions to be taken against any employee making the report.

2. *Acknowledgment Statement.* Each employee must complete and sign from time to time an Acknowledgment Statement to the effect that the employee fully understands the Compliance Program, and acknowledges his or her commitment to comply with the Program as an employee of the Hospital. Each Acknowledgment Statement shall form a part of the personnel file of each employee. It shall be the responsibility of each manager to ensure that all employees under his or her supervision who are materially involved in any of the Hospital's documentation, coding, billing, and competitive practices have executed such an acknowledgment.

## B. Hospital Assessment of Employee Performance Under Compliance Program

1. *Violation of Applicable Law or Regulation.* If an employee violates any law or regulation in the course of his or her employment, the employee will be subject to sanctions by the Hospital.

2. *Other Violation of the Compliance Program.* In addition to direct participation in an illegal act, employees will be subject to disciplinary actions by the Hospital for failure to adhere to the principles and policies set forth in this Compliance Program. Examples of actions or omissions that will subject an employee to discipline on this basis include, but are not limited to, the following:

   a.  a breach of the Hospital's Policy;

   b.  failure to report a suspected or actual violation of law or a breach of the Policy;

   c.  failure to make, or falsification of, any certification required under the Compliance Program;

    d.  lack of attention or diligence on the part of supervisory personnel that directly or indirectly leads to a violation of law; and/or

    e.  direct or indirect retaliation against an employee who reports a violation of the Compliance Program or a breach of the Policy.

3.  *Possible Sanctions.* The possible sanctions include, but are not limited to, termination, suspension, demotion, reduction in pay, reprimand, and/or retraining. Employees who engage in intentional or reckless violation of law, regulation, or this Compliance Program will be subject to more severe sanctions than accidental transgressors.

## C.  Employee Evaluation

Employee participation in, and adherence to, the Compliance Program and related activities will be an element of each employee's annual personnel evaluations including, without limitation, annual personnel evaluations of Hospital supervisors and managers. As such, it will affect decisions concerning compensation, promotion, and retention.

## D.  Nonemployment or Retention of Sanctioned Individuals

The Hospital shall not knowingly employ any individual, or contract with any person or entity, who has been convicted of a criminal offense related to healthcare or who is listed by a federal agency as debarred, excluded, or otherwise ineligible for participation in federally funded healthcare programs. In addition, until resolution of such criminal charges or proposed debarment or exclusion, any individual who is charged with criminal offenses related to healthcare or proposed for exclusion or debarment shall be removed from direct responsibility for, or involvement in, documentation, coding, billing, or competitive practices. If resolution results in conviction, debarment, or exclusion of the individual, the Hospital shall terminate its employment of such individual.

# V. RESPONSE TO REPORTS OF VIOLATIONS

The Hospital, along with its legal counsel where necessary, shall promptly respond to and investigate all allegations of wrongdoing of Hospital employees, whether such allegations are received through the hotline or in any other manner.

## A.  Investigation

On the discovery that a material violation of the law or of the Policy has occurred, the Hospital shall take immediate action to rectify the violation, if possible, and to report the violation to the appropriate regulatory body, if necessary, and to appropriately sanction the culpable employee(s) of the Hospital.

Promptly after any discovered material violation is addressed, the Hospital shall, with the assistance of the Compliance Coordinator, amend this Policy in any manner the Hospital or the Compliance Coordinator feels will prevent any similar violation(s) in the future.

If an investigation of an alleged violation is undertaken and the Compliance Coordinator believes the integrity of the investigation may be at stake because of the presence of employees under investigation, the employee(s) allegedly involved in the misconduct shall, at the discretion of the Compliance Coordinator, be removed from his/her/their current work activity until the investigation is completed. In addition, the Hospital and the Compliance Coordinator shall take any steps necessary to prevent the destruction of documents or other evidence relevant to the investigation. Once an investigation is completed, if disciplinary action is warranted, it shall be immediate and imposed in accordance with the Hospital's written standards of disciplinary action.

# VI. AUDITING AND MONITORING

## A. Importance of Auditing and Monitoring

It is critical to the Hospital's compliance with the Policy for the Hospital to conduct regular auditing and monitoring of the activities of the Hospital and its employees to identify and promptly rectify any potential barriers to such compliance.

## B. Regular Audits

Regular, periodic audits, as periodically as the Compliance Coordinator shall prescribe, shall be conducted with the assistance of the Hospital's legal counsel at the Compliance Coordinator's direction. Such audits shall evaluate the Hospital's compliance with its Compliance Program and determine what, if any, compliance issues exist. Such audits shall be designed and implemented to ensure compliance with the Hospital's Compliance Program and all applicable federal and state laws.

Compliance audits shall be conducted in accordance with the comprehensive audit procedures established by the Compliance Coordinator and shall include, at a minimum:

1. interviews conducted by the Hospital's legal counsel with personnel involved in management, operations, and other related activities;
2. reviews, at least annually, of whether the Compliance Program's elements have been satisfied (e.g., whether there has been appropriate dissemination of the Compliance Program's standards, training, disciplinary actions, etc.);

3. random reviews of Hospital records with special attention given to procedures relating to documentation, coding, billing, the giving and receiving of remuneration to induce referrals, and engagement in certain business affiliations or pricing arrangements that may affect competition; and
4. reviews of written materials and documentation used by the Hospital.

All compliance audit procedures shall be conducted with the assistance of the Hospital's legal counsel and all investigations, and the results thereof, are confidential.

## C. Formal Audit Reports

Formal audit reports shall be prepared with the assistance of the Hospital's legal counsel and submitted to the Compliance Coordinator and [THE GOVERNING BODY] to ensure that management is aware of the results and can take whatever steps necessary to correct past problems and deter them from recurring. The audit or other analytical reports shall specifically identify areas where corrective actions are needed and should identify in which cases, if any, subsequent audits or studies would be advisable to ensure that the recommended corrective actions have been implemented and are successful.

## D. Compliance with Applicable Fraud Alerts

The Compliance Coordinator shall regularly and periodically monitor the issuance of fraud alerts by the Office of the Inspector General of the Department of Health and Human Services. Any and all fraud alerts so issued shall be carefully considered by the Compliance Coordinator and by the Hospital's legal counsel. The Hospital shall revise and amend this Compliance Program, as necessary, in accordance with such fraud alerts. In addition, the Hospital shall immediately cease and correct any conduct applicable to the Hospital and criticized in any such a fraud alert.

## E. Retention of Records and Reports

The Hospital shall document its efforts to comply with applicable statutes, regulations and federal healthcare program requirements. All records and reports created in conjunction with the Hospital's adherence to the Compliance Policy are confidential and shall be maintained by the Hospital, through the Compliance Coordinator, in a secure location until such time as the Compliance Coordinator, through consultation with the Hospital's legal counsel, determines that the destruction of such documentation is appropriate.

**This Compliance Program has been adopted by [THE GOVERNING BODY] as of the _____.**

# Acknowledgment

I hereby acknowledge that I have received and reviewed _____
(the Hospital)'s Corporate Compliance Program, including its Statement of
Policy on Ethical Practices (Policy). I fully understand that, as an employee, I
have an obligation to fully adhere to these policies and principles.

In particular, I hereby acknowledge and affirm that:

1. I fully understand the Hospital Policy and the Compliance Program, and
   I acknowledge my commitment to comply with the Hospital Policy and
   Compliance Program as an employee of the Hospital.
2. When I have a concern about a possible violation of Hospital Policy, I
   will promptly report the concern to the Compliance Coordinator in
   accordance with the Compliance Program.


_____          _____
         Date                            Employee's signature


                                _____
                                  Printed name of Employee

# Acknowledgment—Compliance

The undersigned independent contractor, or employee of independent contractor, as the case may be, (Contractor) acknowledges that he or she has received and reviewed _____ (the Hospital)'s Compliance Program, including its Statement of Policy on Ethical Practices (Policy). Contractor fully understands the Hospital Policy and Compliance Program and is committed to comply with the Hospital Policy and Compliance Program as long as Contractor (or Contractor's employer, as the case may be) is engaged by the Hospital. When Contractor has a concern about a possible violation of Hospital Policy, Contractor will promptly report the concern to the Compliance Coordinator in accordance with the Compliance Program.


_____          _____
Date                                              Contractor's signature


                                   _____
                                   Printed name of Contractor

# Physician Acknowledgment—Compliance

The undersigned physician (Physician) acknowledges that he or she has received and reviewed _____ (the Hospital)'s Compliance Program, including its Statement of Policy on Ethical Practices (Policy). Physician fully understands the Hospital Policy and Compliance Program and is committed to comply with the Hospital Policy and Compliance Program as long as Physician has admitting privileges at the Hospital. When Physician has a concern about a possible violation of Hospital Policy, Physician will promptly report the concern to the Compliance Coordinator in accordance with the Compliance Program.

Physician acknowledges that the Hospital may furnish to all admitting physicians and their staff, from time to time, training in the federal requirements for determining, accurately documenting, and supporting the principal and secondary diagnoses and the major procedures performed on the patient, as attested by Physician in the medical record pursuant to 42 C.F.R. § 412.46. Such training shall be furnished for one or more of the following purposes: (1) to promote compliance with the Physician's obligations under 42 C.F.R. § 412.46, (2) to promote compliance with Hospital Policy pursuant to the Compliance Program, and/or (3) to satisfy the training standard imposed on the Hospital under proposed 42 C.F.R. § 482.125(c) for the Hospital's continued participation in the Medicare and Medicaid programs.

Physician and Hospital each acknowledges that such training is not intended to, and will not, induce referrals from Physician to the Hospital. To the extent that such training may be deemed to constitute remuneration or compensation under any applicable law or regulation, the benefit resulting from such training to the Physician is consistent with fair market value of the services rendered by the Physician in documenting and attesting to the medical records which support the Hospital's billings. The term of this arrangement is at least one year and shall continue thereafter as long as Physician has admitting privileges at the Hospital.

_____      _____

       Date                                   Physician's signature

                             _____

                                Printed name of Physician

# THE OFFICE OF INSPECTOR GENERAL'S COMPLIANCE PROGRAM GUIDANCE FOR HOSPITALS

[Bracketed references to sections of *Managing Healthcare Compliance*]

## I. INTRODUCTION

The Office of Inspector General (OIG) of the Department of Health and Human Services (HHS) continues in its efforts to promote voluntarily developed and implemented compliance programs for the health care industry. The following compliance program guidance is intended to assist hospitals and their agents and subproviders (referred to collectively in this document as "hospitals") develop effective internal controls that promote adherence to applicable federal and state law, and the program requirements of federal, state and private health plans. The adoption and implementation of voluntary compliance programs significantly advance the prevention of fraud, abuse and waste in these health care plans while at the same time furthering the fundamental mission of all hospitals, which is to provide quality care to patients. **[3.6]**

Within this document, the OIG intends to provide first, its general views on the value and fundamental principles of hospital compliance programs, and, second, specific elements that each hospital should consider when developing and implementing an effective compliance program. While this document presents basic procedural and structural guidance for designing a compliance program, it is not in itself a compliance program. Rather, it is a set of guidelines for a hospital interested in implementing a compliance program to consider. The recommendations and guidelines provided in this document must be considered depending upon their applicability to each particular hospital.

Fundamentally, compliance efforts are designed to establish a culture within a hospital that promotes prevention, detection and resolution of instances of conduct that do not conform to federal and state law, and federal, state and private payor health care program requirements, as well as the hospital's ethical and business policies. In practice, the compliance program should effectively articulate and demonstrate the organization's commitment to the compliance process. The existence of benchmarks that demonstrate implementation and achievements are essential to any effective compliance program. **[7.4]** Eventually, a compliance program should become part of the fabric of routine hospital operations.

Specifically, compliance programs guide a hospital's governing body (e.g., Boards of Directors or Trustees), Chief Executive Officer (CEO), managers, other employees and physicians and other health care professionals in the efficient management and operation of a hospital. They are especially critical as an internal control in the reimbursement and payment areas, where claims and billing operations are often the source of fraud and abuse and, therefore, historically have been the focus of government regulation, scrutiny and sanctions. **[Chapter 13]**

It is incumbent upon a hospital's corporate officers and managers to provide ethical leadership to the organization and to assure that adequate systems are in place to facilitate ethical and legal conduct. Indeed, many hospitals and hospital organizations have adopted mission statements articulating their commitment to high ethical standards. A formal compliance program, as an additional element in this process, offers a hospital a further concrete method that may improve quality of care and reduce waste. Compliance programs also provide a central coordinating mechanism for furnishing and disseminating information and guidance on applicable federal and state statutes, regulations and other requirements.

Adopting and implementing an effective compliance program requires a substantial commitment of time, energy and resources by senior management and the hospital's governing body.[1] Programs hastily constructed and implemented without appropriate ongoing monitoring will likely be ineffective and could result in greater harm or liability to the hospital than no program at all. While it may require significant additional resources or reallocation of existing resources to implement an effective compliance program, the OIG believes that the long term benefits of implementing the program outweigh the costs.

## A. BENEFITS OF A COMPLIANCE PROGRAM

In addition to fulfilling its legal duty to ensure that it is not submitting false or inaccurate claims to government and private payors, a hospital may gain numerous additional benefits by implementing an effective compliance program. Such programs make good business sense in that they help a hospital fulfill its fundamental care-giving mission to patients and the community, and assist hospitals in identifying weaknesses in internal systems and management. Other important potential benefits include the ability to:

- concretely demonstrate to employees and the community at large the hospital's strong commitment to honest and responsible provider and corporate conduct;
- provide a more accurate view of employee and contractor behavior relating to fraud and abuse;
- identify and prevent criminal and unethical conduct;
- tailor a compliance program to a hospital's specific needs;
- improve the quality of patient care;
- create a centralized source for distributing information on health care statutes, regulations and other program directives related to fraud and abuse and related issues;
- develop a methodology that encourages employees to report potential problems;
- develop procedures that allow the prompt, thorough investigation of alleged misconduct by corporate officers, managers, employees, independent contractors, physicians, other health care professionals and consultants;
- initiate immediate and appropriate corrective action; and
- through early detection and reporting, minimize the loss to the Government from false claims, and thereby reduce the hospital's exposure to civil damages and penalties, criminal sanctions, and administrative remedies, such as program exclusion.[2]

Overall, the OIG believes that an effective compliance program is a sound investment on the part of a hospital.

The OIG recognizes that the implementation of a compliance program may not entirely eliminate fraud, abuse and waste from the hospital system. However, a sincere effort by hospitals to comply with applicable federal and state standards, as well as the requirements of private health care programs, through the establishment of an effective compliance program, significantly reduces the risk of unlawful or improper conduct.

## B. APPLICATION OF COMPLIANCE PROGRAM GUIDANCE

There is no single "best" hospital compliance program, given the diversity within the industry. The OIG understands the variances and complexities within the hospital industry and is sensitive to the differences among large urban medical centers, community hospitals, small, rural hospitals, specialty hospitals, and other types of hospital organizations and systems. However, elements of this guidance can be used by all hospitals, regardless of size, location or corporate structure, to establish an effective compliance program. We recognize that some hospitals may not be able to adopt certain elements to the same comprehensive degree that others with more extensive resources may achieve. This guidance represents the OIG's suggestions on how a hospital can best establish internal controls and monitoring to correct and prevent fraudulent activities. By no means should the contents of this guidance be viewed as an exclusive discussion of the advisable elements of a compliance program.

The OIG believes that input and support by representatives of the major hospital trade associations is critical to the development and success of this compliance program guidance. Therefore, in drafting this guidance, the OIG received and considered input from various hospital and medical associations, as well as professional practice organizations. Further, we took into consideration previous OIG publications, such as *Special Fraud Alerts* and *Management Advisory Reports*, the recent findings and recommendations in reports issued by OIG's Office of Audit Services and Office of Evaluation and Inspections, as well as the experience of past and recent fraud investigations related to hospitals conducted by OIG's Office of Investigations and the Department of Justice.

As appropriate, this guidance may be modified and expanded as more information and knowledge is obtained by the OIG, and as changes in the law, and in the rules, policies and procedures of the federal, state and private health plans occur. The OIG understands that hospitals will need adequate time to react to these modifications and expansions to make any necessary changes to their voluntary compliance programs. We recognize that hospitals are already accountable for complying with an extensive set of statutory and other legal requirements, far more specific and complex than what we have referenced in this document. We also recognize that the development and implementation of compliance programs in hospitals often raise sensitive and complex legal and managerial issues.[3] **[3.9]** However, the OIG wishes to offer what it believes is critical guidance for providers who are sincerely attempting to comply with the relevant health care statutes and regulations.

## II. COMPLIANCE PROGRAM ELEMENTS

The elements proposed by these guidelines are similar to those of the clinical laboratory model compliance program published by the OIG in February 1997[4] and our corporate integrity agreements.[5] The elements represent a guide—a process that can be used by hospitals, large or small, urban or rural, for-profit or not-for-profit. Moreover, the elements can be incorporated into the managerial structure of multi-hospital and integrated delivery systems. As we stated in our clinical laboratory plan, these suggested guidelines can be tailored to fit the needs and financial realities of a particular hospital. The OIG is cognizant that with regard to compliance programs, one model is not suitable to every hospital. Nonetheless, the OIG believes that every hospital, regardless of size or structure, can benefit from the principles espoused in this guidance.

The OIG believes that every effective compliance program must begin with a formal commitment by the hospital's governing body to include *all* of the applicable elements listed below. These elements are based on the seven steps of the Federal Sentencing Guidelines.[6] Further, we believe that every hospital can implement most of our recommended elements that expand upon the seven steps of the Federal Sentencing Guidelines.[7] We recognize that full implementation of all elements may not be immediately feasible for all hospitals. However, as a first step, a good faith and meaningful commitment on the part of the hospital administration, especially the governing body and the CEO, will substantially contribute to a program's successful implementation.

At a minimum, comprehensive compliance programs should include the following seven elements:

1. the development and distribution of written standards of conduct, as well as written policies and procedures that promote the hospital's commitment to compliance (e.g., by including adherence to compliance as an element in evaluating managers and employees) and that address specific areas of potential fraud, such as claims development and submission processes, code gaming, and financial relationships with physicians and other health care professionals; [**Chapter 4**]

2. the designation of a chief compliance officer and other appropriate bodies (e.g., a corporate compliance committee), charged with the responsibility of operating and monitoring the compliance program and who report directly to the CEO and the governing body; [**Chapter 5**]

3. the development and implementation of regular, effective education and training programs for all affected employees; [**Chapter 6**]

4. the maintenance of a process, such as a hotline, to receive complaints, and the adoption of procedures to protect the anonymity of complainants and to protect whistleblowers from retaliation; [**Chapter 8**]

5. the development of a system to respond to allegations of improper/illegal activities and the enforcement of appropriate disciplinary action against employees who have violated internal compliance policies, applicable statutes, regulations or federal health care program requirements; [**Chapter 9**]

6. the use of audits and/or other evaluation techniques to monitor compliance and assist in the reduction of identified problem areas; [**Chapter 7**] and

7. the investigation and remediation of identified systemic problems and the development of policies addressing the non-employment or retention of sanctioned individuals. [**Chapter 10**]

# A. WRITTEN POLICIES AND PROCEDURES

Every compliance program should require the development and distribution of written compliance policies that identify specific areas of risk to the hospital. These policies should be developed under the direction and supervision of the chief compliance officer and compliance committee, and, at a minimum, should be provided to all individuals who are affected by the particular policy at issue, including the hospital's agents and independent contractors.

## 1. Standards of Conduct

Hospitals should develop standards of conduct [**4.1**] for all affected employees that include a clearly delineated commitment to compliance by the hospital's senior management[8] and its divisions, including affiliated providers operating under the hospital's control,[9] hospital-based physicians and other health care professionals (e.g., utilization review managers, nurse anesthetists, physician assistants and physical therapists). Standards should articulate the hospital's commitment to comply with all federal and state standards, with an emphasis on preventing fraud and abuse. [**4.1**] They should state the organization's mission, goals, and ethical requirements of compliance and reflect a carefully crafted, clear expression of expectations for all hospital governing body members, officers, managers, employees, physicians, and, where appropriate, contractors and other agents. Standards should be distributed to, and comprehensible by, all employees (e.g., translated into other languages and written at appropriate reading levels, where appropriate). Further, to assist in ensuring that employees continuously meet the expected high standards set forth in the code of conduct, any employee handbook delineating or expanding upon these standards of conduct should be regularly updated as applicable statutes, regulations and federal health care program requirements are modified.[10]

## 2. Risk Areas

The OIG believes that a hospital's written policies and procedures should take into consideration the regulatory exposure for each function or department of the hospital. Consequently, we recommend that the individual policies and procedures be coordinated with the appropriate training and educational programs with an emphasis on areas of special concern that have been identified by the OIG through its investigative and audit functions.[11] Some of the special areas of OIG concern include:[12] [**4.2, 4.3 and Table 4.1**]

- Billing for items or services not actually rendered;[13] [**13.20**]
- Providing medically unnecessary services;[14] [**13.14**]
- Upcoding;[15] [**4.4, 13.3 through 13.9**]
- "DRG creep";[16] [**4.4, 6.4, 13.3 through 13.9**]
- Outpatient services rendered in connection with inpatient stays;[17] [**13.11**]

- Teaching physician and resident requirements for teaching hospitals; **[13.10]**
- Duplicate billing;[18] **[13.20]**
- False cost reports;[19] **[13.9 and 13.20]**
- Unbundling;[20] **[13.12]**
- Billing for discharge in lieu of transfer;[21] **[13.20]**
- Patients' freedom of choice;[22]
- Credit balances—failure to refund; **[10.2]**
- Hospital incentives that violate the anti-kickback statute or other similar federal or state statute or regulation;[23] **[Chapter 14]**
- Joint ventures;[24] **[Chapter 15]**
- Financial arrangements between hospitals and hospital-based physicians;[25] **[4.3]**
- Stark physician self-referral law; **[Chapter 14]**
- Knowing failure to provide covered services or necessary care to members of a health maintenance organization; and
- Patient dumping.[26]

Additional risk areas should be assessed as well by hospitals and incorporated into the written policies and procedures and training elements developed as part of their compliance programs.

## 3. CLAIM DEVELOPMENT AND SUBMISSION PROCESS

A number of the risk areas identified above, pertaining to the claim development and submission process, have been the subject of administrative proceedings, as well as investigations and prosecutions under the civil False Claims Act and criminal statutes. Settlement of these cases often has required the defendants to execute corporate integrity agreements, in addition to paying significant civil damages and/or criminal fines and penalties. These corporate integrity agreements have provided the OIG with a mechanism to advise hospitals concerning what it feels are acceptable practices to ensure compliance with applicable federal and state statutes, regulations, and program requirements. The following recommendations include a number of provisions from various corporate integrity agreements. While these recommendations include examples of effective policies, each hospital should develop its own specific policies tailored to fit its individual needs.

With respect to reimbursement claims, a hospital's written policies and procedures should reflect and reinforce current federal and state statutes and regulations regarding the submission of claims and Medicare cost reports. The policies must create a mechanism for the billing or reimbursement staff to communicate effectively and accurately with the clinical staff. Policies and procedures should:

- provide for proper and timely documentation of all physician and other professional services prior to billing to ensure that only accurate and properly documented services are billed;
- emphasize that claims should be submitted only when appropriate documentation supports the claims and only when such documentation is maintained and available for audit and review. The documentation, which may include patient records, should record the length of time spent in conducting the activity leading to the record entry, and the identity of the individual providing the service. The hospital should consult with its medical staff to establish other appropriate documentation guidelines;
- state that, consistent with appropriate guidance from medical staff, physician and hospital records and medical notes used as a basis for a claim submission should be appropriately organized in a legible form so they can be audited and reviewed;
- indicate that the diagnosis and procedures reported on the reimbursement claim should be based on the medical record and other documentation, and that the documentation necessary for accurate code assignment should be available to coding staff; and
- provide that the compensation for billing department coders and billing consultants should not provide any financial incentive to improperly upcode claims.

The written policies and procedures concerning proper coding should reflect the current reimbursement principles set forth in applicable regulations[27] and should be developed in tandem with private payor and organizational standards. Particular attention should be paid to issues of medical necessity, appropriate diagnosis codes, DRG coding, individual Medicare Part B claims (including evaluation and management coding) and the use of patient discharge codes.[28] **[6.2 and 13.6]**

**a. Outpatient services rendered in connection with an inpatient stay** Hospitals should implement measures designed to demonstrate their good faith efforts to comply with the Medicare billing rules for outpatient services rendered in connection with an inpatient stay. **[13.11]** Although not a guard against intentional wrongdoing, the adoption of the following measures are advisable:

- installing and maintaining computer software that will identify those outpatient services that may not be billed separately from an inpatient stay; or
- implementing a periodic manual review to determine the appropriateness of billing each outpatient service claim, to be conducted by one or more appropriately trained individuals familiar with applicable billing rules; or
- with regard to each inpatient stay, scrutinizing the propriety of any potential bills for outpatient services rendered to that patient at the hospital, within the applicable time period.

In addition to the pre-submission undertakings described above, the hospital may implement a post-submission testing process, as follows:

- implement and maintain a periodic post-submission random testing process that examines or re-examines previously submitted claims for accuracy;
- inform the fiscal intermediary and any other appropriate government fiscal agents of the hospital's testing process; and
- advise the fiscal intermediary and any other appropriate government fiscal agents in accordance with current regulations or program instructions with respect to return of overpayments of any incorrectly submitted or paid claims and, if the claim has already been paid, promptly reimburse the fiscal intermediary and the beneficiary for the amount of the claim paid by the government payor and any applicable deductibles or copayments, as appropriate.

**b. Submission of claims for laboratory services**  A hospital's policies should take reasonable steps to ensure that all claims for clinical and diagnostic laboratory testing services are accurate and correctly identify the services ordered by the physician (or other authorized requestor) and performed by the laboratory. **[13.12]** The hospital's written policies and procedures should require, at a minimum,[29] that:

- the hospital bills for laboratory services only after they are performed;
- the hospital bills only for medically necessary services;
- the hospital bills only for those tests actually ordered by a physician and provided by the hospital laboratory;
- the CPT or HCPCS code used by the billing staff accurately describes the service that was ordered by the physician and performed by the hospital laboratory;
- the coding staff: (1) only submit diagnostic information obtained from qualified personnel and (2) contact the appropriate personnel to obtain diagnostic information in the event that the individual who ordered the test has failed to provide such information; and
- where diagnostic information is obtained from a physician or the physician's staff after receipt of the specimen and request for services, the receipt of such information is documented and maintained.

**c. Physicians at teaching hospitals**  Hospitals should ensure the following with respect to all claims submitted on behalf of teaching physicians: **[13.10]**

- only services actually provided may be billed;
- every physician who provides or supervises the provision of services to a patient should be responsible for the correct documentation of the services that were rendered;

- the appropriate documentation must be placed in the patient record and signed by the physician who provided or supervised the provision of services to the patient;
- every physician is responsible for assuring that in cases where that physician provides evaluation and management (E&M) services, a patient's medical record includes appropriate documentation of the applicable key components of the E&M service provided or supervised by the physician (e.g., patient history, physician examination, and medical decision making), as well as documentation to adequately reflect the procedure or portion of the service performed by the physician; and
- every physician should document his or her presence during the key portion of any service or procedure for which payment is sought.

**d. Cost reports** With regard to cost report issues, the written policies should include procedures that seek to ensure full compliance with applicable statutes, regulations and program requirements and private payor plans. **[13.9 and 13.20]** Among other things, the hospital's procedures should ensure that:

- costs are not claimed unless based on appropriate and accurate documentation;
- allocations of costs to various cost centers are accurately made and supportable by verifiable and auditable data;
- unallowable costs are not claimed for reimbursement;
- accounts containing both allowable and unallowable costs are analyzed to determine the unallowable amount that should not be claimed for reimbursement;
- costs are properly classified;
- fiscal intermediary prior year audit adjustments are implemented and are either not claimed for reimbursement or claimed for reimbursement and clearly identified as protested amounts on the cost report;
- all related parties are identified on Form 339 submitted with the cost report and all related party charges are reduced to cost;
- requests for exceptions to TEFRA (Tax Equity and Fiscal Responsibility Act of 1982) limits and the Routine Cost Limits are properly documented and supported by verifiable and auditable data;
- the hospital's procedures for reporting of bad debts on the cost report are in accordance with federal statutes, regulations, guidelines and policies;
- allocations from a hospital chain's home office cost statement to individual hospital cost reports are accurately made and supportable by verifiable and auditable data; and
- procedures are in place and documented for notifying promptly the Medicare fiscal intermediary (or any other applicable payor, e.g., TRICARE [formerly CHAMPUS] and Medicaid) of errors discovered after the submission of the hospital cost report, and where applicable, after the submission of a hospital chain's home office cost statement.

With regard to bad debts claimed on the Medicare cost report, see also section six, below, on Bad Debts.

## 4. MEDICAL NECESSITY—REASONABLE AND NECESSARY SERVICES

A hospital's compliance program should provide that claims should only be submitted for services that the hospital has reason to believe are medically necessary and that were ordered by a physician[30] or other appropriately licensed individual. [13.14]

As a preliminary matter, the OIG recognizes that licensed health care professionals must be able to order any services that are appropriate for the treatment of their patients. [13.15] However, Medicare and other government and private health care plans will only pay for those services that meet appropriate medical necessity standards (in the case of Medicare, i.e., "reasonable and necessary" services). Providers may not bill for services that do not meet the applicable standards. The hospital is in a unique position to deliver this information to the health care professionals on its staff. Upon request, a hospital should be able to provide documentation, such as patients' medical records and physicians' orders, to support the medical necessity of a service that the hospital has provided. The compliance officer should ensure that a clear, comprehensive summary of the "medical necessity" definitions and rules of the various government and private plans is prepared and disseminated appropriately.

## 5. ANTI-KICKBACK AND SELF-REFERRAL CONCERNS

The hospital should have policies and procedures in place with respect to compliance with federal and state anti-kickback statutes, as well as the Stark physician self-referral law.[31] [Chapter 14] Such policies should provide that:

- all of the hospital's contracts and arrangements with referral sources comply with all applicable statutes and regulations;
- the hospital does not submit or cause to be submitted to the federal health care programs claims for patients who were referred to the hospital pursuant to contracts and financial arrangements that were designed to induce such referrals in violation of the anti-kickback statute, Stark physician self-referral law or similar federal or state statute or regulation; and
- the hospital does not enter into financial arrangements with hospital-based physicians that are designed to provide inappropriate remuneration to the hospital in return for the physician's ability to provide services to federal health care program beneficiaries at that hospital.[32] [Tables 14.2A, B, and C]

Further, the policies and procedures should reference the OIG's safe harbor regulations, clarifying those payment practices that would be immune from prosecution under the anti-kickback statute. *See* 42 C.F.R. § 1001.952.

## 6. BAD DEBTS

A hospital should develop a mechanism[33] to review, at least annually: 1) whether it is properly reporting bad debts to Medicare; and 2) all Medicare bad debt expenses claimed, to ensure that the hospital's procedures are in accordance with applicable federal and state statutes, regulations, guidelines and policies. In addition, such a review should ensure that the hospital has appropriate and reasonable mechanisms in place regarding beneficiary deductible or co-payment collection efforts and has not claimed as bad debts any routinely waived Medicare copayments and deductibles, which waiver also constitutes a violation of the anti-kickback statute. [**Chapter 14**] Further, the hospital may consult with the appropriate fiscal intermediary as to bad debt reporting requirements, if questions arise.

## 7. CREDIT BALANCES

The Hospital should institute procedures to provide for the timely and accurate reporting of Medicare and other federal health care program credit balances. [**10.2**] For example, a hospital may redesignate segments of its information system to allow for the segregation of patient accounts reflecting credit balances. The hospital could remove these accounts from the active accounts and place them in a holding account pending the processing of a reimbursement claim to the appropriate program. A hospital's information system should have the ability to print out the individual patient accounts that reflect a credit balance in order to permit simplified tracking of credit balances.

In addition, a hospital should designate at least one person (e.g., in the Patient Accounts Department or reasonable equivalent thereof) as having the responsibility for the tracking, recording and reporting of credit balances. Further, a comptroller or an accountant in the hospital's Accounting Department (or reasonable equivalent thereof) may review reports of credit balances and reimbursements or adjustments on a monthly basis as an additional safeguard.

## 8. RETENTION OF RECORDS

Hospital compliance programs should provide for the implementation of a records system. This system should establish policies and procedures regarding the creation, distribution, retention, storage, retrieval and destruction of documents. The two types of documents developed under this system should include: 1) all records and documentation (e.g., clinical and medical records and claims documentation) required either by federal or state law for participation in federal health care programs (e.g., Medicare's conditions of participation requirement that hospital records regarding Medicare claims be retained for a minimum of five years, see 42 C.F.R. § 482.24(b)(1) and *HCFA Hospital Manual* § 413(C)(12-91)); and 2) all records necessary to protect the integrity of the hospital's compliance process and confirm the effectiveness of the program (e.g., documentation that employees were adequately trained; reports from the hospital's hotline, including the nature and results of any investigation that was conducted; modifications to the compliance program; self-disclosures; and the results of the hospital's auditing and monitoring efforts).[34]

## 9. Compliance as an Element of a Performance Plan

Compliance programs should require that the promotion of, and adherence to, the elements of the compliance program be a factor in evaluating the performance of managers and supervisors. **[9.1]** They, along with other employees, should be periodically trained in new compliance policies and procedures. In addition, all managers and supervisors involved in the coding, claims and cost report development and submission processes should:

- discuss with all supervised employees the compliance policies and legal requirements applicable to their function;
- inform all supervised personnel that strict compliance with these policies and requirements is a condition of employment; and
- disclose to all supervised personnel that the hospital will take disciplinary action up to and including termination or revocation of privileges for violation of these policies or requirements.

In addition to making performance of these duties an element in evaluations, the compliance officer or hospital management should include in the hospital's compliance program a policy that managers and supervisors will be sanctioned for failure to instruct adequately their subordinates or for failing to detect noncompliance with applicable policies and legal requirements, where reasonable diligence on the part of the manager or supervisor would have led to the discovery of any problems or violations and given the hospital the opportunity to correct them earlier.

## B. DESIGNATION OF A COMPLIANCE OFFICER AND A COMPLIANCE COMMITTEE

### 1. Compliance Officer

Every hospital should designate a compliance officer **[5.7]** to serve as the focal point for compliance activities. This responsibility may be the individual's sole duty or added to other management responsibilities, depending upon the size and resources of the hospital and the complexity of the task. Designating a compliance officer with the appropriate authority is critical to the success of the program, necessitating the appointment of a high-level official in the hospital with direct access to the hospital's governing body and the CEO.[35] **[5.1]** The officer should have sufficient funding and staff to perform his or her responsibilities fully. Coordination and communication are the key functions of the compliance officer with regard to planning, implementing, and monitoring the compliance program.

The compliance officer's primary responsibilities [5.9] should include:

- overseeing and monitoring the implementation of the compliance program;[36]
- reporting on a regular basis to the hospital's governing body, CEO and compliance committee on the progress of implementation, and assisting these components in establishing methods to improve the hospital's efficiency and quality of services, and to reduce the hospital's vulnerability to fraud, abuse and waste;
- periodically revising the program in light of changes in the needs of the organization, and in the law and policies and procedures of government and private payor health plans;
- developing, coordinating, and participating in a multifaceted educational and training program that focuses on the elements of the compliance program, and seeks to ensure that all appropriate employees and management are knowledgeable of, and comply with, pertinent federal and state standards;
- ensuring that independent contractors and agents who furnish medical services to the hospital are aware of the requirements of the hospital's compliance program with respect to coding, billing, and marketing, among other things;
- coordinating personnel issues with the hospital's Human Resources office (or its equivalent) to ensure that the National Practitioner Data Bank and *Cumulative Sanction Report*[37] have been checked with respect to all employees, medical staff and independent contractors;
- assisting the hospital's financial management in coordinating internal compliance review and monitoring activities, including annual or periodic reviews of departments;
- independently investigating and acting on matters related to compliance, including the flexibility to design and coordinate internal investigations (e.g., responding to reports of problems or suspected violations) and any resulting corrective action with all hospital departments, providers and sub-providers,[38] agents and, if appropriate, independent contractors; and [5.9]
- developing policies and programs that encourage managers and employees to report suspected fraud and other improprieties without fear of retaliation.

The compliance officer must have the authority to review all documents and other information that are relevant to compliance activities, including, but not limited to, patient records, billing records, and records concerning the marketing efforts of the facility and the hospital's arrangements with other parties, including employees, professionals on staff, independent contractors, suppliers, agents, and hospital-based physicians, etc. This policy enables the compliance officer to review contracts and obligations (seeking the advice of legal counsel, where appropriate) that may contain referral and payment issues that could violate the anti-kickback statute, as well as the physician self-referral prohibition and other legal or regulatory requirements.

## 2. COMPLIANCE COMMITTEE

The OIG recommends that a compliance committee be established to advise the compliance officer and assist in the implementation of the compliance program.[39] **[5.8]** The committee's functions should include:

- analyzing the organization's industry environment, the legal requirements with which it must comply, and specific risk areas;
- assessing existing policies and procedures that address these areas for possible incorporation into the compliance program;
- working with appropriate hospital departments to develop standards of conduct and policies and procedures to promote compliance with the institution's program;
- recommending and monitoring, in conjunction with the relevant departments, the development of internal systems and controls to carry out the organization's standards, policies and procedures as part of its daily operations;
- determining the appropriate strategy/approach to promote compliance with the program and detection of any potential violations, such as through hotlines and other fraud reporting mechanisms; and
- developing a system to solicit, evaluate and respond to complaints and problems.

The committee may also address other functions as the compliance concept becomes part of the overall hospital operating structure and daily routine.

## C. CONDUCTING EFFECTIVE TRAINING AND EDUCATION

The proper education and training of corporate officers, managers, employees, physicians and other health care professionals, and the continual retraining of current personnel at all levels, are significant elements of an effective compliance program. As part of their compliance programs, hospitals should require personnel to attend specific training on a periodic basis, including appropriate training in federal and state statutes, regulations and guidelines, and the policies of private payors, **[13.19]** and training in corporate ethics, which emphasizes the organization's commitment to compliance with these legal requirements and policies.

These training programs should include sessions highlighting the organization's compliance program, summarizing fraud and abuse laws, coding requirements, claim development and submission processes **[Chapters 13 and 14]** and marketing practices **[Chapter 15]** that reflect current legal and program standards.**[6.1]** The organization must take steps to communicate effectively its standards and procedures to all affected employees, physicians, independent contractors and other significant agents **[6.3]**, e.g., by requiring participation in training programs and disseminating publications that explain in a practical manner specific requirements.[40] Managers of specific departments or groups can assist in identifying areas that require training and in carrying out such training. Training instructors may come from outside or inside the organization. New employees should be targeted for training early in their employment.[41] Any formal training undertaken by the hospital as part of the compliance program should be documented by the compliance officer.

A variety of teaching methods **[6.6]**, such as interactive training, and training in several different languages, particularly where a hospital has a culturally diverse staff, should be implemented so that all affected employees are knowledgeable of the institution's standards of conduct and procedures for alerting senior management to problems and concerns. Targeted training should be provided to corporate officers, managers and other employees whose actions affect the accuracy of the claims submitted to the Government, such as employees involved in the coding, billing, cost reporting and marketing processes. Given the complexity and interdependent relationships of many departments, proper coordination and supervision of this process by the compliance officer is important. In addition to specific training in the risk areas identified in section II.A.2, above, primary training to appropriate corporate officers, managers and other hospital staff should include such topics **[6.1]** as:

- Government and private payor reimbursement principles;
- general prohibitions on paying or receiving remuneration to induce referrals;
- proper confirmation of diagnoses;
- submitting a claim for physician services when rendered by a non-physician (i.e., the "incident to" rule and the physician physical presence requirement);
- signing a form for a physician without the physician's authorization;
- alterations to medical records;
- prescribing medications and procedures without proper authorization;
- proper documentation of services rendered; and
- duty to report misconduct. **[8.1 and 8.3]**

Clarifying and emphasizing these areas of concern through training and educational programs are particularly relevant to a hospital's marketing and financial personnel, in that the pressure to meet business goals may render these employees vulnerable to engaging in prohibited practices.

The OIG suggests that all relevant levels of personnel be made part of various educational and training programs of the hospital. Employees should be required to have a minimum number of educational hours per year, as appropriate, as part of their employment responsibilities.[42] For example, for certain employees involved in the billing and coding functions, periodic training in proper DRG coding and documentation of medical records should be required.[43] In hospitals with high employee turnover, periodic training updates are critical.

The OIG recommends that attendance and participation in training programs be made a condition of continued employment and that failure to comply with training requirements should result in disciplinary action, including possible termination, when such failure is serious. Adherence to the provisions of the compliance program, such as training requirements, should be a factor in the annual evaluation of each employee.[44] The hospital should retain adequate records of its training of employees, including attendance logs and material distributed at training sessions.

Finally, the OIG recommends that hospital compliance programs address the need for periodic professional education courses that may be required by statute and regulation for certain hospital personnel.

## D. DEVELOPING EFFECTIVE LINES OF COMMUNICATION

### 1. ACCESS TO THE COMPLIANCE OFFICER

An open line of communication between the compliance officer and hospital personnel is equally important to the successful implementation of a compliance program and the reduction of any potential for fraud, abuse and waste. **[8.1]** Written confidentiality and non-retaliation policies should be developed and distributed to all employees to encourage communication and the reporting of incidents of potential fraud.[45] The compliance committee should also develop several independent reporting paths for an employee to report fraud, waste or abuse so that such reports cannot be diverted by supervisors or other personnel.

The OIG encourages the establishment of a procedure so that hospital personnel may seek clarification from the compliance officer or members of the compliance committee in the event of any confusion or question with regard to a hospital policy or procedure. Questions and responses should be documented and dated and, if appropriate, shared with other staff so that standards, policies and procedures can be updated and improved to reflect any necessary changes or clarifications. The compliance officer may want to solicit employee input in developing these communication and reporting systems.

### 2. HOTLINES AND OTHER FORMS OF COMMUNICATION

The OIG encourages the use of hotlines (including anonymous hotlines), e-mails, written memoranda, newsletters, and other forms of information exchange to maintain these open lines of communication. **[8.4]** If the hospital establishes a hotline, the telephone number should be made readily available to all employees and independent contractors, possibly by conspicuously posting the telephone number in common work areas.[46] Employees should be permitted to report matters on an anonymous basis. Matters reported through the hotline or other communication sources that suggest substantial violations of compliance policies, regulations or statutes should be documented and investigated promptly to determine their veracity. A log should be maintained by the compliance officer that records such calls, including the nature of any investigation and its results. Such information should be included in reports to the governing body, the CEO and compliance committee. Further, while the hospital should always strive to maintain the confidentiality of an employee's identity, it should also explicitly communicate that there may be a point where the individual's identity may become known or may have to be revealed in certain instances when governmental authorities become involved. **[8.5]**

The OIG recognizes that assertions of fraud and abuse by employees who may have participated in illegal conduct or committed other malfeasance raise numerous complex legal and management issues that should be examined on a case-by-case basis. The compliance officer should work closely with legal counsel, who can provide guidance regarding such issues.

## E. ENFORCING STANDARDS THROUGH WELL-PUBLICIZED DISCIPLINARY GUIDELINES

### 1. DISCIPLINE POLICY AND ACTIONS

An effective compliance program should include guidance regarding disciplinary action for corporate officers, managers, employees, physicians and other health care professionals who have failed to comply with the hospital's standards of conduct, policies and procedures, or federal and state laws, or those who have otherwise engaged in wrongdoing, which have the potential to impair the hospital's status as a reliable, honest and trustworthy health care provider.

The OIG believes that the compliance program should include a written policy statement setting forth the degrees of disciplinary actions that may be imposed upon corporate officers, managers, employees, physicians and other health care professionals for failing to comply with the hospital's standards and policies and applicable statutes and regulations. **[9.1]** Intentional or reckless noncompliance should subject transgressors to significant sanctions. Such sanctions could range from oral warnings to suspension, privilege revocation (subject to any applicable peer review procedures), termination or financial penalties, as appropriate. **[9.1]** The written standards of conduct should elaborate on the procedures for handling disciplinary problems and those who will be responsible for taking appropriate action. Some disciplinary actions can be handled by department managers, while others may have to be resolved by a senior hospital administrator. Disciplinary action may be appropriate where a responsible employee's failure to detect a violation is attributable to his or her negligence or reckless conduct. Personnel should be advised by the hospital that disciplinary action will be taken on a fair and equitable basis. Managers and supervisors should be made aware that they have a responsibility to discipline employees in an appropriate and consistent manner.

It is vital to publish and disseminate the range of disciplinary standards for improper conduct and to educate officers and other hospital staff regarding these standards. The consequences of noncompliance should be consistently applied and enforced, in order for the disciplinary policy to have the required deterrent effect. All levels of employees should be subject to the same disciplinary action for the commission of similar offenses. The commitment to compliance applies to all personnel levels within a hospital. The OIG believes that corporate officers, managers, supervisors, medical staff and other health care professionals should be held accountable for failing to comply with, or for the foreseeable failure of their subordinates to adhere to, the applicable standards, laws, and procedures. **[9.2]**

## 2. NEW EMPLOYEE POLICY

For all new employees who have discretionary authority to make decisions that may involve compliance with the law or compliance oversight, hospitals should conduct a reasonable and prudent background investigation, including a reference check, as part of every such employment application.[47] **[3.7, 9.3]** The application should specifically require the applicant to disclose any criminal conviction, as defined by 42 U.S.C. § 1320a-7(i), or exclusion action. Pursuant to the compliance program, hospital policies should prohibit the employment of individuals who have been recently convicted of a criminal offense related to health care or who are listed as debarred, excluded or otherwise ineligible for participation in federal health care programs (as defined in 42 U.S.C. § 1320a-7b(f)).[48] **[9.4]** In addition, pending the resolution of any criminal charges or proposed debarment or exclusion, the OIG recommends that such individuals should be removed from direct responsibility for or involvement in any federal health care program.[49] With regard to current employees or independent contractors, if resolution of the matter results in conviction, debarment or exclusion, the hospital should terminate its employment or other contract arrangement with the individual or contractor.

## F. AUDITING AND MONITORING

An ongoing evaluation process is critical to a successful compliance program. The OIG believes that an effective program should incorporate thorough monitoring of its implementation and regular reporting to senior hospital or corporate officers.[50] Compliance reports created by this ongoing monitoring, including reports of suspected noncompliance, should be maintained by the compliance officer and shared with the hospital's senior management and the compliance committee.

Although many monitoring techniques are available, one effective tool to promote and ensure compliance is the performance of regular, periodic compliance audits by internal or external auditors who have expertise in federal and state health care statutes, regulations and federal health care program requirements. The audits should focus on the hospital's programs or divisions, including external relationships with third-party contractors, specifically those with substantive exposure to government enforcement actions. At a minimum, these audits should be designed to address the hospital's compliance with laws governing kickback arrangements, the physician self-referral prohibition, CPT/HCPCS ICD-9 coding, claim development and submission, reimbursement, cost reporting and marketing. [7.1] In addition, the audits and reviews should inquire into the hospital's compliance with specific rules and polices [sic] that have been the focus of particular attention on the part of the Medicare fiscal intermediaries or carriers, and law enforcement, as evidenced by OIG *Special Fraud Alerts*, OIG audits and evaluations, and law enforcement's initiatives. *See* section II.A.2, *supra*. In addition, the hospital should focus on any areas of concern that have been identified by any entity, i.e., federal, state, or internally, specific to the individual hospital.

Monitoring techniques may include sampling protocols that permit the compliance officer to identify and review variations from an established baseline.[51] Significant variations from the baseline should trigger a reasonable inquiry to determine the cause of the deviation. If the inquiry determines that the deviation occurred for legitimate, explainable reasons, the compliance officer, hospital administrator or manager may want to limit any corrective action or take no action. If it is determined that the deviation was caused by improper procedures, misunderstanding of rules, including fraud and systemic problems, the hospital should take prompt steps to correct the problem. [7.4] Any overpayments discovered as a result of such deviations should be returned promptly to the affected payor, with appropriate documentation and a thorough explanation of the reason for the refund.[52]

Monitoring techniques may also include a review of any reserves the hospital has established for payments that it may owe to Medicare, Medicaid, TRICARE or other federal health care programs. Any reserves discovered that include funds that should have been paid to Medicare or another government program should be paid promptly, regardless of whether demand has been made for such payment.

An effective compliance program should also incorporate periodic (at least annual) reviews of whether the program's compliance elements have been satisfied, e.g., whether there has been appropriate dissemination of the program's standards, training, ongoing educational programs and disciplinary actions, among others. This process will verify actual conformance by all departments with the compliance program. Such reviews could support a determination that appropriate records have been created and maintained to document the implementation of an effective program. However, when monitoring discloses that deviations were not detected in a timely manner due to program deficiencies, appropriate modifications must be implemented. Such evaluations, when developed with the support of management, can help ensure compliance with the hospital's policies and procedures.

As part of the review process, the compliance officer or reviewers should consider techniques [7.7] such as:

- on-site visits;
- interviews with personnel involved in management, operations, coding, claim development and submission, patient care, and other related activities;
- questionnaires developed to solicit impressions of a broad cross-section of the hospital's employees and staff;
- reviews of medical and financial records and other source documents that support claims for reimbursement and Medicare cost reports;
- reviews of written materials and documentation prepared by the different divisions of a hospital; and
- trend analyses, or longitudinal studies, that seek deviations, positive or negative, in specific areas over a given period.

The reviewers should:

- be independent of physicians and line management;
- have access to existing audit and health care resources, relevant personnel and all relevant areas of operation;
- present written evaluative reports on compliance activities to the CEO, governing body and members of the compliance committee on a regular basis, but no less than annually; and
- specifically identify areas where corrective actions are needed.

With these reports, hospital management can take whatever steps are necessary to correct past problems and prevent them from reoccurring. In certain cases, subsequent reviews or studies would be advisable to ensure that the recommended corrective actions have been implemented successfully.

The hospital should document its efforts to comply with applicable statutes, regulations and federal health care program requirements. For example, where a hospital, in its efforts to comply with a particular statute, regulation or program requirement, requests advice from a government agency (including a Medicare fiscal intermediary or carrier) charged with administering a federal health care program, the hospital should document and retain a record of the request and any written or oral response. This step is extremely important if the hospital intends to rely on that response to guide it in future decisions, actions or claim reimbursement requests or appeals. Maintaining a log of oral inquiries between the hospital and third parties represents an additional basis for establishing documentation on which the organization may rely to demonstrate attempts at compliance. Records should be maintained demonstrating reasonable reliance and due diligence in developing procedures that implement such advice.

## G. RESPONDING TO DETECTED OFFENSES AND DEVELOPING CORRECTIVE ACTION INITIATIVES

### 1. VIOLATIONS AND INVESTIGATIONS

Violations of a hospital's compliance program, failures to comply with applicable federal or state law, and other types of misconduct threaten a hospital's status as a reliable, honest and trustworthy provider capable of participating in federal health care programs. Detected but uncorrected misconduct can seriously endanger the mission, reputation, and legal status of the hospital. Consequently, upon reports or reasonable indications of suspected noncompliance, it is important that the chief compliance officer or other management officials initiate prompt steps to investigate the conduct in question to determine whether a material violation of applicable law or the requirements of the compliance program has occurred, and if so, take steps to correct the problem.[53] As appropriate, such steps may include an immediate referral to criminal and/or civil law enforcement authorities, a corrective action plan,[54] a report to the Government,[55] and the submission of any overpayments, if applicable. **[10.1]**

Where potential fraud or False Claims Act liability is not involved, the OIG recognizes that HCFA regulations and contractor guidelines already include procedures for returning overpayments to the Government as they are discovered. However, even if the overpayment detection and return process is working and is being monitored by the hospital's audit or coding divisions, the OIG still believes that the compliance officer needs to be made aware of these overpayments, violations or deviations and look for trends or patterns that may demonstrate a systemic problem. **[10.2]**

Depending upon the nature of the alleged violations, an internal investigation will probably include interviews and a review of relevant documents. Some hospitals should consider engaging outside counsel, auditors, or health care experts to assist in an investigation. Records of the investigation should contain documentation of the alleged violation, a description of the investigative process, copies of interview notes and key documents, a log of the witnesses interviewed and the documents reviewed, the results of the investigation, e.g., any disciplinary action taken, and the corrective action implemented. While any action taken as the result of an investigation will necessarily vary depending upon the hospital and the situation, hospitals should strive for some consistency by utilizing sound practices and disciplinary protocols. Further, after a reasonable period, the compliance officer should review the circumstances that formed the basis for the investigation to determine whether similar problems have been uncovered. **[10.1]**

If an investigation of an alleged violation is undertaken and the compliance officer believes the integrity of the investigation may be at stake because of the presence of employees under investigation, those subjects should be removed from their current work activity until the investigation is completed (unless an internal or Government-led undercover operation is in effect). In addition, the compliance officer should take appropriate steps to secure or prevent the destruction of documents or other evidence relevant to the investigation. If the hospital determines that disciplinary action is warranted, it should be prompt and imposed in accordance with the hospital's written standards of disciplinary action.

## 2. REPORTING

If the compliance officer, compliance committee or management official discovers credible evidence of misconduct from any source and, after a reasonable inquiry, has reason to believe that the misconduct may violate criminal, civil or administrative law, then the hospital promptly should report the existence of misconduct to the appropriate governmental authority[56] within a reasonable period, but not more than sixty (60) days[57] after determining that there is credible evidence of a violation.[58] **[10.4]** Prompt reporting will demonstrate the hospital's good faith and willingness to work with governmental authorities to correct and remedy the problem. In addition, reporting such conduct will be considered a mitigating factor by the OIG in determining administrative sanctions (e.g., penalties, assessments, and exclusion), if the reporting provider becomes the target of an OIG investigation.[59]

When reporting misconduct to the Government, a hospital should provide all evidence relevant to the alleged violation of applicable federal or state law(s) and potential cost impact. The compliance officer, under advice of counsel, and with guidance from the governmental authorities, could be requested to continue to investigate the reported violation. Once the investigation is completed, the compliance officer should be required to notify the appropriate governmental authority of the outcome of the investigation, including a description of the impact of the alleged violation on the operation of the applicable health care programs or their beneficiaries. If the investigation ultimately reveals that criminal or civil violations have occurred, the appropriate federal and state officials[60] should be notified immediately.

As previously stated, the hospital should take appropriate corrective action, including prompt identification and restitution of any overpayment to the affected payor and the imposition of proper disciplinary action. Failure to repay overpayments within a reasonable period of time could be interpreted as an intentional attempt to conceal the overpayment from the Government, thereby establishing an independent basis for a criminal violation with respect to the hospital, as well as any individuals who may have been involved.[61] For this reason, hospital compliance programs should emphasize that overpayments obtained from Medicare or other federal health care programs should be promptly returned to the payor that made the erroneous payment.[62]

## III. CONCLUSION

Through this document, the OIG has attempted to provide a foundation to the process necessary to develop an effective and cost-efficient hospital compliance program. As previously stated, however, each program must be tailored to fit the needs and resources of an individual hospital, depending upon its particular corporate structure, mission, and employee composition. The statutes, regulations and guidelines of the federal and state health insurance programs, as well as the policies and procedures of the private health plans, should be integrated into every hospital's compliance program.

The OIG recognizes that the health care industry in this country, which reaches millions of beneficiaries and expends about a trillion dollars, is constantly evolving. However, the time is right for hospitals to implement a strong voluntary compliance program concept in health care. As stated throughout this guidance, compliance is a dynamic process that helps to ensure that hospitals and other health care providers are better able to fulfill their commitment to ethical behavior, as well as meet the changes and challenges being imposed upon them by Congress and private insurers. Ultimately, it is OIG's hope that a voluntarily created compliance program will enable hospitals to meet their goals, improve the quality of patient care, and substantially reduce fraud, waste and abuse, as well as the cost of health care to federal, state and private health insurers.

## Notes

1. Indeed, recent case law suggests that the failure of a corporate Director to attempt in good faith to institute a compliance program in certain situations may be a breach of a Director's fiduciary obligation. *See, e.g., In re Caremark International Inc. Derivative Litigation*, 698 A.2d 959 (Ct. Chanc. Del. 1996).

2. The OIG, for example, will consider the existence of an *effective* compliance program that pre-dated any Governmental investigation when addressing the appropriateness of administrative penalties. Further, the False Claims Act, 31 U.S.C. §§ 3729-3733, provides that a person who has violated the Act, but who voluntarily discloses the violation to the Government, in certain circumstances will be subject to not less than double, as opposed to treble, damages. *See* 31 U.S.C. § 3729(a).

3. Nothing stated herein should be substituted for, or used in lieu of, competent legal advice from counsel.

4. *See* 62 Fed. Reg. 9435 (3/3/97).

5. Corporate integrity agreements are executed as part of a civil settlement between the health care provider and the Government to resolve a case arising under the False Claims Act (FCA), including the *qui tam* provisions of the FCA, based on allegations of health care fraud or abuse. These OIG-imposed programs are in effect for a period of three to five years and require many of the elements included in this compliance guidance.

6. *See* United States Sentencing Commission Guidelines, *Guidelines Manual*, 8A1.2, comment. (n.3(k)).

7. Current HCFA reimbursement principles provide that certain of the costs associated with the creation of a voluntarily established compliance program may be allowable costs on certain types of hospitals' cost reports. These allowable costs, of course, must at a minimum be *reasonable* and related to patient care. *See generally* 42 U.S.C. § 1395x(v)(1)(A) (definition of reasonable cost); 42 C.F.R. §§ 413.9(a), (b)(2) (costs related to patient care). In contrast, however, costs specifically associated with the implementation of a corporate integrity agreement in response to a Government investigation resulting in a civil or criminal judgment or settlement are unallowable, and are also made specifically and expressly unallowable in corporate integrity agreements and civil fraud settlements. **[2.4]**

8. The OIG strongly encourages high-level involvement by the hospital's governing body, chief executive officer, chief operating officer, general counsel, and chief financial officer, as well as other medical personnel, as appropriate, in the development of standards of conduct. Such involvement should help communicate a strong and explicit statement of compliance goals and standards.

9. E.g., skilled nursing facilities, home health agencies, psychiatric units, rehabilitation units, outpatient clinics, clinical laboratories, dialysis facilities.

10. The OIG recognizes that not all standards, policies and procedures need to be communicated to all employees. However, the OIG believes that the bulk of the standards that relate to complying with fraud and abuse laws and other ethical areas should be addressed and made part of all affected employees' training. The hospital must appropriately decide which additional educational programs should be limited to the different levels of employees, based on job functions and areas of responsibility. **[4.5, 6.3]**

11. The OIG periodically issues Special Fraud Alerts setting forth activities believed to raise legal and enforcement issues. Hospital compliance programs should require that the legal staff, chief compliance officer, or other appropriate personnel, carefully consider any and all Special Fraud Alerts issued by the OIG that relate to hospitals. Moreover, the compliance programs should address the ramifications of failing to cease and correct any conduct criticized in such a Special Fraud Alert, if applicable to hospitals, or to take reasonable action to prevent such conduct from reoccurring in the future. If appropriate, a hospital should take the steps described in Section G regarding investigations, reporting and correction of identified problems.

12. The OIG's work plan is currently available on the Internet at *www.dhhs.gov/progorg/oig*.

13. Billing for services not actually rendered involves submitting a claim that represents that the provider performed a service all or part of which was simply not performed. This form of billing fraud occurs in many health care entities, including hospitals and nursing homes, and represents a significant part of the OIG's investigative caseload.

14. A claim requesting payment for medically unnecessary services intentionally seeks reimbursement for a service that is not warranted by the patient's current and documented medical condition. *See* 42 U.S.C. § 1395y(a)(1)(A) ("no payment may be made under part A or

part B for any expenses incurred for items or services which . . . are not reasonable and necessary for the diagnosis or treatment of illness or injury or to improve the functioning of the malformed body member"). On every HCFA claim form, a physician must certify that the services were medically necessary for the health of the beneficiary.

15. "Upcoding" reflects the practice of using a billing code that provides a higher payment rate than the billing code that actually reflects the service furnished to the patient. Upcoding has been a major focus of the OIG's enforcement efforts. In fact, the Health Insurance Portability and Accountability Act of 1996 added another civil monetary penalty to the OIG's sanction authorities for upcoding violations. *See* 42 U.S.C. § 1320a-7a(a)(1)(A).

16. Like upcoding, "DRG creep" is the practice of billing using a Diagnosis Related Group (DRG) code that provides a higher payment rate than the DRG code that accurately reflects the service furnished to the patient.

17. Hospitals that submit claims for non-physician outpatient services that were already included in the hospital's inpatient payment under the Prospective Payment System (PPS) are in effect submitting duplicate claims.

18. Duplicate billing occurs when the hospital submits more than one claim for the same service or the bill is submitted to more than one primary payor at the same time. Although duplicate billing can occur due to simple error, systematic or repeated double billing may be viewed as a false claim, particularly if any overpayment is not promptly refunded.

19. As another example of health care fraud, the submission of false cost reports is usually limited to certain Part A providers, such as hospitals, skilled nursing facilities and home health agencies, which are reimbursed in part on the basis of their self-reported operating costs. An OIG audit report on the misuse of fringe benefits and general and administrative costs identified millions of dollars in unallowable costs that resulted from providers' lack of internal controls over costs included in their Medicare cost reports. In addition, the OIG is aware of practices in which hospitals inappropriately shift certain costs to cost centers that are below their reimbursement cap and shift non-Medicare related costs to Medicare cost centers.

20. "Unbundling" is the practice of submitting bills piecemeal or in fragmented fashion to maximize the reimbursement for various tests or procedures that are required to be billed together and therefore at a reduced cost.

21. Under the Medicare regulations, when a prospective payment system (PPS) hospital transfers a patient to another PPS hospital, only the hospital to which the patient was transferred may charge the full DRG; the transferring hospital should charge Medicare only a per diem amount.

22. This area of concern is particularly important for hospital discharge planners referring patients to home health agencies, DME suppliers or long term care and rehabilitation providers.

23. Excessive payment for medical directorships, free or below market rents or fees for administrative services, interest-free loans and excessive payment for intangible assets in physician practice acquisitions are examples of arrangements that may run afoul of the anti-kickback statute. *See* 42 U.S.C. § 1320a-7b(b) and 59 Fed. Reg. 65372 (12/19/94). **[14.2 through 14.4]**

24. Equally troubling to the OIG is the proliferation of business arrangements that may violate the anti-kickback statute. Such arrangements are generally established between those in a position to refer business, such as physicians, and those providing items or services for which a federal health care program pays. Sometimes established as "joint ventures," these arrangements may take a variety of forms. The OIG currently has a number of investigations and audits underway that focus on such areas of concern. **[Chapter 14]**

25. Another OIG concern with respect to the anti-kickback statute is hospital financial arrangements with hospital-based physicians that compensate physicians for less than the fair market value of services they provide to hospitals or require physicians to pay more than market value for services provided by the hospital. *See* OIG *Management Advisory Report: Financial Arrangements Between Hospitals and Hospital-Based Physicians.* OEI-09-89-0030, October 1991. Examples of such arrangements that may violate the anti-kickback statute are token or no payment for Part A supervision and management services; requirements to donate equipment to hospitals; and excessive charges for billing services. **[4.3]**

26. The patient anti-dumping statute, 42 U.S.C. § 1395dd, requires that all Medicare participating hospitals with an emergency department: 1) provide for an appropriate medical screening examination to determine whether or not an individual requesting such examination has an emergency medical condition; and 2) if the person has such a condition, (a) stabilize that condition; or (b) appropriately transfer the patient to another hospital.

27. The official coding guidelines are promulgated by HCFA, the National Center for Health Statistics, the American Medical Association and the American Health Information Management Association. *See* International Classification of Diseases, 9th Revision, Clinical Modification (ICD9-CM); 1998 Health Care Financing Administration Common Procedure Coding System (HCPCS); and Physicians' Current Procedural Terminology (CPT).

28. The failure of hospital staff to: (i) document items and services rendered; and (ii) properly submit them for reimbursement is a major area of potential fraud and abuse in federal health care programs. The OIG has undertaken numerous audits, investigations, inspections and national enforcement initiatives aimed at reducing potential and actual fraud, abuse and waste. Recent OIG audit reports, which have focused on issues such as hospital patient transfers incorrectly paid as discharges, and hospitals' general and administrative costs, continue to reveal abusive, wasteful or fraudulent behavior by some hospitals. Our inspection report entitled *Financial Arrangements between Hospitals and Hospital-Based Physicians, see* note 25, *supra,* and our *Special Fraud Alerts on Hospital Incentives to Physicians and Joint Venture Arrangements,* further illustrate how certain business practices may result in fraudulent and abusive behavior.

29. The OIG's *February 1997 Model Compliance Plan for Clinical Laboratories* provides more specific and detailed information than is contained in this section, and hospitals that have clinical laboratories should extract the relevant guidance from both documents.

30. For Medicare reimbursement purposes, a physician is defined as: (1) a doctor of medicine or osteopathy; (2) a doctor of dental surgery or of dental medicine; (3) a podiatrist; (4) an optometrist; and (5) a chiropractor, all of whom must be appropriately licensed by the state. 42 U.S.C. § 1395x(r).

31. Towards this end, the hospital's in-house counsel or compliance officer should, *inter alia,* obtain copies of all OIG regulations, special fraud alerts and advisory opinions concerning the anti-kickback statute, Civil Monetary Penalties Law (CMPL) and Stark physician self-referral law (the fraud alerts and anti-kickback or CMPL advisory opinions are published on HHS-OIG's home page on the Internet), and ensure that the hospital's policies reflect the guidance provided by the OIG.

32. *See* note 25, *supra.*

33. E.g., assigning in-house counsel or contracting with an independent professional organization such as an accounting, law or consulting firm.

34. The creation and retention of such documents and reports may raise a variety of legal issues, such as patient privacy and confidentiality. These issues are best discussed with legal counsel.

35. The OIG believes that there is some risk to establishing an independent compliance function

if that function is subordinate to the hospital's general counsel, or comptroller or similar hospital financial officer. Free standing compliance functions help to ensure independent and objective legal reviews and financial analyses of the institution's compliance efforts and activities. By separating the compliance function from the key management positions of general counsel or chief hospital financial officer (where the size and structure of the hospital make this a feasible option), a system of checks and balances is established to more effectively achieve the goals of the compliance program. **[5.1 through 5.6]**

36. For multi-hospital organizations, the OIG encourages coordination with each hospital owned by the corporation or foundation through the use of a headquarter's compliance officer, communicating with parallel positions in each facility, or regional office, as appropriate.

37. The *Cumulative Sanction Report* is an OIG-produced report available on the Internet at *www.dhhs.gov/progorg/oig*. It is updated on a regular basis to reflect the status of health care providers who have been excluded from participation in the Medicare and Medicaid programs. In addition, the General Services Administration maintains a monthly listing of debarred contractors on the Internet at *www.arnet.gov/epls*. Also, once the database established by the Health Care Fraud and Abuse Data Collection Act of 1996 is fully operational, the hospital should regularly request information from this databank as part of its employee screening process.

38. E.g., skilled nursing facilities and home health agencies.

39. The compliance committee benefits from having the perspectives of individuals with varying responsibilities in the organization, such as operations, finance, audit, human resources, utilization review, social work, discharge planning, medicine, coding and legal, as well as employees and managers of key operating units. **[5.8]**

40. Some publications, such as OIG's *Management Advisory Report* entitled "Financial Arrangements between Hospitals and Hospital-Based Physicians," *Special Fraud Alerts*, audit and inspection reports, and advisory opinions, as well as the annual OIG work plan, are readily available from the OIG and could be the basis for standards, educational courses and programs for appropriate hospital employees.

41. Certain positions, such as those involving the coding of medical services, create a greater organizational legal exposure, and therefore require specialized training. One recommendation would be for a hospital to attempt to fill such positions with individuals who have the appropriate educational background and training.

42. Currently, the OIG is monitoring approximately 165 corporate integrity agreements that require many of these training elements. The OIG usually requires a minimum of one to three hours annually for basic training in compliance areas. More is required for specialty fields such as billing and coding. **[6.3]**

43. Accurate coding depends upon the quality and completeness of the physician's documentation. Therefore, the OIG believes that active staff physician participation in educational programs focusing on coding and documentation should be emphasized by the hospital. **[6.2 and 6.3]**

44. In addition, where feasible, the OIG believes that a hospital's outside contractors, including physician corporations, should be afforded the opportunity to participate in, or develop their own, compliance training and educational programs, which complement the hospital's standards of conduct, compliance requirements, and other rules and regulations. **[6.3, 6.5]**

45. The OIG believes that whistleblowers should be protected against retaliation, a concept embodied in the provisions of the False Claims Act. In many cases, employees sue their

employers under the False Claims Act's *qui tam* provisions out of frustration because of the company's failure to take action when a questionable, fraudulent or abusive situation was brought to the attention of senior corporate officials. **[8.2 and 13.17]**

46. Hospitals should also post in a prominent, available area the HHS-OIG Hotline telephone number, 1-800-HHS-TIPS (447-8477), in addition to any company hotline number that may be posted. **[8.4]**

47. *See* note 37, *supra.*

48. Likewise, hospital compliance programs should establish standards prohibiting the execution of contracts with companies that have been recently convicted of a criminal offense related to health care or that are listed by a federal agency as debarred, excluded, or otherwise ineligible for participation in federal health care programs.

49. Prospective employees who have been officially reinstated into the Medicare and Medicaid programs by the OIG may be considered for employment upon proof of such reinstatement.

50. Even when a hospital is owned by a larger corporate entity, the regular auditing and monitoring of the compliance activities of an individual hospital must be a key feature in any annual review. Appropriate reports on audit findings should be periodically provided and explained to a parent-organization's senior staff and officers. **[7.3]**

51. The OIG recommends that when a compliance program is established in a hospital, the compliance officer, with the assistance of department managers, should take a "snapshot" of their operations from a compliance perspective. This assessment can be undertaken by outside consultants, law or accounting firms, or internal staff, with authoritative knowledge of health care compliance requirements. This "snapshot," often used as part of benchmarking analyses, becomes a baseline for the compliance officer and other managers to judge the hospital's progress in reducing or eliminating potential areas of vulnerability. For example, it has been suggested that a baseline level include the frequency and percentile levels of various diagnosis codes and the increased billing of complications and co-morbidities. **[7.4]**

52. In addition, when appropriate, as referenced in section G.2, below, reports of fraud or systemic problems should also be made to the appropriate governmental authority.

53. Instances of non-compliance must be determined on a case-by-case basis. The existence, or amount, of a *monetary* loss to a health care program is not solely determinative of whether or not the conduct should be investigated and reported to governmental authorities. In fact, there may be instances where there is no monetary loss at all, but corrective action and reporting are still necessary to protect the integrity of the applicable program and its beneficiaries.

54. Advice from the hospital's in-house counsel or an outside law firm may be sought to determine the extent of the hospital's liability and to plan the appropriate course of action.

55. The OIG currently maintains a voluntary disclosure program that encourages providers to report suspected fraud. The concept of voluntary self-disclosure is premised on a recognition that the Government alone cannot protect the integrity of the Medicare and other federal health care programs. Health care providers must be willing to police themselves, correct underlying problems and work with the Government to resolve these matters. The OIG's voluntary self-disclosure program has four prerequisites: (1) the disclosure must be on behalf of an entity and not an individual; (2) the disclosure must be truly voluntary (i.e., no pending proceeding or investigation); (3) the entity must disclose the nature of the wrongdoing and the harm to the federal programs; and (4) the entity must not be the subject of a bankruptcy proceeding before or after the self-disclosure. **[10.3]**

56. I.e., Federal and/or state law enforcement having jurisdiction over such matter. Such governmental authority would include DOJ and OIG with respect to Medicare and Medicaid violations giving rise to causes of actions under various criminal, civil and administrative false claims statutes. **[10.4]**

57. To qualify for the "not less than double damages" provision of the False Claims Act, the report must be provided to the Government within thirty (30) days after the date when the hospital first obtained the information. 31 U.S.C. § 3729(a). **[10.5]**

58. The OIG believes that some violations may be so serious that they warrant immediate notification to governmental authorities, prior to, or simultaneous with, commencing an internal investigation, e.g., if the conduct: (1) is a clear violation of criminal law; (2) has a significant adverse effect on the quality of care provided to program beneficiaries (in addition to any other legal obligations regarding quality of care); or (3) indicates evidence of a systemic failure to comply with applicable laws, an existing corporate integrity agreement, or other standards of conduct, regardless of the financial impact on federal health care programs. **[10.5]**

59. The OIG has published criteria setting forth those factors that the OIG takes into consideration in determining whether it is appropriate to exclude a health care provider from program participation pursuant to 42 U.S.C. § 1320a-7(b)(7) for violations of various fraud and abuse laws. *See* 62 Fed. Reg. 67,392 (12/24/97). **[10.5]**

60. Appropriate federal and state authorities include the Criminal and Civil Divisions of the Department of Justice, the U.S. Attorney in the hospital's district, and the investigative arms for the agencies administering the affected federal or state health care programs, such as the state Medicaid Fraud Control Unit, the Defense Criminal Investigative Service, and the Offices of Inspector General of the Department of Health and Human Services, the Department of Veterans Affairs and the Office of Personnel Management (which administers the Federal Employee Health Benefits Program). **[10.4]**

61. *See* 42 U.S.C. § 1320a-7b(a)(3). **[10.4]**

62. Normal repayment channels as described in HCFA's manuals and guidances are the appropriate vehicle for repaying identified overpayments. Hospitals should consult with its fiscal intermediary or HCFA for any further guidance regarding these repayment channels. Interest will be assessed, when appropriate. *See* 42 C.F.R. § 405.376.

# COMPLIANCE-RELATED INTERNET LINKS

American Bar Association Health Law Section
(frequent educational programs)                    www.abanet.org/health/home.html

American College of Healthcare Executives
(publications and programs directed
to executives)                                                            www.ache.org

American Hospital Association
(check for updates on hospital advocacy and
litigation with the U.S. Department of Justice)                            www.aha.org

American Health Lawyers Association
(more education)                                              www.healthlawyers.org

Association of American Medical Colleges
(effective advocacy for teaching hospitals
on PATH audits)                                                          www.aamc.org

Columbia/HCA Healthcare Corporation
(comprehensive compliance policies
and procedures)                                          www.columbia-hca.com/ethics

Health Care Financing Administration
(program manuals are now available online)                                www.hcfa.gov

Health HIPPO
(a wealth of information, including
a fraud and abuse page)                                              hippo.findlaw.com

Healthcare Financial Management Association
(even more education)                                                    www.hfma.org

J. A. Thomas & Associates, Inc.
(hospital and physician consultants
focusing on clinical documentation)                                  www.jathomas.com

Modern Healthcare
(good current events)                                        www.modernhealthcare.com

Office of Inspector General of the
Department of Health and Human Services
(primary site for fraud and
abuse developments)                                          www.dhhs.gov/progorg/oig

Withrow, McQuade & Olsen, LLP
(includes online version of Appendix A,
Form Compliance Program)                                              www.wmolaw.com

## GLOSSARY OF ACRONYMS

| | |
|---|---|
| AICPA | American Institure of Certified Public Accountants |
| BBA | Balanced Budget Act of 1997 |
| CEO | chief executive officer |
| CFO | chief financial officer |
| CMPL | Civil Monetary Penalties Law |
| CPT | Current Procedural Terminology |
| DOJ | U.S. Department of Justice |
| DRG | diagnosis-related group |
| FCA | False Claims Act |
| FTC | Federal Trade Commission |
| GAO | U.S. General Accounting Office |
| GME | graduate medical education |
| HCFA | Health Care Financing Administration |
| HCPCS | Health Care Financing Administration Common Procedural Coding System |
| HHS | Department of Health and Human Services |
| HIM | Health Information Management |
| HIPAA | Health Insurance Portability and Accountability Act of 1996 |
| ICD-9-CM | International Classification of Diseases, Ninth Revision, Clinical Modification |
| IPA | individual practice association |
| OIG | Office of Inspector General of the Department of Health and Human Services |
| PATH | physicians at teaching hospitals |
| PHO | physician-hospital organization |
| PPO | preferred provider organization |
| PPS | prospective payment system |
| RICO | Racketeer Influenced Corrupt Organizations Act |

# Index

NME. *See* National Medical Enterprises
Non-fee information, provision of to
healthcare purchasers, antitrust safety
zone for, 144*t*, 148-49

Office of Inspector General, HHS
(OIG)
on anti-kickback statute, 122
areas of special concern, 28-30, 46
compliance focus on, 90-91
for home health agencies, 29*t*
for hospitals, 28*t*
reduced list of, 32-33
on background investigations, 69
on compliance guidance, need for
analysis of, 25
on compliance officers, 35
and compliance programs, 9-10
*Cumulative Sanction Report,* 69
enforcement by, 8-9
on False Claims Act, 105
on healthcare fraud, 3-4
Home Health Guidance. *See*
Compliance Program Guidance
for Home Health Agencies
Hospital Guidance. *See* Compliance
Program Guidance for Hospitals
Internet address of, 207
on lawyers as compliance officers, 39
*Management Advisory Report,* 1991, 30
on medically unnecessary services, 102
on PATH, 99
reporting to, 73
on reporting to government, 75
on snapshots, 57
on training, 47
on unbundling, 100-101
on written standards of conduct, 27
zero tolerance policy on healthcare
fraud, 4, 55
Office of Personnel Management,
reporting to, 73
Ohio Hospital Association, 104
OIG. *See* Office of Inspector General,
HHS
Organizations. *See also* Corporations

culpability of, 19-20
compliance programs and, 17-18

PATH. *See* Physician(s), at teaching
hospitals
Patient abuse risk, anti-kickback statute/
Stark exceptions on, 117-18
Patient care, as OIG area of special
concern, 28*t*-29*t*
Pattern (or practice), 31-32, 95
definition of, 96
Penalties. *See also* Fines
under anti-kickback statute, 112-13
for antitrust violations, 142
for noncompliance, 67-68
for violation of criminal provisions of
Social Security Act, 94, 98
*Per se* standard, 140
Personal services, anti-kickback safe
harbors/Stark exceptions on, 130
PHO. *See* Physician-hospital organization
Physician(s)
acknowledgement of written compliance program by, 175
education of
on anti-kickback/Stark issues,
122-24
on under-reimbursement, 48-49
involvement in compliance process, 103
nonemployed, legal concerns about,
49, 103
OIG areas of special concern and,
28*t*-29*t*
Stark and, 114, 122-24, 136-37
in tax-exempt organizations, 124
at teaching hospitals (PATH), 98-99
and billing fraud, 108
Hospital Guidance on, 185-86
Physician-hospital organization (PHO),
152
Physician network joint ventures,
antitrust safety zone for, 146*t*, 150-52
Policy statements, on antitrust issues,
142-43
PPO. See Preferred provider organization
PPS. *See* Prospective-payment system

# ABOUT THE AUTHOR

 **Scott C. Withrow** is a founding partner of Withrow, McQuade & Olsen, LLP, in Atlanta, Georgia. He has practiced healthcare and corporate law for 15 years, representing clients that include hospitals, home health agencies, physicians and group practices, physician-hospital organizations, and physician practice management companies. He is a member of the American Bar Association's Health Law Section and the Georgia Academy of Healthcare Attorneys, serves on the editorial board of Aspen Publishers' *Home Health Care Revenue Report*, and has spoken frequently on the topic of healthcare compliance. Mr. Withrow has published articles in *The Practical Lawyer*, Leader Publications' *Health Care Fraud & Abuse Newsletter*, and elsewhere.

Prior to commencing his legal career, Mr. Withrow worked as a certified public accountant for a Big 5 accounting firm. He earned his undergraduate degree in accounting from the University of Virginia's McIntire School of Commerce and his law degree from Vanderbilt University.